IMAGES
of America

VIRGINIA IN THE CIVIL WAR

On the Cover: Pictured are two gentlemen in Richmond, framed by the spoils of war. The once-handsome city, demolished following five long years of fighting, was but a shell of its former self. Hundreds of Confederate cannons lay as silent as the men they had put into the grave. The year was 1865, and the war was over; the scars of a nation had just begun to heal. (Courtesy of the Library of Congress.)

IMAGES
of America

VIRGINIA IN THE CIVIL WAR

Joseph D'Arezzo

ARCADIA
PUBLISHING

ISBN 978-1-4671-1575-9

Published by Arcadia Publishing
Charleston, South Carolina

Printed in the United States of America

Library of Congress Control Number: 2015951130

For all general information, please contact Arcadia Publishing:
Telephone 843-853-2070
Fax 843-853-0044
E-mail sales@arcadiapublishing.com
For customer service and orders:
Toll-Free 1-888-313-2665

Visit us on the Internet at www.arcadiapublishing.com

To the Americans from the North and South who fought and died in the Commonwealth of Virginia.

Contents

Acknowledgments

I am particularly grateful to the participants in the American Civil War who understood the importance of history and took the time to immortalize their experience in writings, photographs, and official records. Further credit is due to the countless historians who have attempted to preserve and accurately interpret the stories of those who fought. I am also thankful to all of my professors, especially Dr. David Dillard, who guided me through my formal education in the field of history. The Library of Congress has done a superb job of preserving many important photographs, which shape our perceptions of the conflict. Unless otherwise noted, all images are courtesy of the Library of Congress. I am particularly appreciative of Cedar Creek Battlefield Foundation for its support and generosity in this endeavor. I wish to thank my dad, Mark D'Arezzo, for always challenging my perceptions of the past and for igniting a passion for history in my brother Charles and me. I could not have done this without him. Finally, I would like to thank all of my loved ones, including my mother and beloved Hannah.

Introduction

"We the People of the United States, in Order to form a more perfect Union"—these hallowed words touch on man's innate desire to create a society founded in justice. This idea, immortalized by the framers of the US Constitution, reverberates to this day, as America continues to strive to achieve that "more perfect Union." The 1860s brought about significant changes for the American populace as the nation rapidly expanded west. Since the earliest European settlers arrived on the continent, people had yearned to tame the western frontier. When England became more involved in its colonial acquisitions in North America, westward expansion began to increase. The continent seemed to stretch forever, and colonists welcomed the idea of acquiring new land and, with it, the freedom to create their own destinies. As tensions rose with England, colonists began to express dangerously radical ideas of individual liberties that were unlike anything to which European society was accustomed. Tensions quickly evolved into violent conflict, and within a few years, the British colonies had achieved independence. Some of the former colonies, like Virginia, had ascended to what the founders regarded as sovereign states. These states were bound by a federal government that saw each state as an independent territory with the freedom to operate unimpeded. This system worked well for some time, but, by the late 1850s, the powers of the individual states had become a point of contention on Capitol Hill. Following American independence, territories in the west sought statehood, resulting in a fierce debate in Congress.

The Northern states had the benefit of an industrialized economy, while the South, with its agrarian production base, was dependent on massive numbers of workers to harvest cash crops, such as tobacco. Since the Colonial period, the English had imported slaves to augment shortages on farms. This institution continued until the 1850s and was an integral part of the Southern economy. With the prospect of new territories achieving statehood, concerns arose in Congress as to whether these states would prohibit slavery or continue to allow it. This issue came to a head when Missouri wished to be added to the Union. The prospect of its admittance threatened to upset the balance in Congress between free states and slave states. As pressure mounted to disallow the admittance of new slave states, the Southern states began to push for an alternative to remaining in the Union.

By the early 1860s, states such as South Carolina initiated the call for secession, arguing that the interests of Southern states would be better served if they created their own confederation, separate from the Union. This effort immediately spurred a groundswell of support across the South, and states such as Virginia joined the cause. Although Virginia elected to sever ties with the Union, a few counties in the northern portion of the state wished to remain a part of the United States. These counties subsequently split from the Commonwealth of Virginia and formed a new state, West Virginia. The boundary between Virginia and its new neighbor figured heavily in the strategies and clashes that occurred over the course of the Civil War. The split allowed the Shenandoah Valley and Richmond to remain in the Confederacy; these regions in turn became prime targets for the Union military.

Although Virginia had elected to join the Confederacy, many Virginians still loved the Union and did not wish to see it dissolved. Gen. Robert E. Lee was an ardent supporter of the Union but, upon hearing of Virginia's secession, could not bear to fight against his home state. He cast his lot with the fledgling nation. Like Lee, thousands of Virginians answered the call of the Confederacy and formed regiments to repel what they perceived as an invasion by the United States.

Virginia was dissimilar to many of the Confederate states, as its geographic layout was something of a hybrid between Deep South cash-crop farming and Northern production. Furthermore, the state's rugged mountains in the west made military operations in the region quite dynamic, as armies were forced to maneuver around various geographic encumbrances, such as numerous rivers and mountain ranges. The Shenandoah Valley, for example, became the sight of many bloody campaigns as Union forces attempted to reach Central Virginia through the region. Likewise, Union armies made attempts to reach Richmond via the numerous waterways, which acted as exposed arteries to the city.

The very decision to place the Confederate capitol in Richmond makes Virginia unique, as the city is within 100 miles of Washington, DC. The capitol was the constant target of Union advances that sought to bring about a quick end to the war by capturing the Confederate seat of power. This warranted the presence of a Confederate army in the region, and the stage was set for Virginia to become the site of many significant battles and bloody clashes. Virginia saw more battles than any other state during the war, and it was the primary operating area for famous officers, such as Lee, Stonewall Jackson, and Phillip Sheridan. By the end of the war, even Ulysses S. Grant was operating in the commonwealth, as he recognized it to be the most critical region at that period.

The civilian population experienced tremendous hardships throughout the war as armies destroyed farmland, barns, and homes throughout the state. Virginia truly was a battleground, and young men from all over the Union converged on the state to fight for their beliefs. Soldiers from every state in the Confederacy and the Union fought in Virginia, many never to return home. In this sense, the battlefields throughout the state truly are hallowed ground. Historians must not make the anachronistic mistake of oversimplifying the motivations of individual soldiers. The men who fought and died in the Old Dominion did so for a wide variety of reasons, ranging from lofty political ideals to simplistic loyalty to one's home state.

This book employs a chronological approach to examining the Civil War in Virginia. Each chapter is dedicated to assessing one year of the war and the major clashes and battles that transpired in that period. Additionally, particular attention is given to localities that had intimate experience with soldiers and the movement of armies. This text attempts to provide a cursory examination of the horrendous experiences the war brought to Virginia, drawing heavily on images preserved in the Library of Congress. The Library of Congress is an excellent resource for finding period photographs that illustrate the experiences of those involved in the war. The photographs found on the following pages are but a few of the extremely powerful images from the period. Each one has a story to tell.

The American Civil War is an immensely complex subject that cannot be distilled into a limited set of arguments or images. Rather, it is an evolving topic that unravels new information over time. Modern historians owe it to those who died to continue to seek the truth regarding the war in order to better understand how it touched places like Virginia and those that fought. Today, the state is home to numerous organizations that endeavor to preserve the hallowed history that the current generation has been charged with protecting. By supporting these organizations, people can touch the past and leave their mark on the continuing history of the war that changed America.

One

THE IMPENDING STORM

The term "civil war" often evokes images of war-torn nation-states that have somehow deviated from the uniquely American constructs of democracy and a modern republic. Bosnia, West Africa, and various banana republics often come to mind. However, America has not been spared from the tumultuous experience of self-dissolution. Within 100 years of the founding of the United States, the nation was experiencing a crisis that resonated with Americans from New England to the Mississippi Delta. Differences about national identity and how the government derives legitimacy from the consent of the governed were central to the secession movement. Southern states seeking to sever their legal union to the North engaged in a constitutional debate that shook the pillars on which this nation was founded. Southerners engaged strong rhetoric that harkened back to the framers of the Constitution and sought to continue the iterative process of government that had been established by the Colonists. Virginia followed other seceding states and soon found itself the target of the Union endeavor to reunite the shattered nation.

It is important to recognize that, in 1861, the government in Washington, DC, saw the Virginia shore across the Potomac River as enemy territory steeped in treason. Conversely, the capital of the fledgling Confederate States of America perceived Washington as the seat of tyranny that the Founding Fathers had vehemently warned against. It is imperative that this history is interpreted objectively so as to understand the struggles and sentiments of the people involved in creating it. Virginia was a war zone, and Americans from all over the continent converged to bleed for the causes they held dearest. The American Civil War was the last major conflict to employ the extraordinarily gruesome Napoleonic tactics of war, and Virginia soon saw the results of such bloody clashes, which forever remind the state of its bid to leave the Union. By the end of 1861, the eyes of the world were on Virginia as they sought to learn the fate of the formerly united nation.

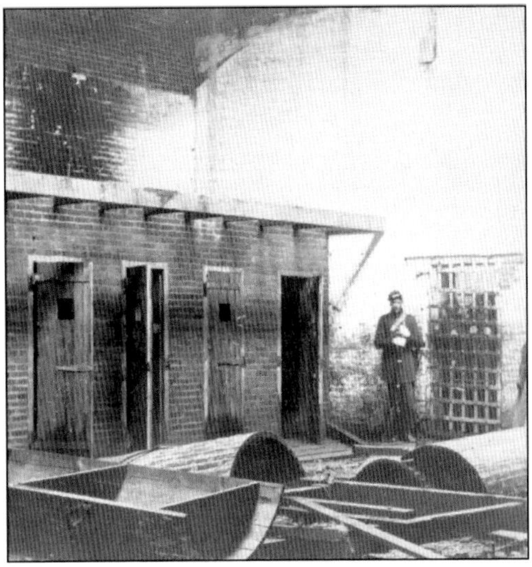

Prior to the war, Alexandria was a burgeoning city along the Potomac River that utilized its unique location on the waterway to assert itself as an economic forerunner in the region. This was in part because roads were cumbersome and not as effective as established waterways for moving goods to market. Slaves were also transported by water to Alexandria and temporarily held in pens, such as those seen here.

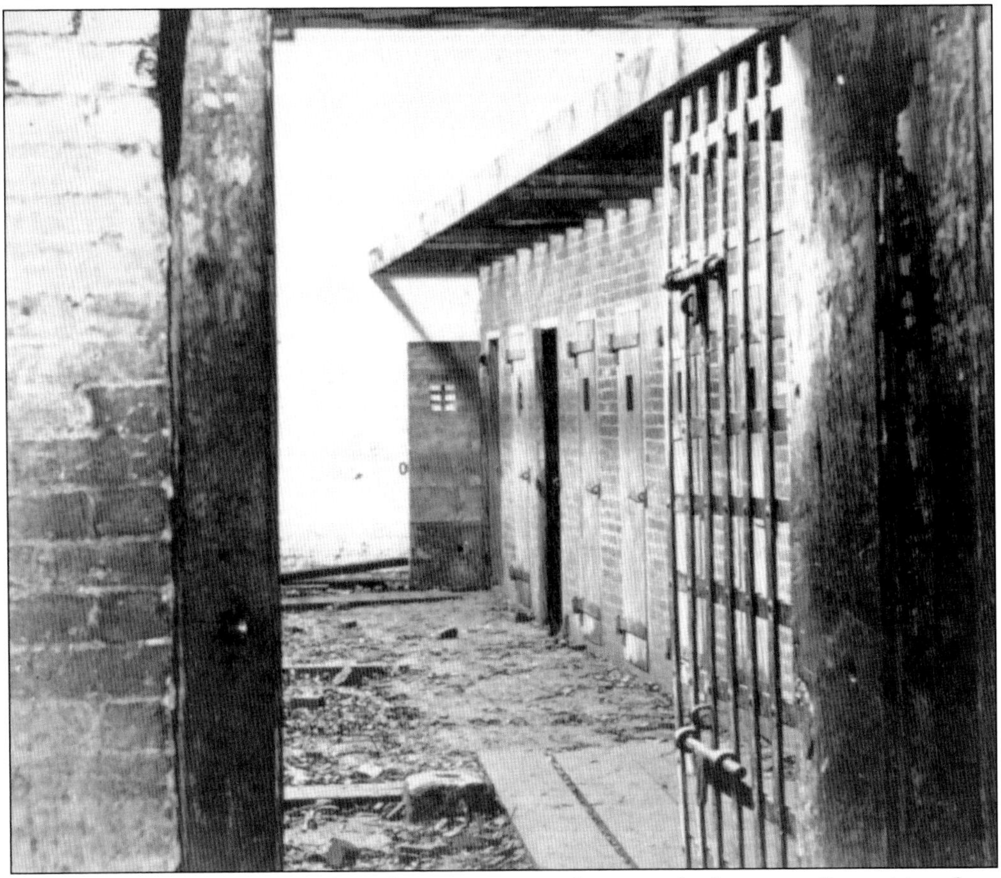

Slaves were an integral part of Alexandria's economy, as the city took advantage of its position along the water. Vessels could sail across the Chesapeake Bay and up the Potomac River to deliver goods and human cargo. Holding cells such as those seen here were common on the city's waterfront. Such images are a reminder that slavery was not limited to the Deep South. It was prevalent throughout Northern Virginia and even existed in states north of the Mason-Dixon line.

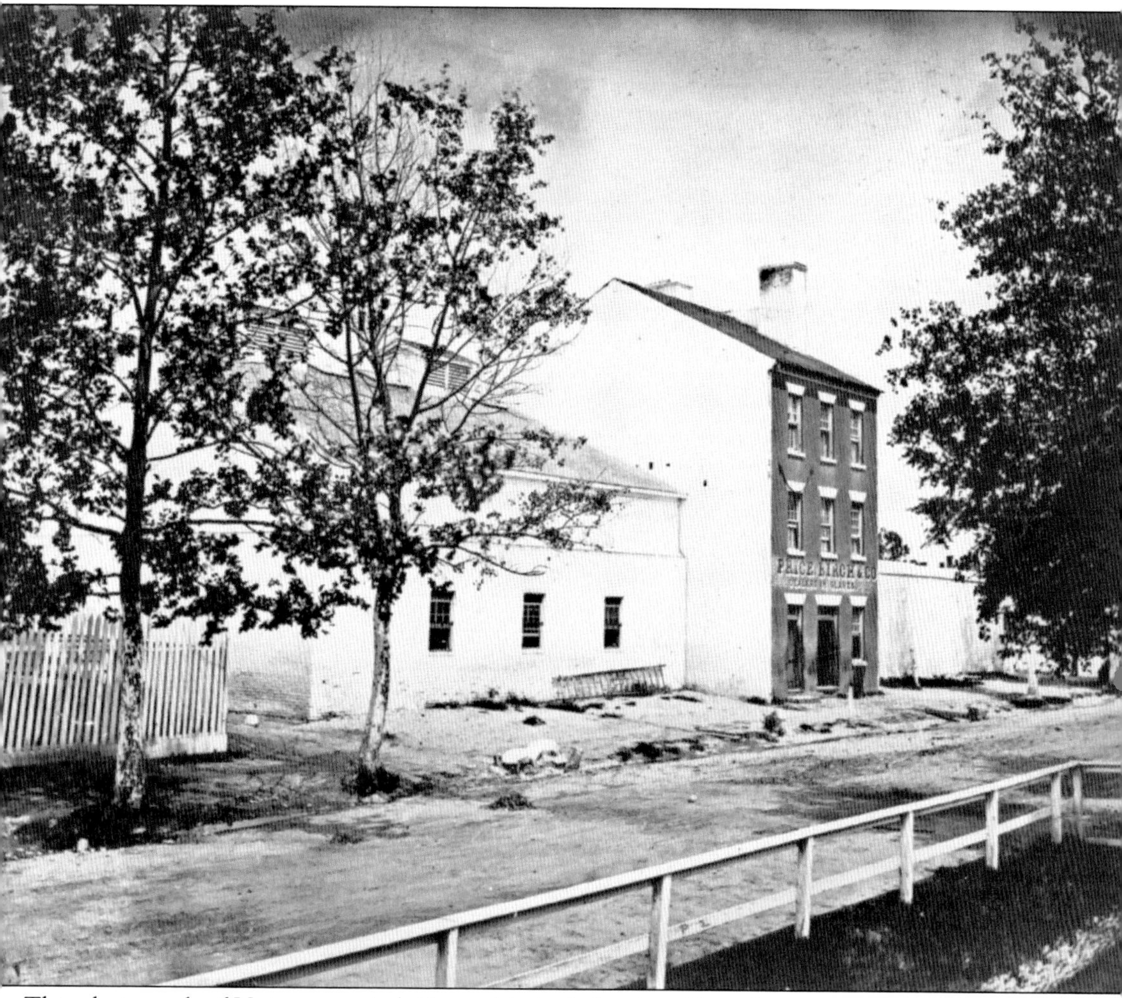

This photograph of Union-occupied Alexandria includes the office of a prominent slave dealer (right). Slave dealers were prevalent throughout what is now Old Town Alexandria. These streets are now home to upscale housing and boutique retail locations, making it difficult to imagine them as industrial warehouses and slave auction houses. Visitors to today's King Street can only imagine the dynamic scenes that occurred here in the early 1860s.

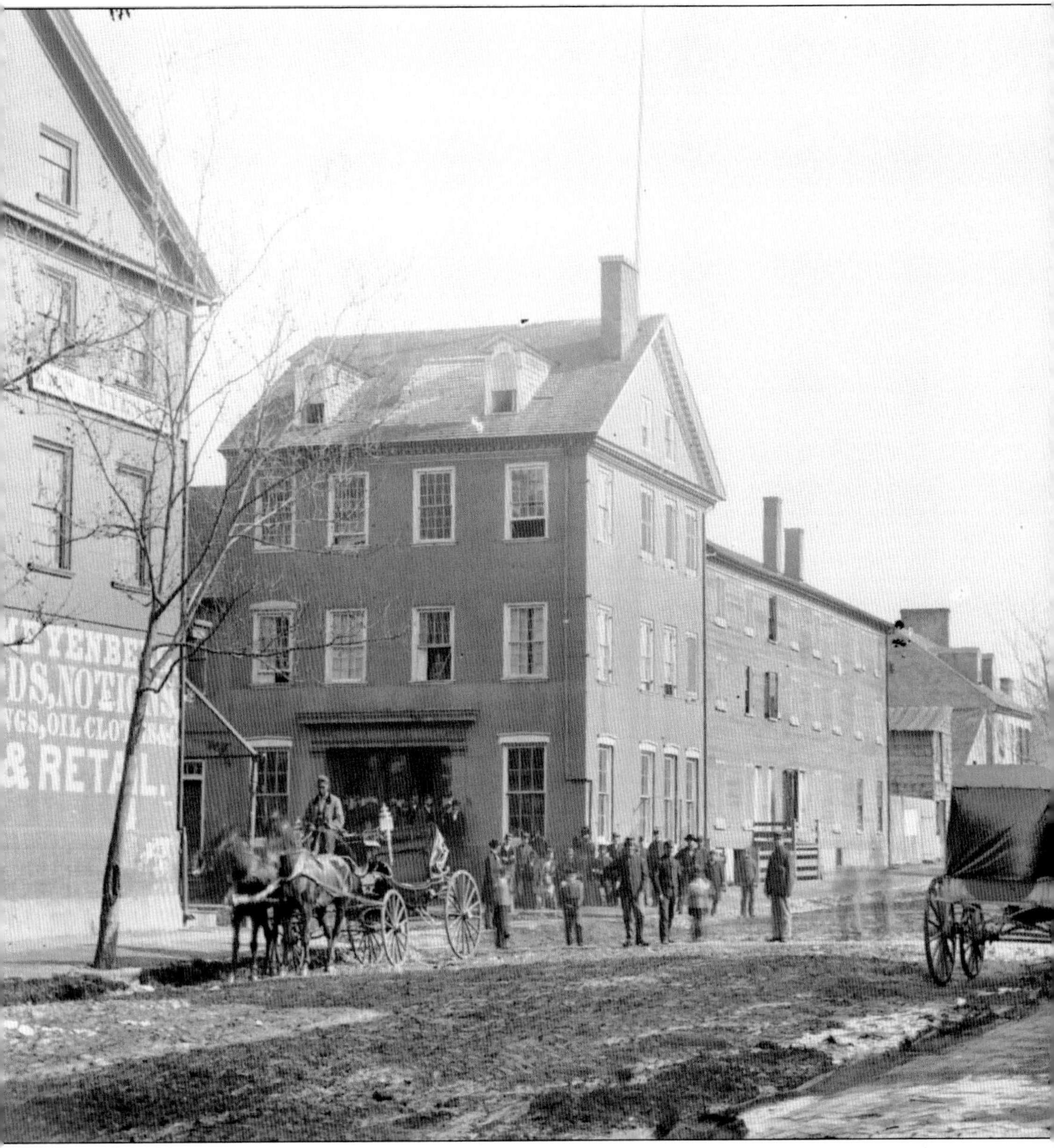

Following Pres. Abraham Lincoln's decision to dispatch an army to impede the South's attempt at secession, Federal troops poured across the Potomac River into Alexandria. This photograph of Union soldiers outside of the Marshall House depicts the somewhat tense interaction between Federal troops and Virginia residents. The Marshall House, located on the corner of King and Pitt Streets, is now the location of a prominent intersection.

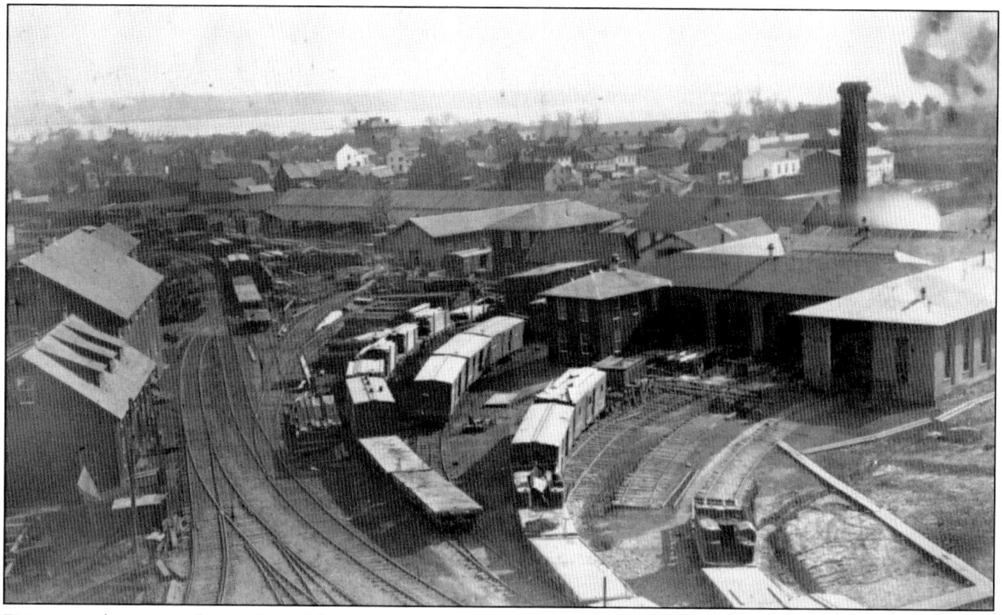

Prior to the war, the railroad began to come into its own as a highly effective and dominant means of transportation. Trains were increasingly used to transport men and material during the antebellum period and would only become more critical as the war progressed. This is the vast rail yard in Alexandria, including machine sheds.

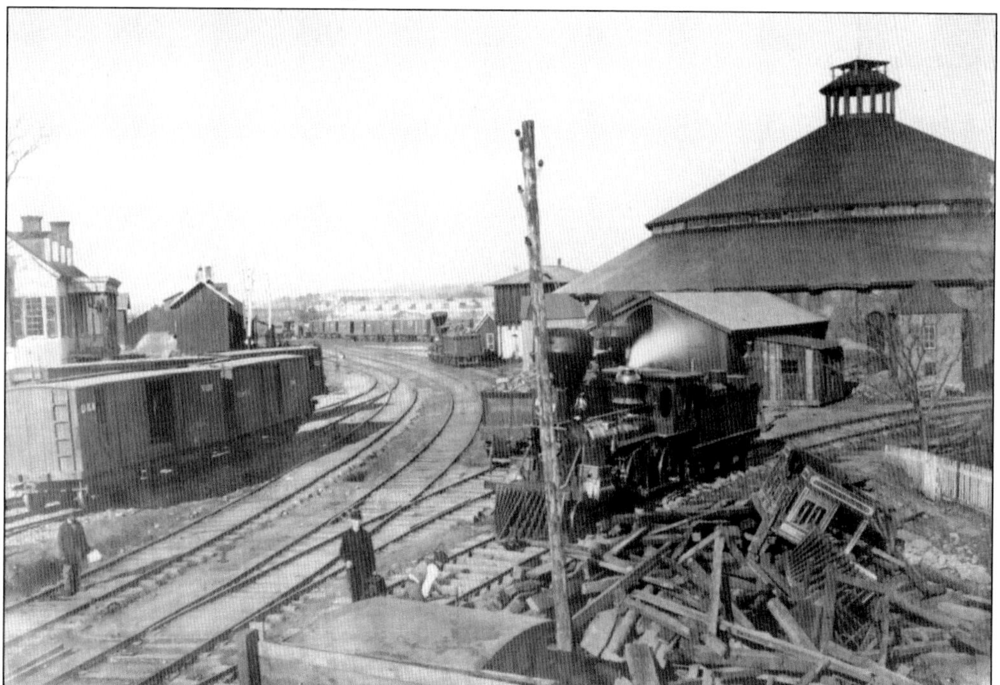

A crucial element at the hub in Alexandria was the massive roundhouse. This state-of-the-art structure allowed mechanics to service and redirect the numerous locomotives that arrived daily. This rail network, along with the extensive wharfs along the Potomac River, made the city an important transportation depot for the Union army throughout the war.

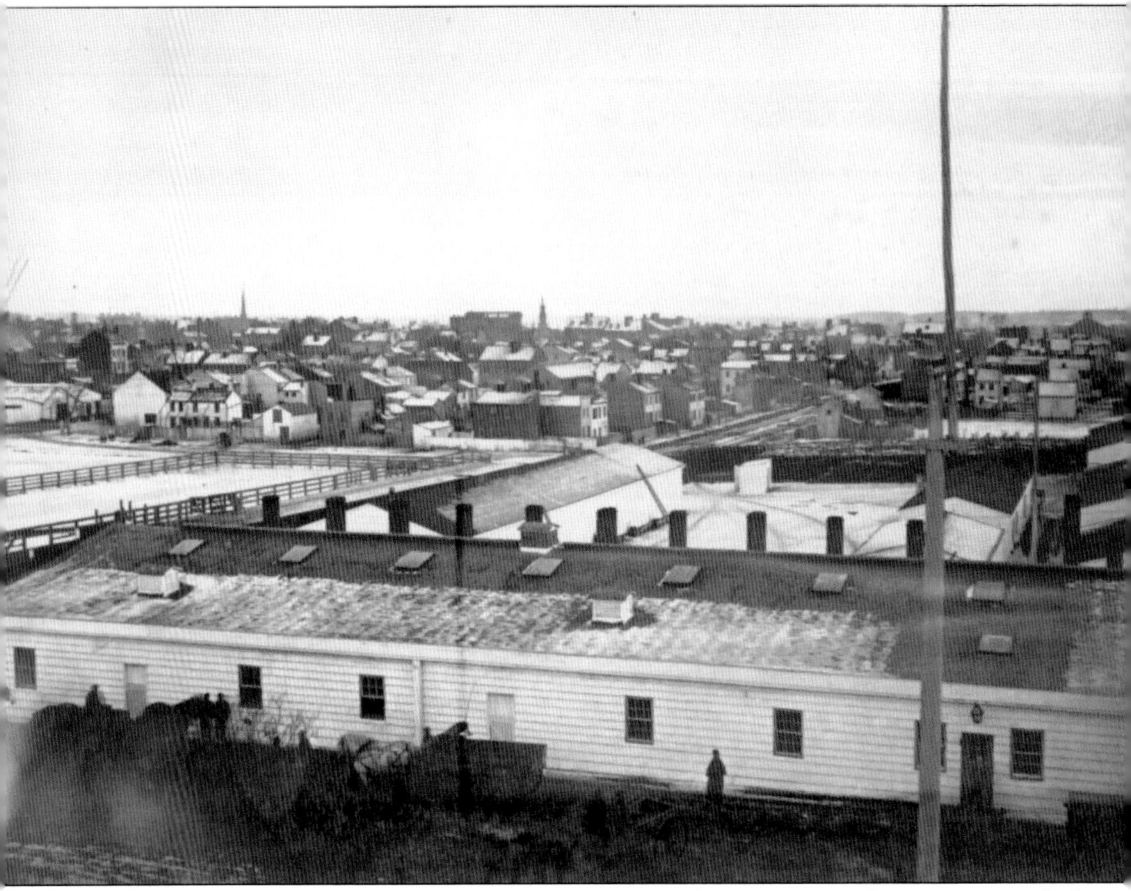

Many historians agree with the old adage, "An army marches on its stomach." It was certainly the case in the Civil War, as soldiers' movements were highly contingent on the proximity of food and supplies. This photograph of the government bakery in Alexandria highlights the immense infrastructure necessary to supply the massive armies fielded by the Union. Such facilities fueled the Union war machine while the Confederate army was often starving and malnourished.

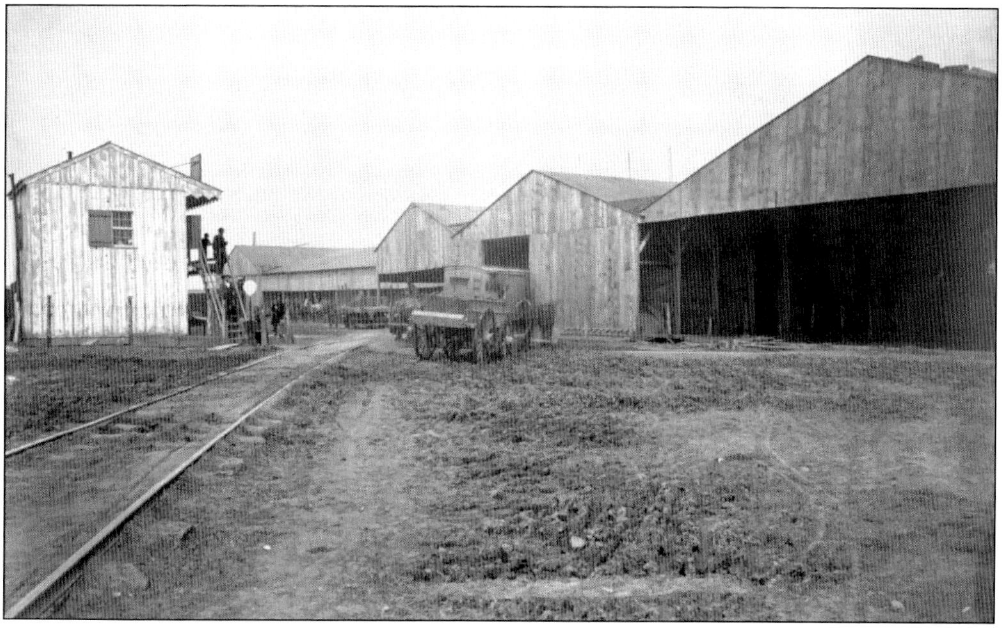

Although waterways and rail lines were preferred methods of transport, they were quite limited by the dynamic geography of Virginia. Trains had not yet eclipsed animal transportation, and large draft animals were utilized by both armies in cavalry and supply roles. This excellent photograph depicts government hay barns, which made up part of the network of military-operated buildings in Alexandria.

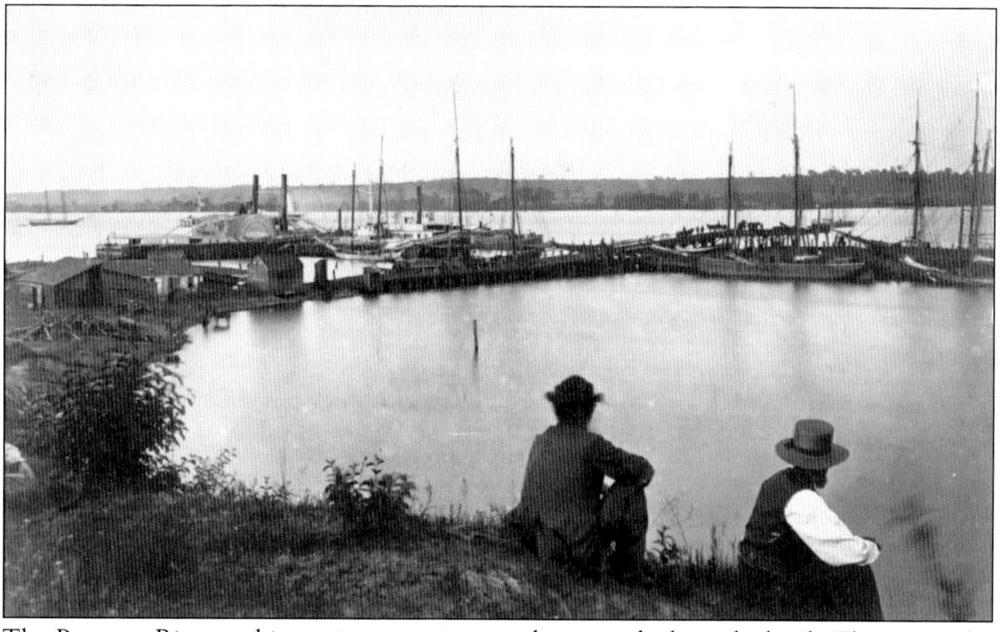

The Potomac River and its various arteries were home to docks and wharfs. This particular coal wharf has a variety of vessels moored to it, emblematic of the drastic changes in watercraft technology during the period. Sailing vessels are accompanied by a steam-powered ship. The use of steam to propel vessels was extensive during the war. Seated in the foreground are two debonair, unidentified gentlemen.

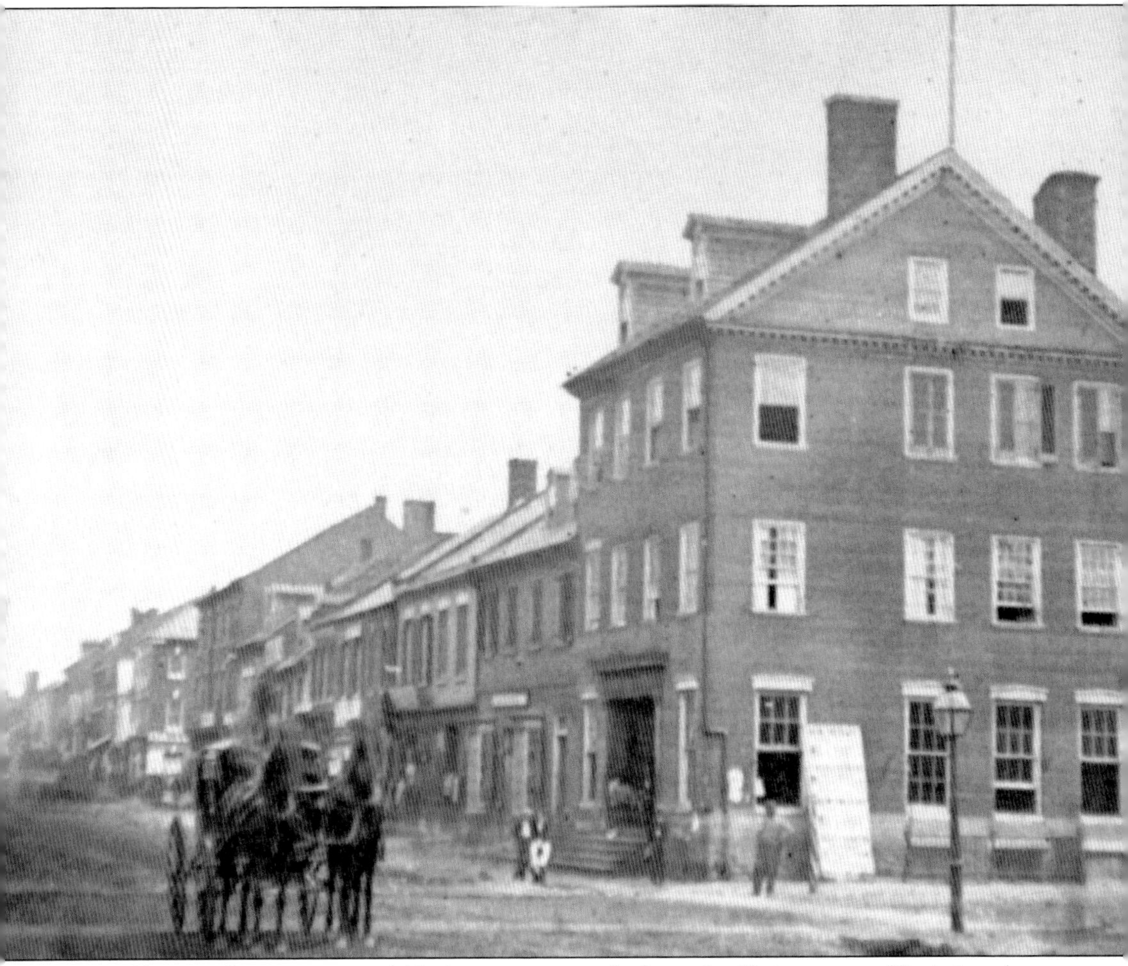

Following the commonwealth's decision to secede from the Union, many Virginians began to express their identity as Confederate nationalists. This intense sense of nationalism certainly existed in Alexandria, where ardent Confederates, such as James W. Jackson, proudly displayed the newly designed Confederate national flag. Jackson showed his support by displaying the flag atop his inn at the Marshall House. Despite Northern Virginia's proximity to Washington, DC, the region was surprisingly pro-Confederate, and many citizens fervently supported the fledgling nation.

Upon his arrival in Alexandria, this Union officer, Col. Elmer Ellsworth of the 11th New York Infantry Regiment, entered the Marshall House and promptly removed the Confederate flag. As he walked down the stairs to the first floor, the innkeeper, James Jackson, shot the colonel at point-blank range. This bloody affair was quickly recognized as involving one of the first conspicuous deaths of the war.

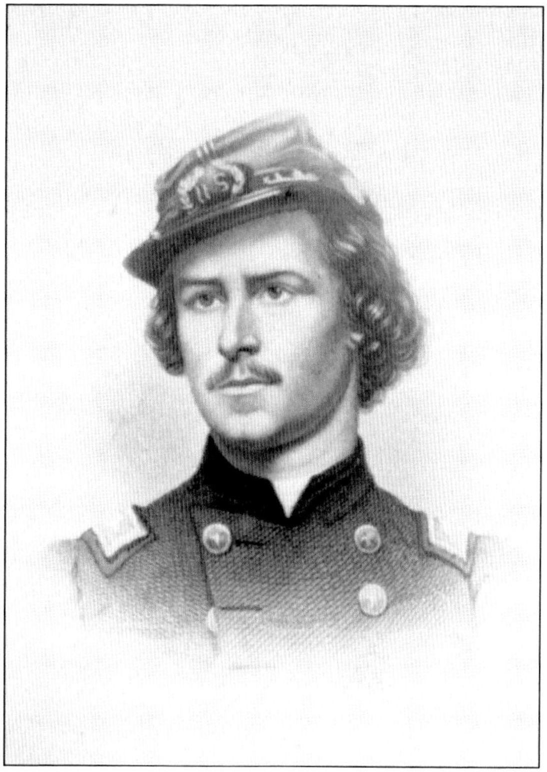

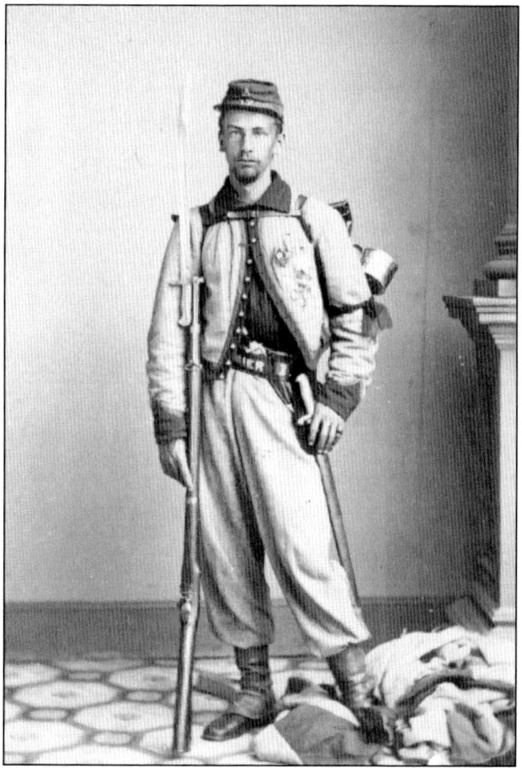

Colonel Ellsworth's death shocked the Union. Many Northerners were surprised to learn that Confederate nationalism was as strong and fervent as their own. In response, an entire regiment was raised and named Ellsworth's Avengers. Pictured is Pvt. F.E. Brownell of the aforementioned unit, formally known as the 11th New York Infantry. Note the flamboyant uniform design, which was adopted by many Northern units.

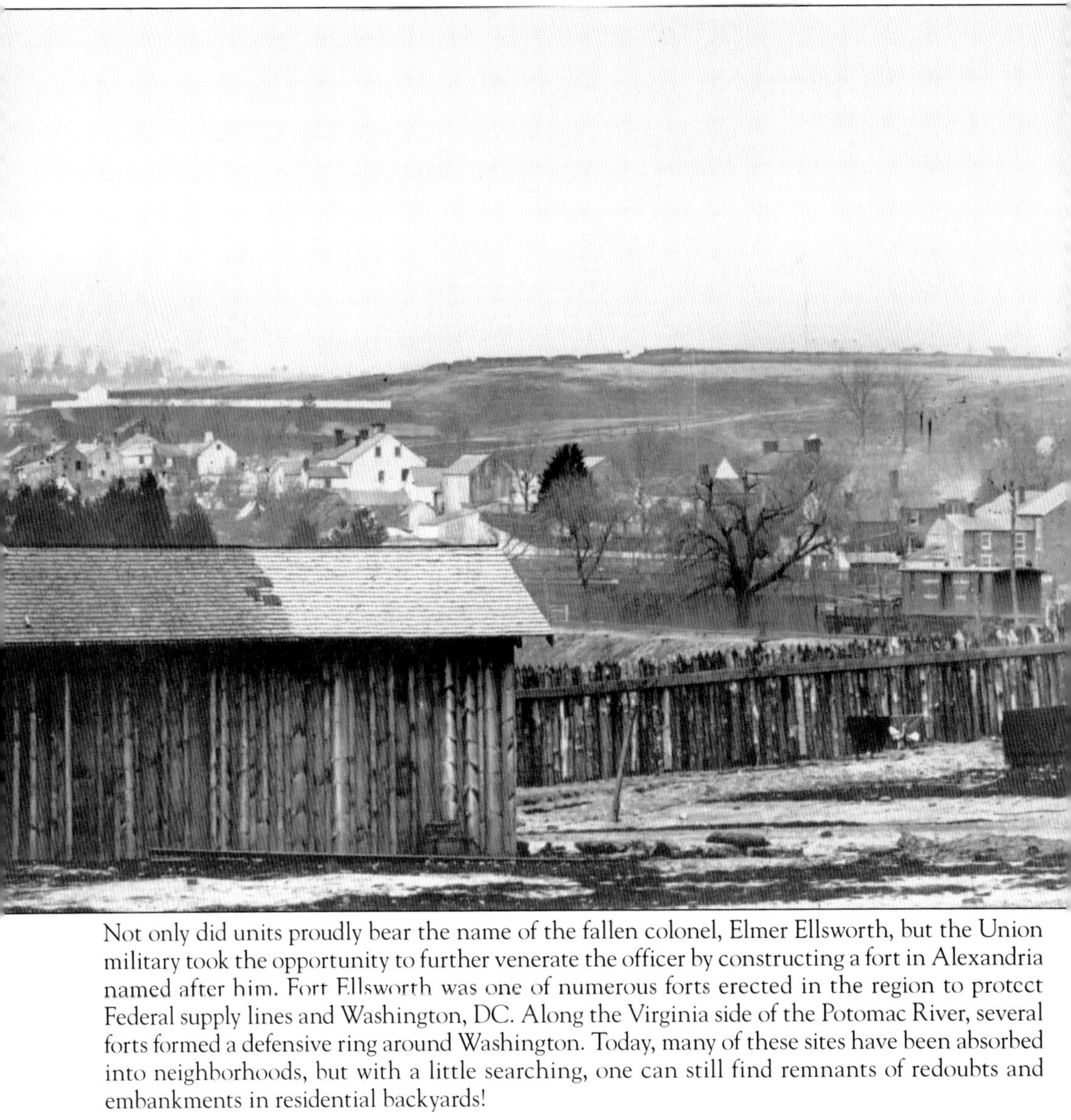

Not only did units proudly bear the name of the fallen colonel, Elmer Ellsworth, but the Union military took the opportunity to further venerate the officer by constructing a fort in Alexandria named after him. Fort Ellsworth was one of numerous forts erected in the region to protect Federal supply lines and Washington, DC. Along the Virginia side of the Potomac River, several forts formed a defensive ring around Washington. Today, many of these sites have been absorbed into neighborhoods, but with a little searching, one can still find remnants of redoubts and embankments in residential backyards!

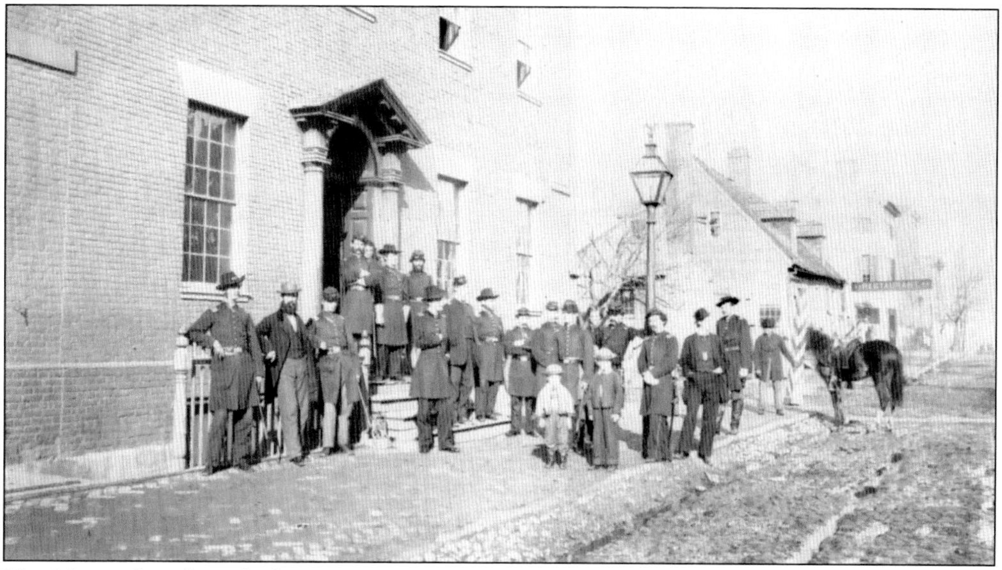

The Union drew heavily from its immense population and utilized its human resources to raise massive armies. Pictured here are officers from the First District Volunteers, one of hundreds of units sent across the Potomac River to fight what they expected to be a rabble of poorly organized Confederate troops. Their naïveté would soon be corrected, as they came to realize that the Confederacy was not a crazed mob, but rather an organized army. In the background is one of the many prominent hotels in Alexandria.

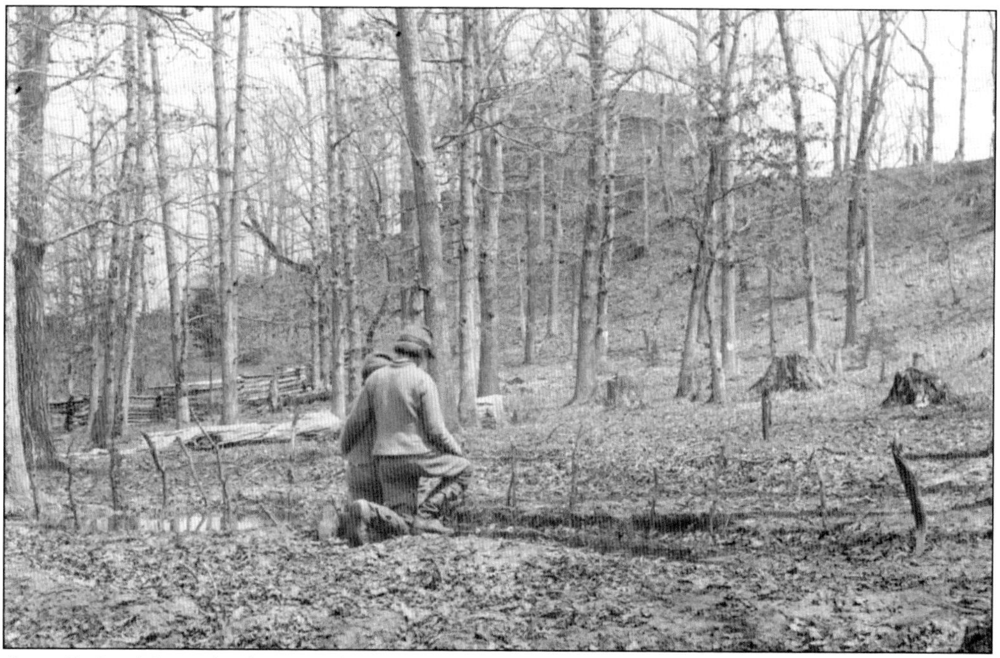

Once Federal forces had amassed on the Virginia side of the river, they began to advance toward an important railroad hub near Manassas, Virginia. However, Confederate forces did not allow this incursion to go unchallenged and swiftly maneuvered to meet the Union army. A dominant local land feature was a stream known as Bull Run. Here, two young men pose after the battle in front of what looks to be hastily dug graves behind Sudley Church.

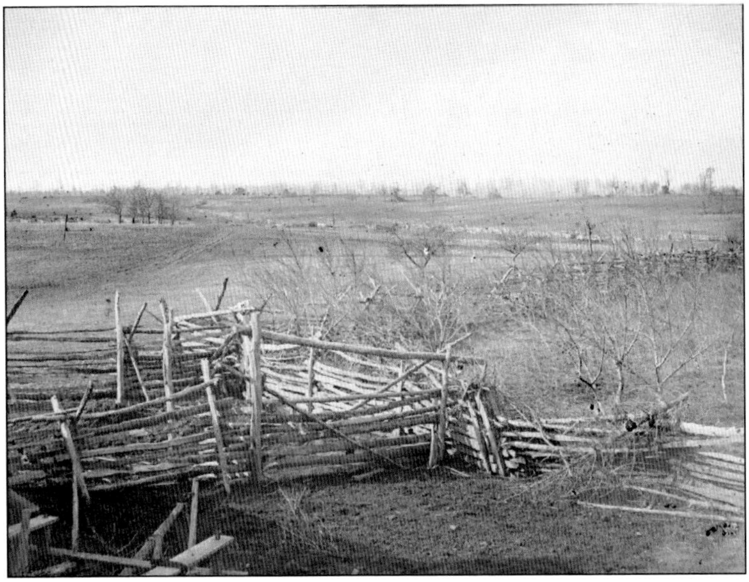

On July 21, 1861, the two armies clashed near Manassas Junction. This skirmish quickly escalated into a full-scale battle, considered by many historians to be the first major land engagement of the American Civil War. This photograph depicts the wide-open spaces over which both armies maneuvered their large columns during the fight.

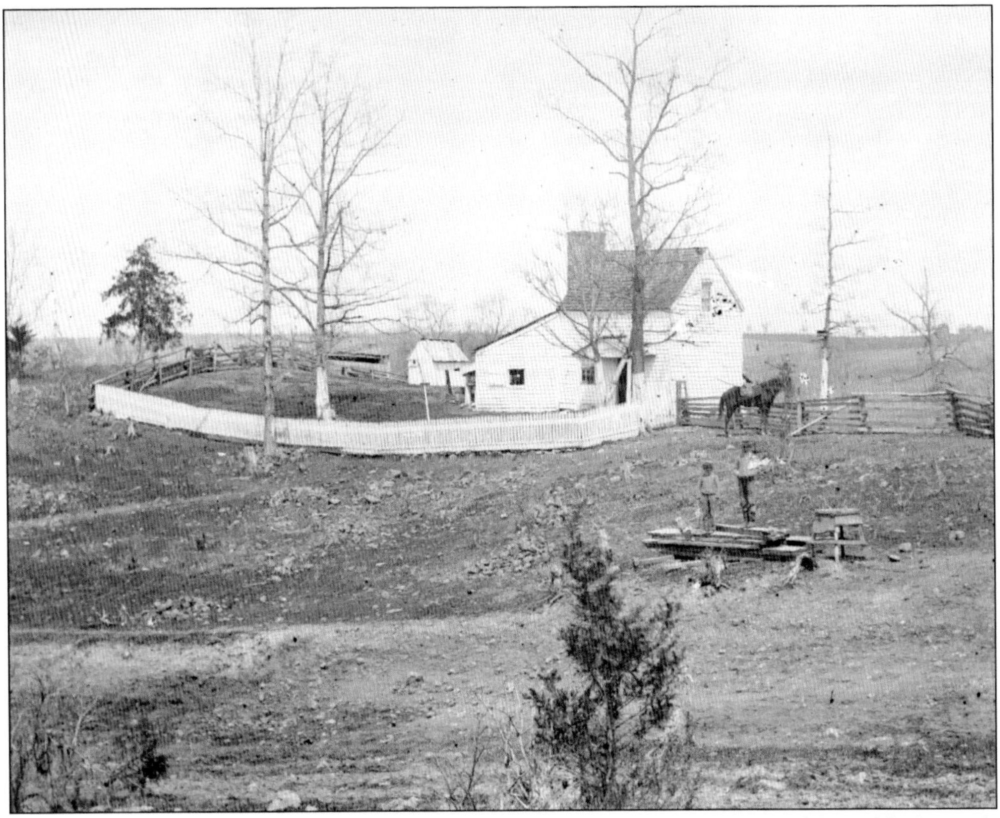

Many folks in the Washington, DC, area suspected that the Union army would quickly dispatch what they imagined to be a poorly assembled band of Confederates. Many Northerners, seeing an opportunity to witness history, hurried to the Manassas battlefield with picnic baskets and other accessories. However, what ensued was far from a small-scale skirmish. Instead, a bloody battle was waged. Shown here is the Robinson House, which bordered the battlefield.

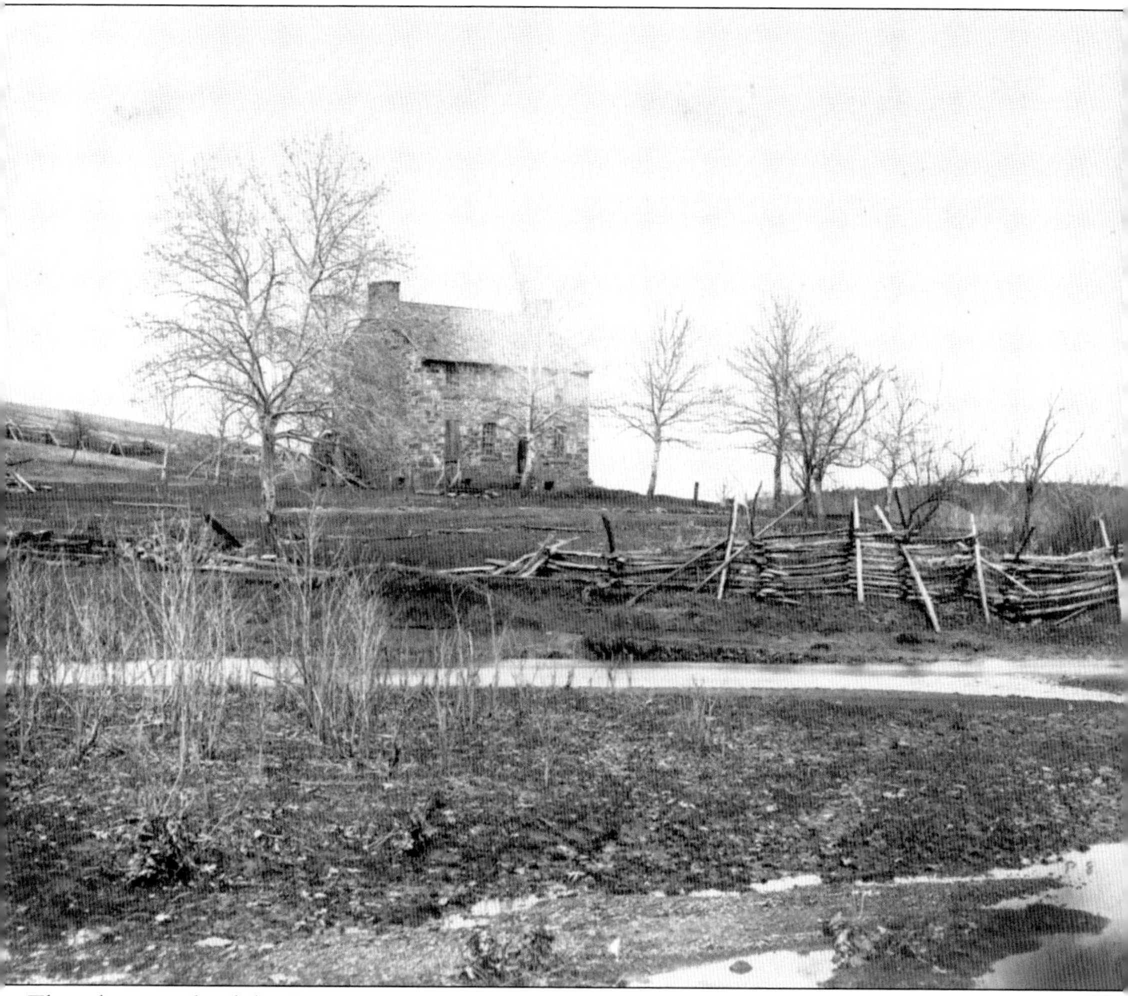

This photograph of the Stone House was taken after the battle. The building, an important landmark during the fight, still stands today, flanked by a busy intersection. However, roughly 150 years ago, this was the sight of bloody fighting that set the tone for the rest of the conflict. Houses like this were important rallying points during battles, and commanders often used them as headquarters and hospitals.

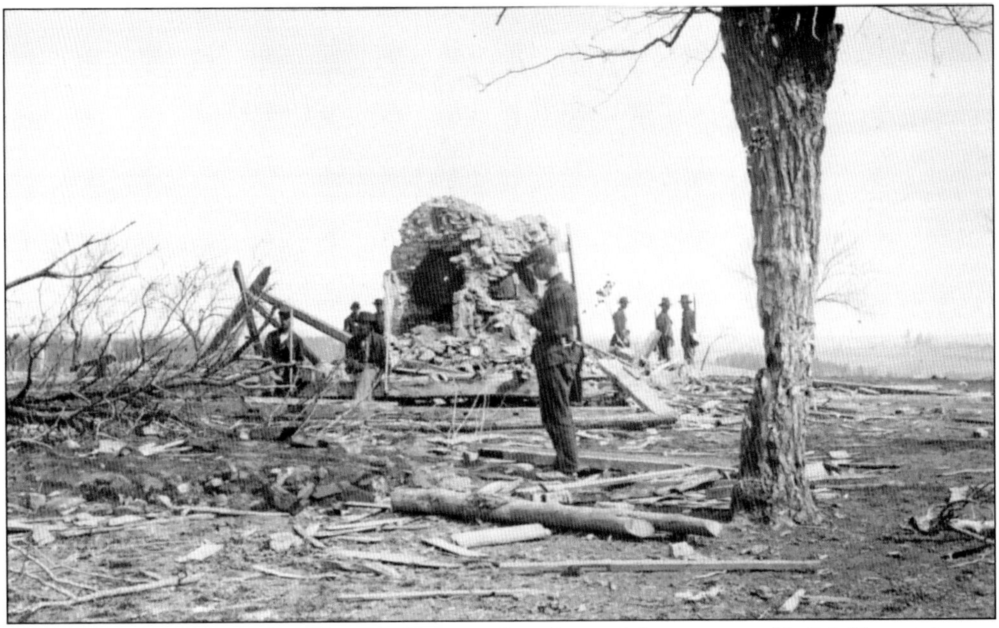

In this sobering photograph, a Union soldier stands in front of the remains of Judith Henry's house. The violent nature of the Battle of First Manassas, and the effectiveness of both Confederate and Union artillery, caused significant collateral damage. Structures such as this often became focal points of military action during battles, as they provided cover from projectiles and would subsequently draw enemy fire.

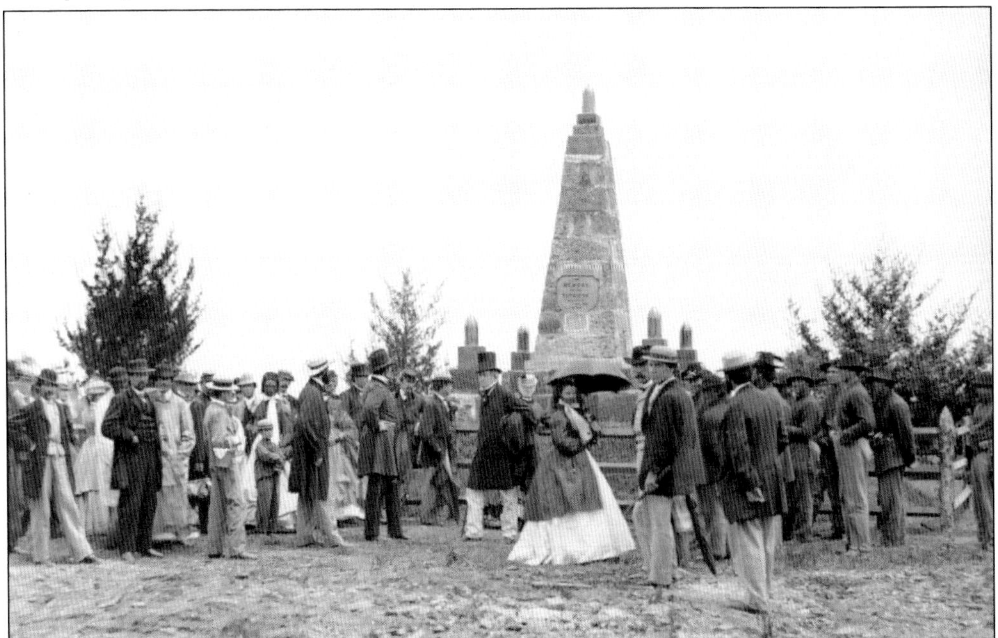

This battle had profound effects on Northern perceptions of the war, as it shattered hopes for a quick and bloodless end to hostilities. The resulting thousands of casualties would be commemorated heavily following the war. The monument seen here, erected soon after the war, is a prominent feature at the Manassas National Battlefield Park today.

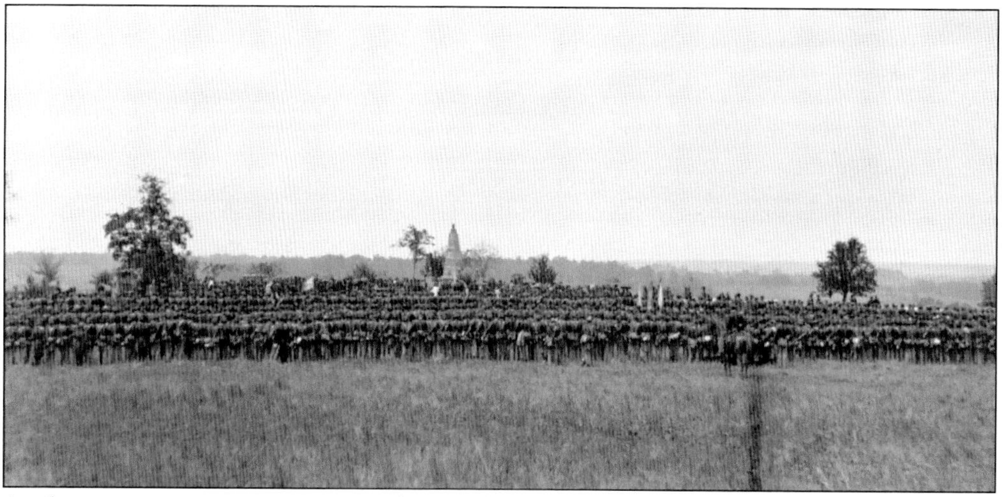

At this commemoration ceremony, thousands of veterans and spectators participated. Such events were immensely popular following the war and were held throughout the state at various battlefields. This monument sits on a portion of the Manassas battlefield that saw some of the heaviest fighting. Despite the hostility that existed during the conflict, many of these events were attended by both Union and Confederate veterans, as those from both sides reminisced about their shared experiences.

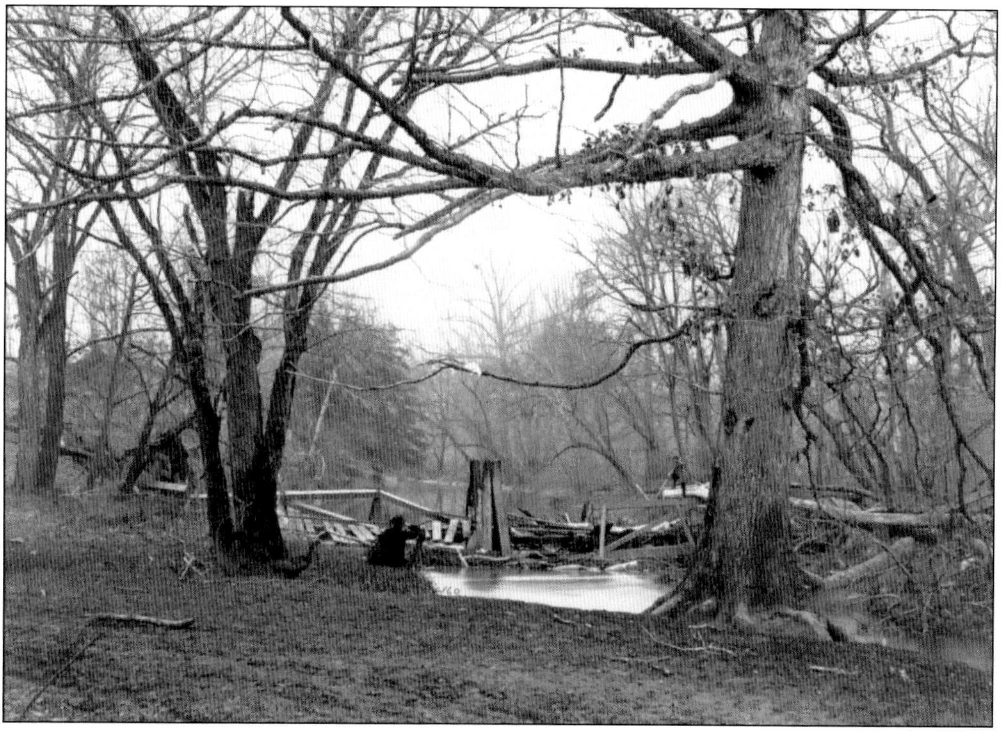

The Civil War in Virginia saw the evolution of military tactics and strategy to adapt to rapid troop movement and improved roads and rail lines. This necessitated that generals adopt destructive tactics, such as the demolition of bridges and various bottlenecks that could be used to benefit the enemy. This dramatic photograph of a destroyed bridge on the Manassas battlefield bears testament to such tactics.

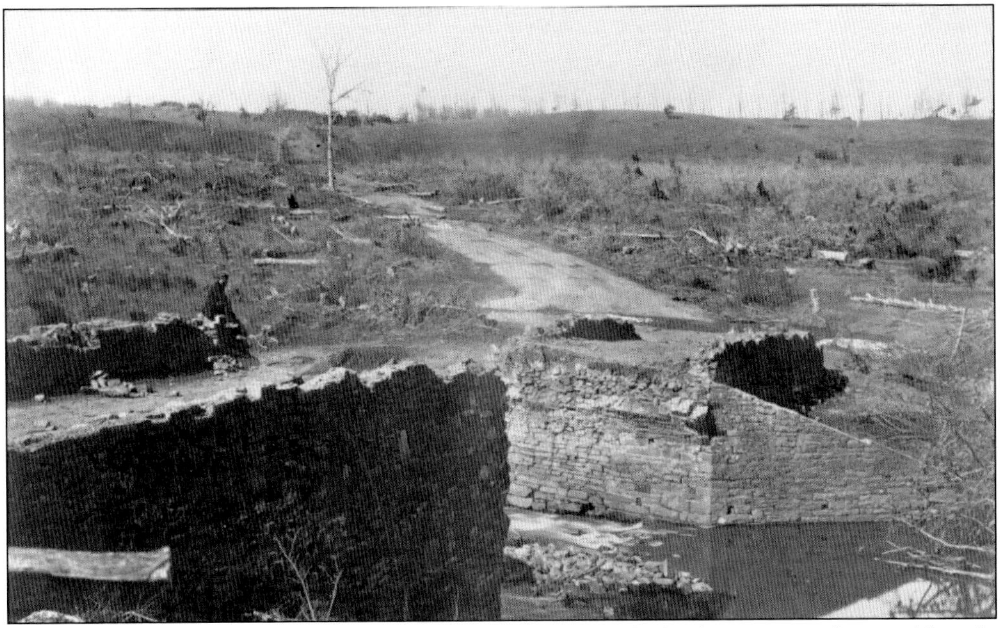

Stone bridges were also the target of preemptive destruction by both armies, as they could easily accommodate the movement of artillery and heavy wagons. In the background, the Manassas battlefield stretches into the distance. The area of fighting was quite large, as highly trained West Point officers on both sides continuously worked to outflank their opponents.

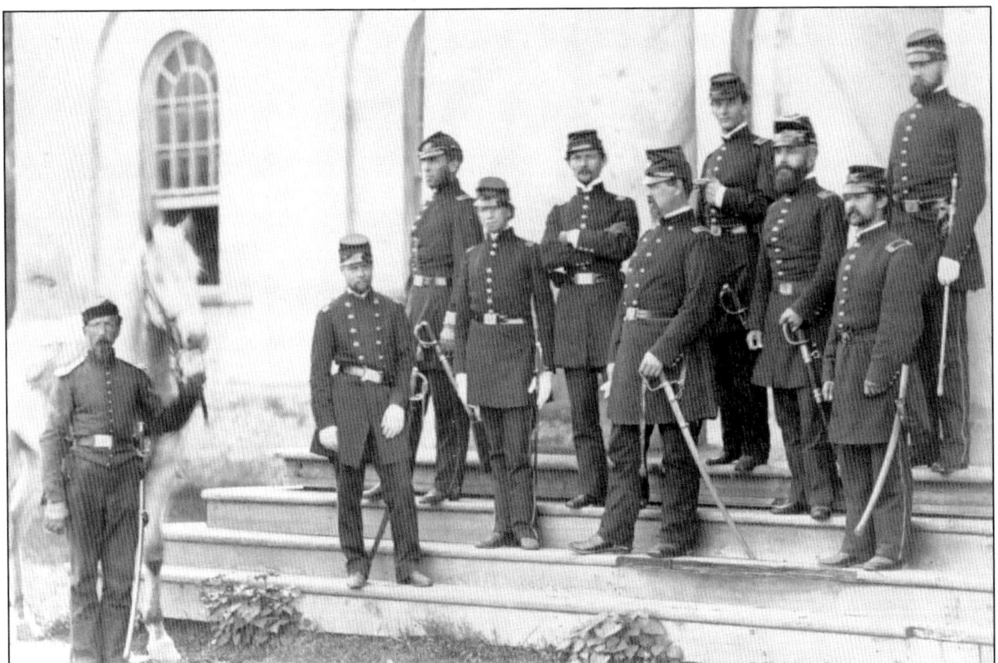

West Point graduates fought for both the Union and the Confederacy in the war and were quickly promoted due to their formal military training. The commanding general of the Union army at Manassas, Irvin McDowell, had over 26,000 troops at his disposal. Here, McDowell (fifth from right) poses with his staff in Arlington, Virginia.

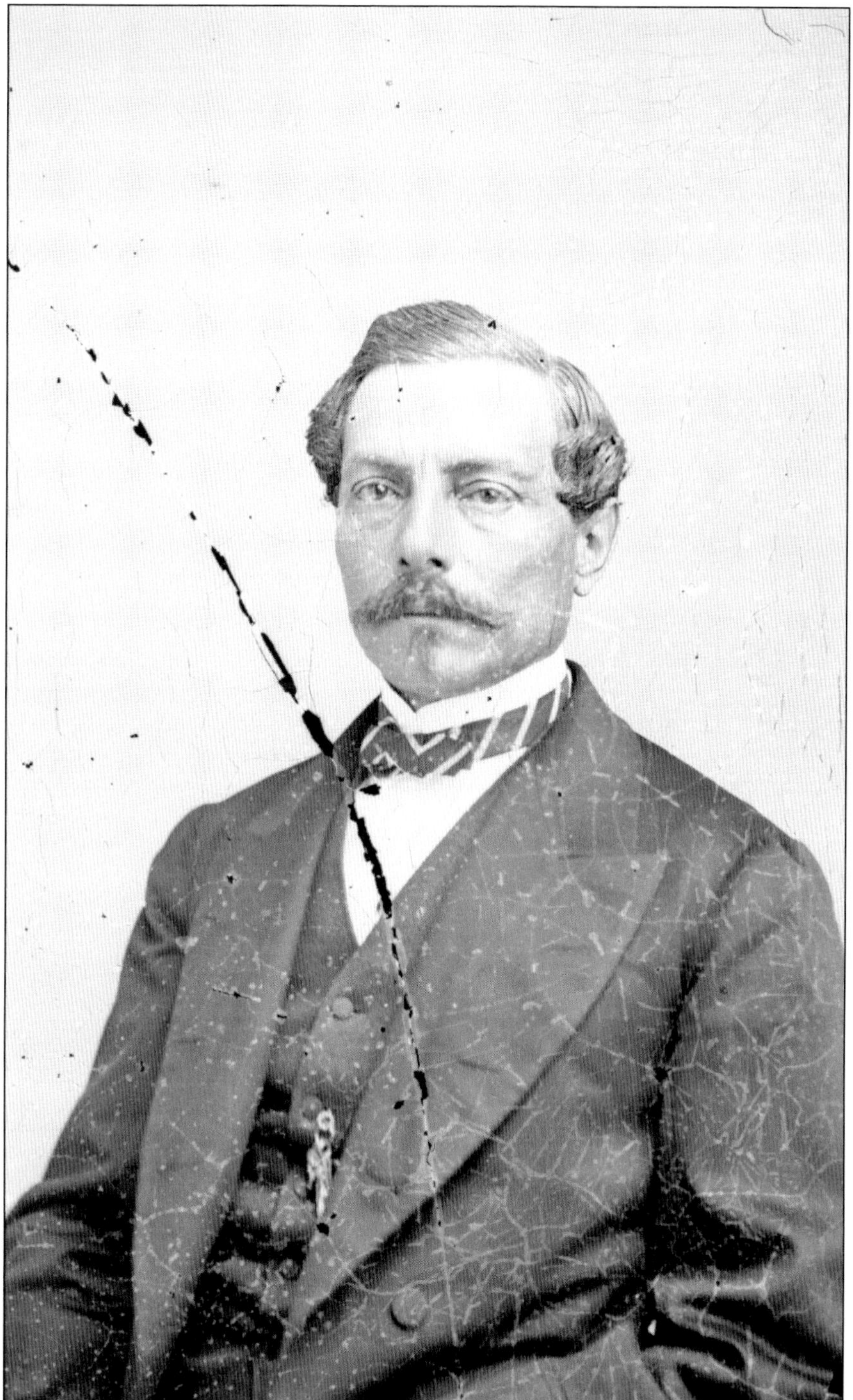

One of McDowell's former West Point classmates, Pierre Gustave Toutant Beauregard, was given command of the Confederate forces that fought at Manassas. These two former students brought their education to bear and quickly created a cauldron of carnage that resulted in many killed and wounded. Here, Beauregard is pictured in less formal, yet quite dapper, civilian attire.

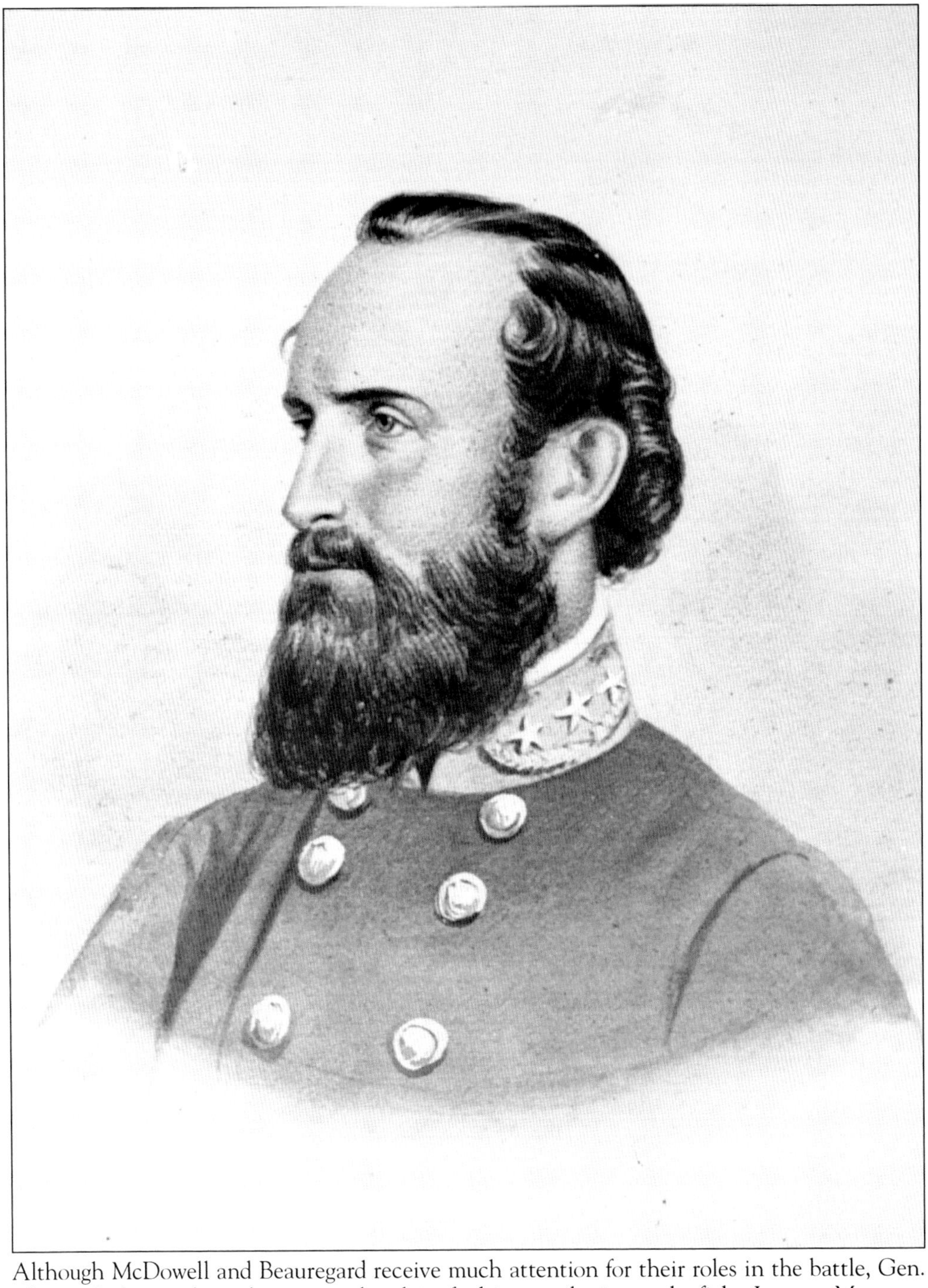

Although McDowell and Beauregard receive much attention for their roles in the battle, Gen. Thomas Jackson achieved intentional acclaim for his contribution to the fight. It was at Manassas that the Confederate general stood tall under withering enemy fire while his troops crouched around him. This act of bravery gained Jackson his moniker, "Stonewall," and led to him becoming one of the most iconic figures of the Civil War.

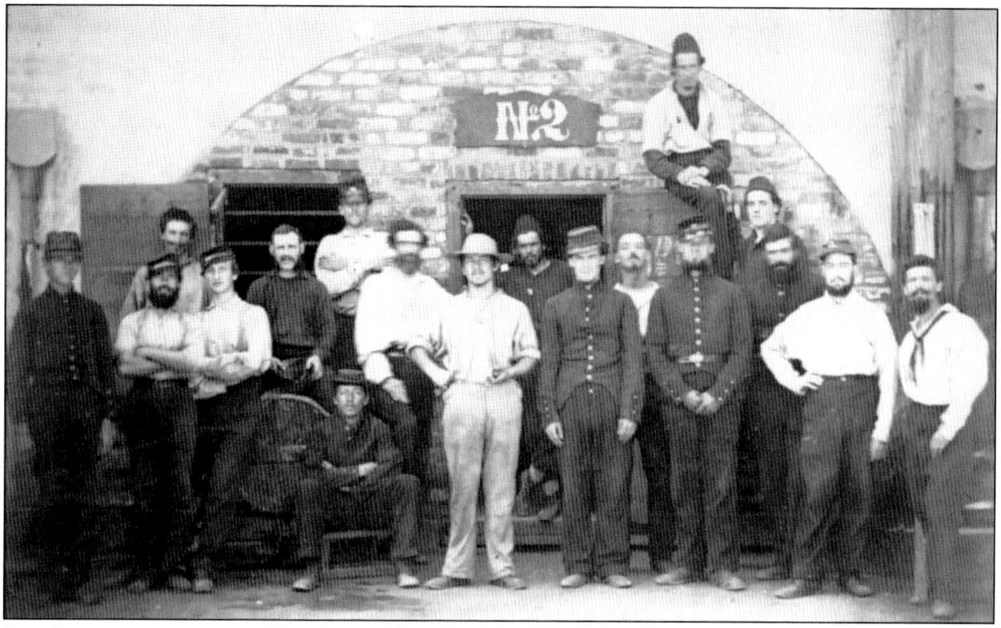

Popular consensus in the North was that the Confederate forces would be quickly repulsed and crushed. The reality, however, was the exact opposite. The Confederates outmaneuvered and outfought the Federals and, by the end of the day, had routed them back to Washington, DC. The Union soldiers shown here were among those who fell captive to the Confederates and were subsequently interned in prisoner-of-war camps throughout the South.

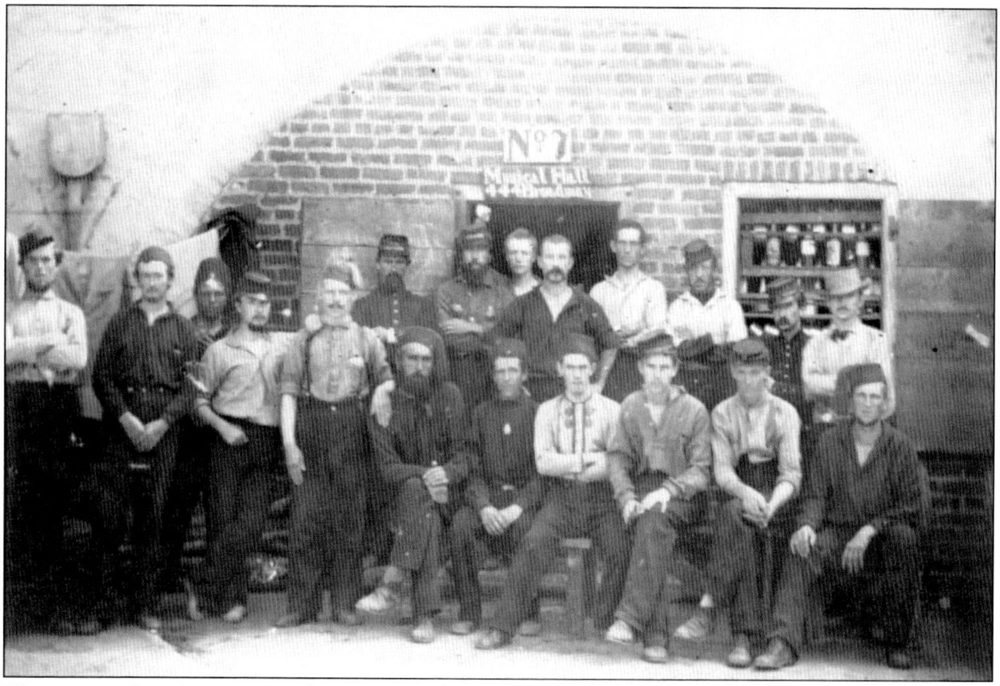

This is another fascinating photograph of Union troops being held in a Southern prisoner-of-war camp. Union forces at Manassas, raised from different states, adhered to different uniform regulations and designs. Note the differences in attire exhibited by these prisoners.

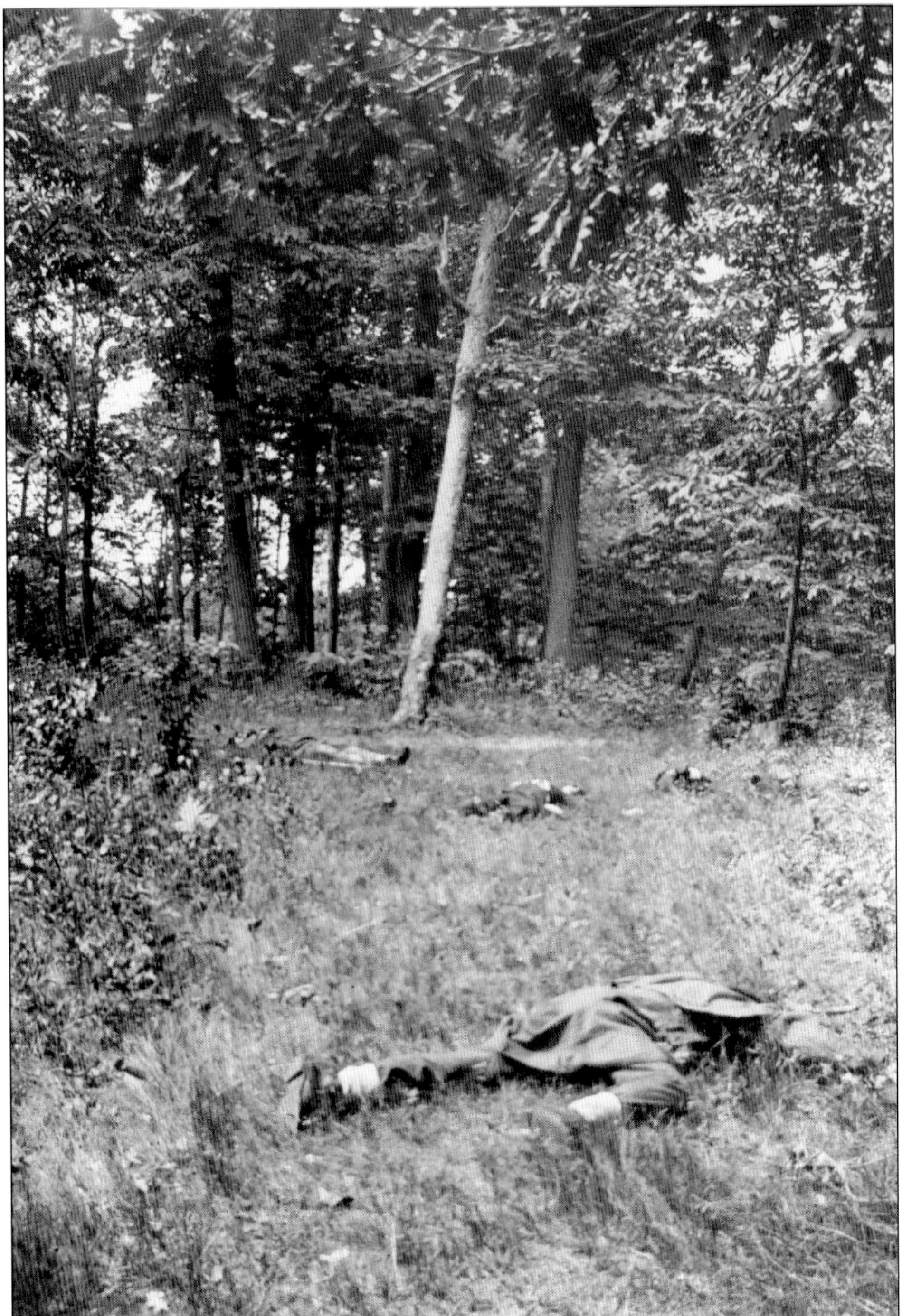

This sobering photograph shows the harsh realities of war. This small clearing, obviously the scene of intense fighting, is strewn with a few dead infantrymen. The carnage at First Manassas (called the First Battle of Bull Run by Northerners) surprised all levels of military leadership. Furthermore, the battlefield encompassed so much territory that it took weeks to gather the dead. In many instances, deceased soldiers remained unburied for weeks.

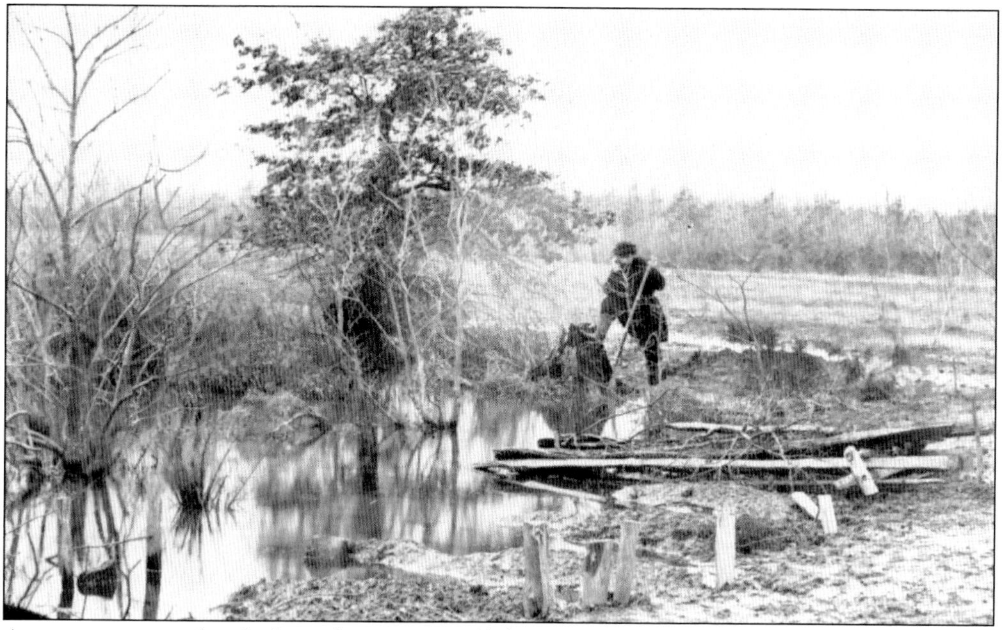

A watery grave and a plank tombstone were all that these fallen soldiers received in the wake of the battle at Manassas. Following many clashes during the war, armies would be forced to quickly extricate themselves from the field, leaving many wounded or dead behind. The cleanup was often left to the local civilian population.

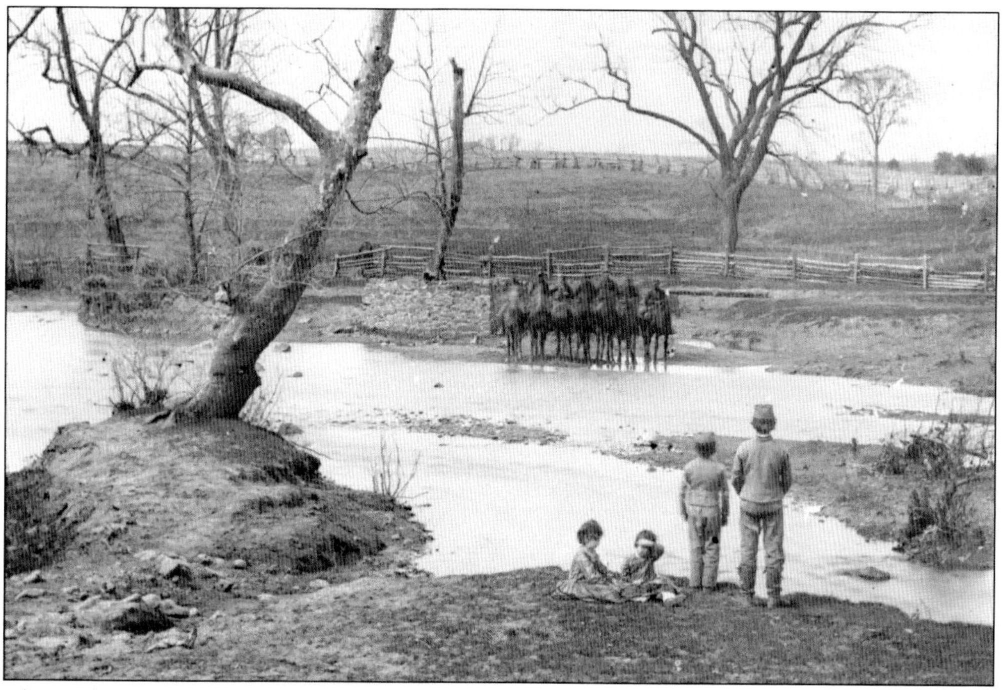

The realities of any civil war often involve close interaction between military and civilian populations. Here, a few young children face a cadre of Federal cavalry across a stream. The photograph was taken somewhere near Sudley Ford following the conclusion of the Battle of First Manassas.

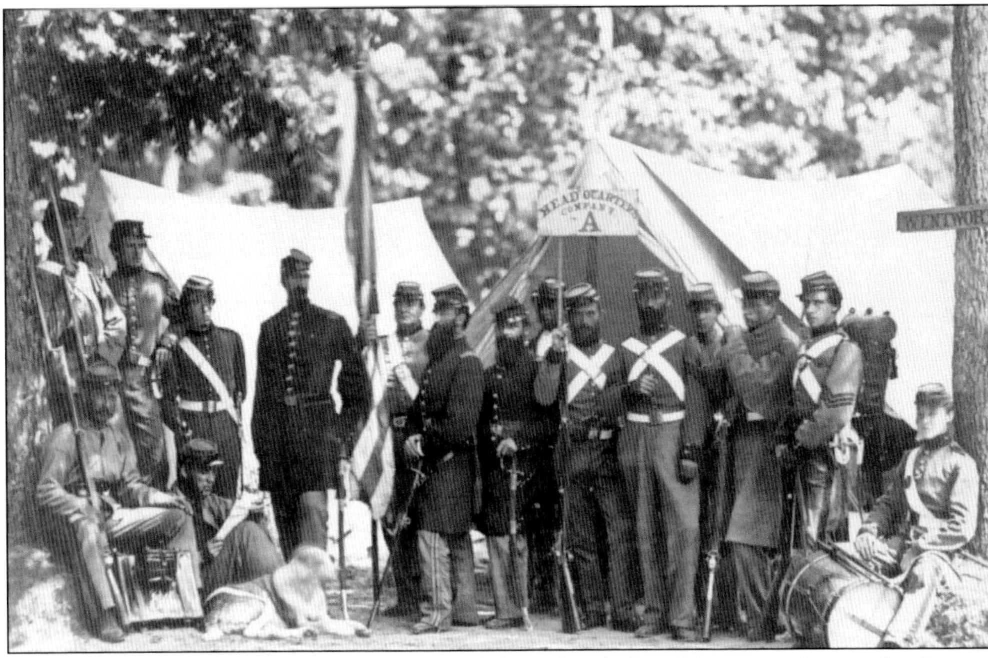

Despite the horrifying bloodshed that resulted from the clash at Manassas, thousands of troops continued to volunteer on both sides. The Union continued to amass units along the Virginia side of the Potomac River, awaiting their next move. Pictured here is Company A of the 8th New York State Militia. This unit, and others like it, were stationed at Arlington, Virginia.

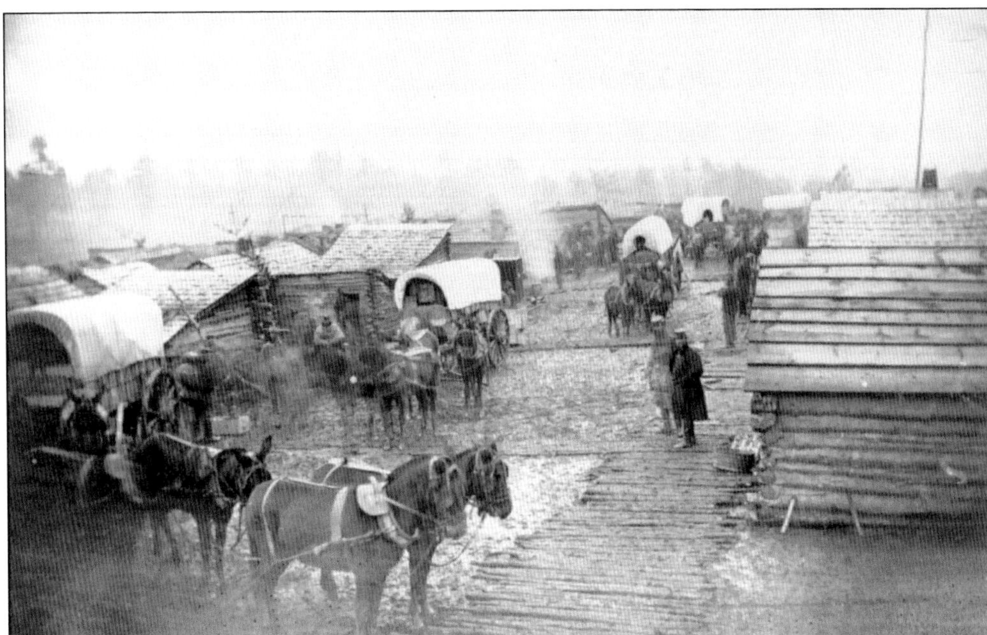

First Manassas was one of the only major battles that occurred in Virginia in the first year of the war. In winter, it was common for armies to construct elaborate camps, as military maneuvers became increasingly difficult to conduct. Shown here are the cold, muddy conditions of a Union camp somewhere near Centerville.

Two

Contested Territory

The year 1862 saw Virginia become the predominant battleground in the eastern theater of the war. Hundreds of thousands of men were engaged on both sides by mid-1862, and each had their own reasons for giving their lives. The motivations for fighting were as numerous as the number of people involved and cannot be distilled into simplistic, easy answers. Passions ran high, and brothers found themselves fighting on opposite sides—more than once, separated by only a few hundred yards on the field of battle. As the year progressed, Pres. Abraham Lincoln began a search for someone to command an army tasked with capturing the Confederate capital at Richmond. After replacing Gen. Irvin McDowell, Lincoln chose George B. McClellan to seize the rebellious Confederate city.

Although Lincoln had high hopes for his generals, the Union and the world were shocked by Robert E. Lee's ability to thwart Federal efforts to destroy the Confederacy in Virginia. In 1862, Lee won numerous decisive victories, spiraling the North's civilian population into progressively lower morale. The Peninsula campaign, Second Manassas, and Fredericksburg resulted in resounding Confederate victories. Foreign powers, including England and France, began to be persuaded to increase their support for the burgeoning Confederacy. Also in 1862, vast technological advances took place. The first ironclad naval vessels clashed at Hampton Roads. The Confederacy gained additional success in the Shenandoah Valley, profoundly affecting the conduct of the war for the next few years. Stonewall Jackson shocked military theorists throughout Europe with his bold techniques, ensuring his position as a hero of the Confederacy and a military genius.

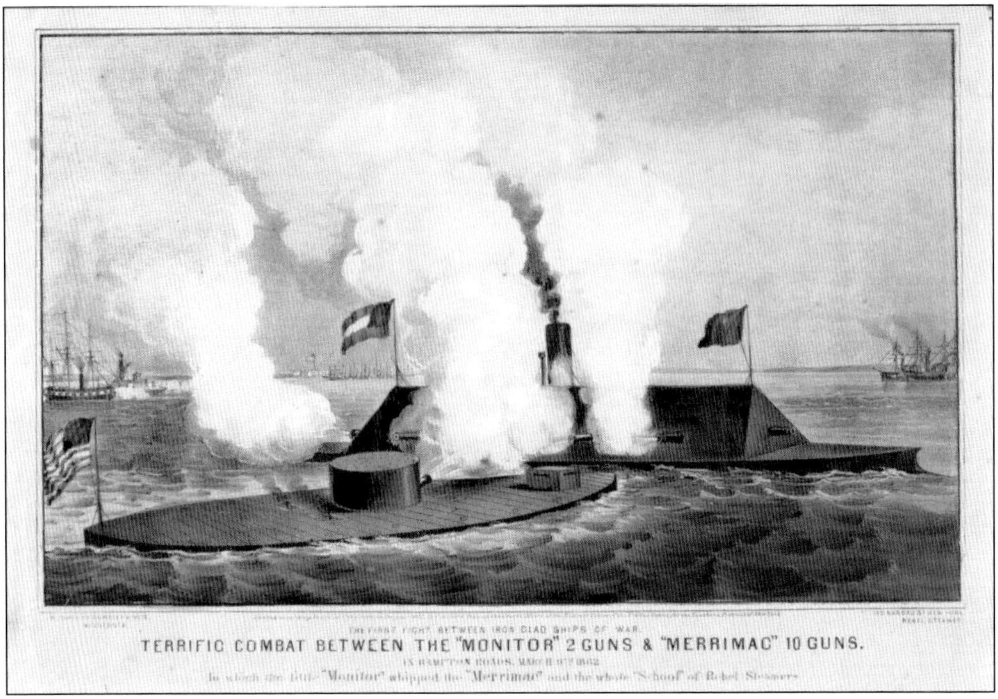

Many people associate the Civil War in Virginia with large-scale infantry engagements, such as Fredericksburg and Petersburg. However, the war also witnessed significant naval action that changed ocean warfare for decades. On March 9, 1862, two state-of-the-art vessels clashed at Hampton Roads, stunning the nation and navies throughout the world. This illustration depicts the battle between the Union-built *Monitor* and the Confederate *Merrimack*.

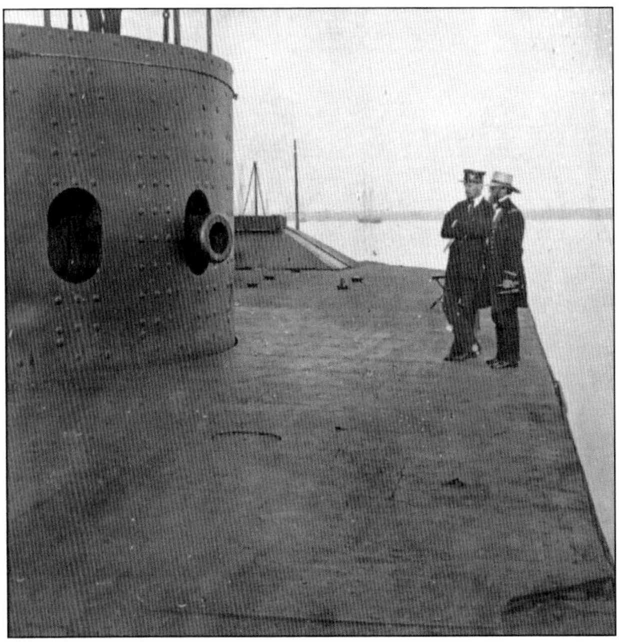

These vessels were the first to utilize iron to create a protective layer against enemy ordnance. The *Monitor* and the *Merrimack* differed in design, but they were similar in that both enjoyed the benefits of thick armor plating. In fact, both vessels were so well constructed that the battle was inconclusive, as neither ship was able to sink the other, despite the firing of hundreds of rounds. This close-up view of the deck of the *Monitor* demonstrates the robustness of its design. The first of their kind, these vessels ushered in a new era of ship design that would culminate during World War II with vessels like the USS *Arizona* and the German battleship *Bismarck*.

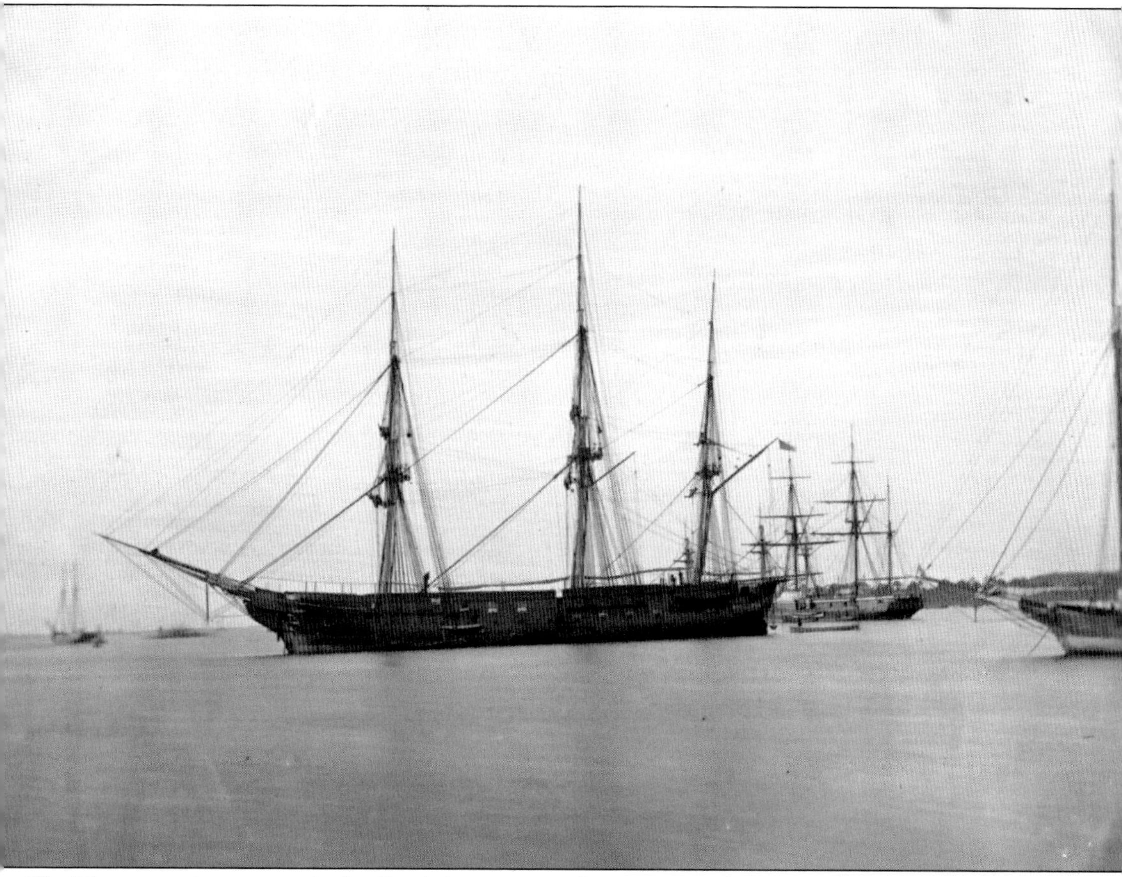

The Union sought to strangle the Confederacy into submission, employing an elaborate blockade at various ports throughout the South. This action was designed to restrict foreign trade to Richmond and Norfolk, thus hampering the Confederate economy. Here, Union sailing vessels near the Chesapeake Bay stand sentry along the waterway once controlled by the Confederacy.

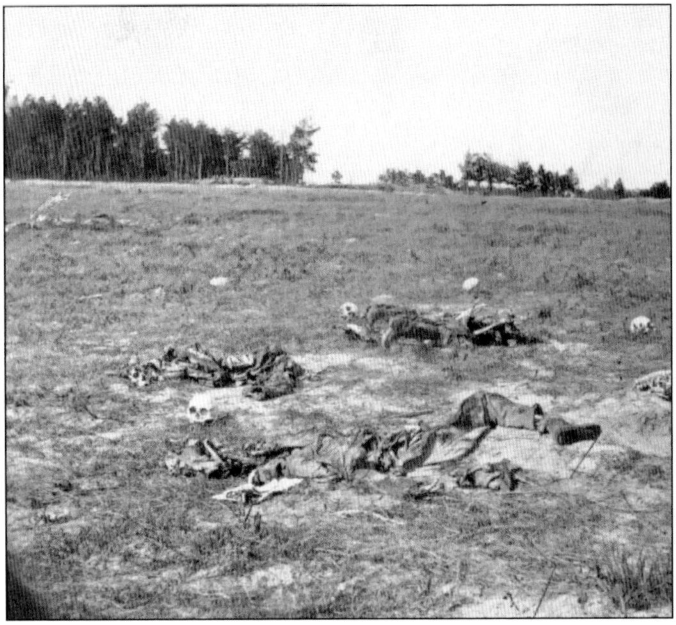

The Union sought to quickly end the war by capturing the Confederate capital at Richmond. To do this, President Lincoln ordered Gen. George B. McClellan to take an army to Richmond, using water routes south of the city. What became known as the Peninsula campaign culminated in seven days of brutal fighting from June 25 to July 1, 1862. Pictured here are unburied bodies from the fighting near Gaines' Mill.

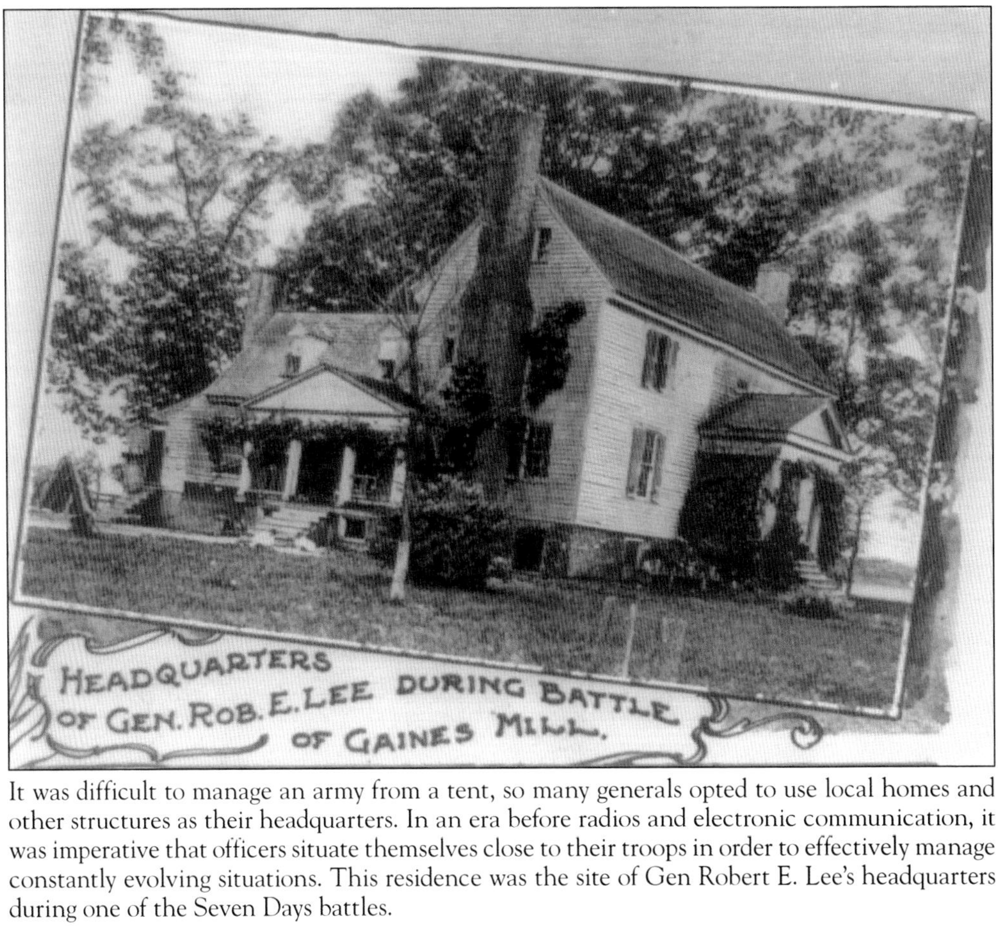

It was difficult to manage an army from a tent, so many generals opted to use local homes and other structures as their headquarters. In an era before radios and electronic communication, it was imperative that officers situate themselves close to their troops in order to effectively manage constantly evolving situations. This residence was the site of Gen Robert E. Lee's headquarters during one of the Seven Days battles.

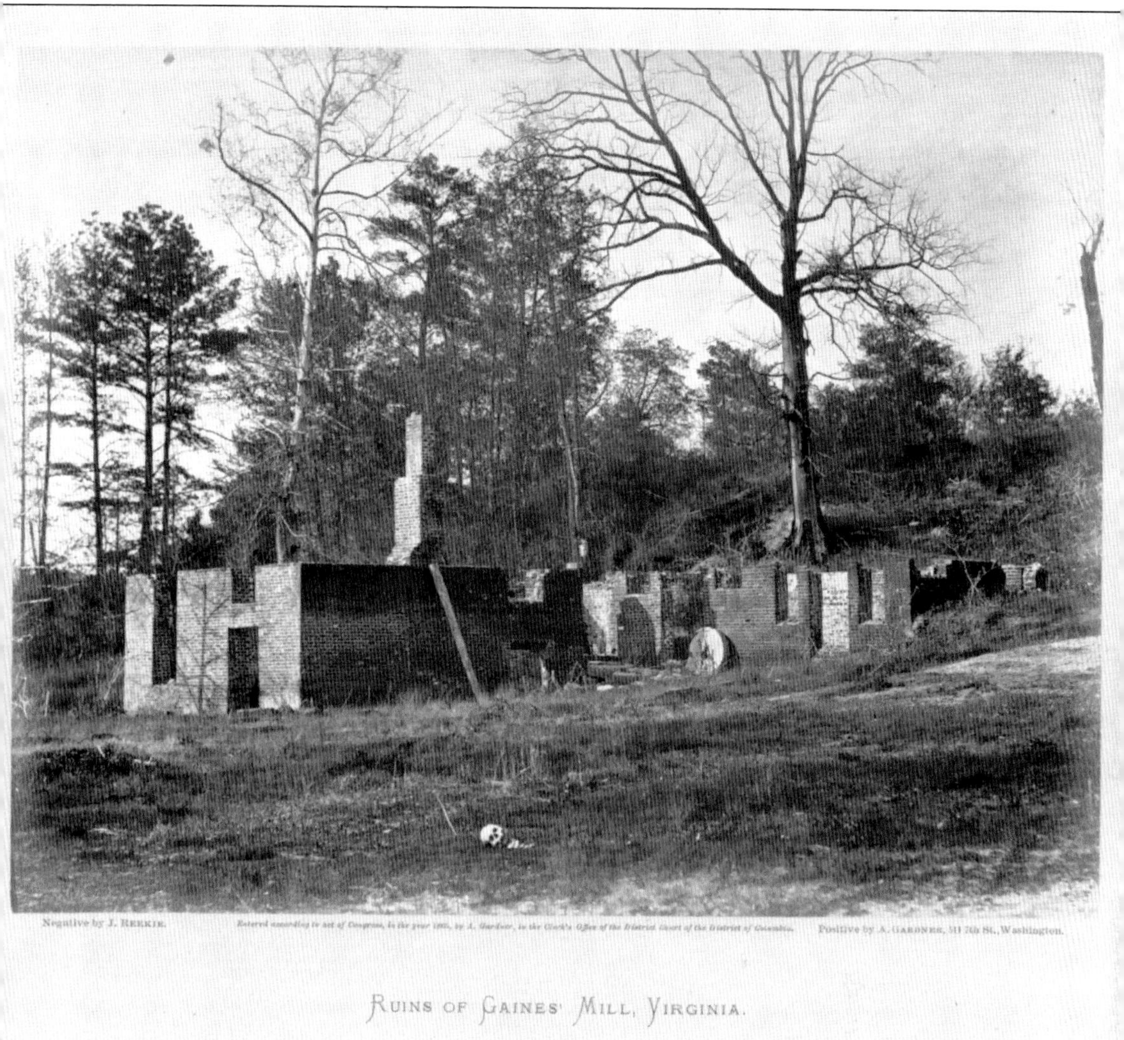

The intense fighting that transpired at Seven Days swept over local farmland and took a tremendous toll on private property. Pictured here are the remnants of Gaines' Mill after it was destroyed by fire. The loss of such a vital part of the local infrastructure was a lasting reminder of the horrors of war. The damage resulting from many battles was never repaired; communities felt the effects of these clashes for decades.

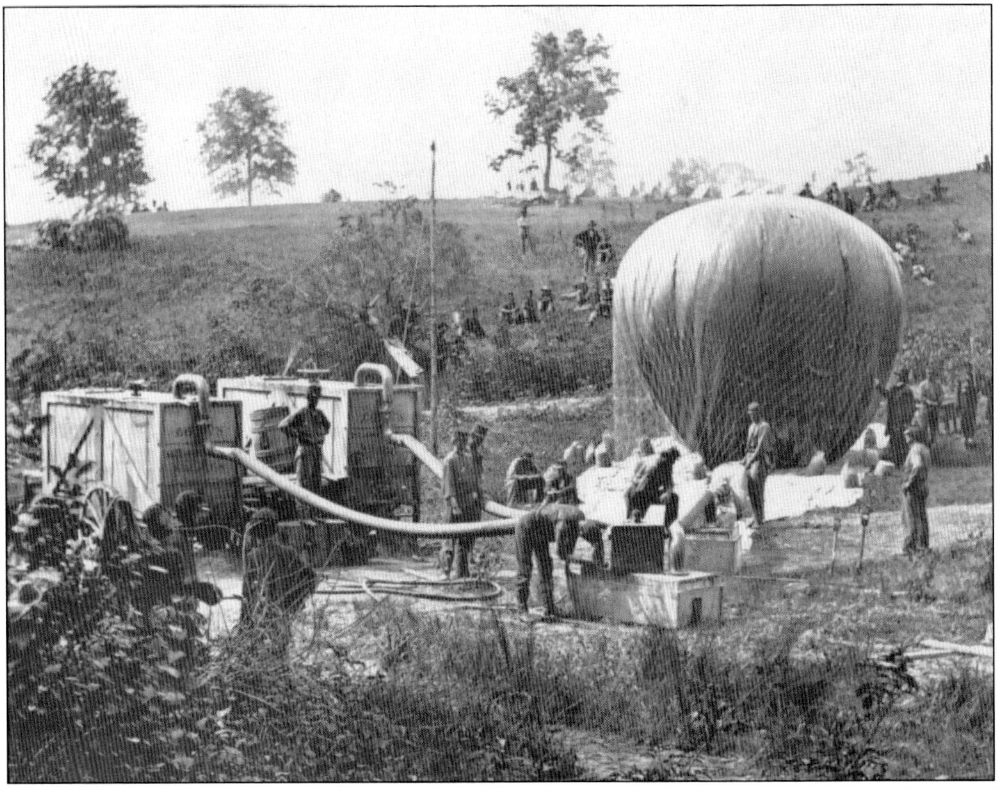

The war in Virginia saw numerous technological innovations and curiosities, including the use of balloons for reconnaissance purposes. Balloons offered generals an opportunity to observe enemy positions and movements often obstructed by topographic obstacles, such as forests and hills. Seen here is one of Thaddeus Lowe's observation balloons during the Seven Days.

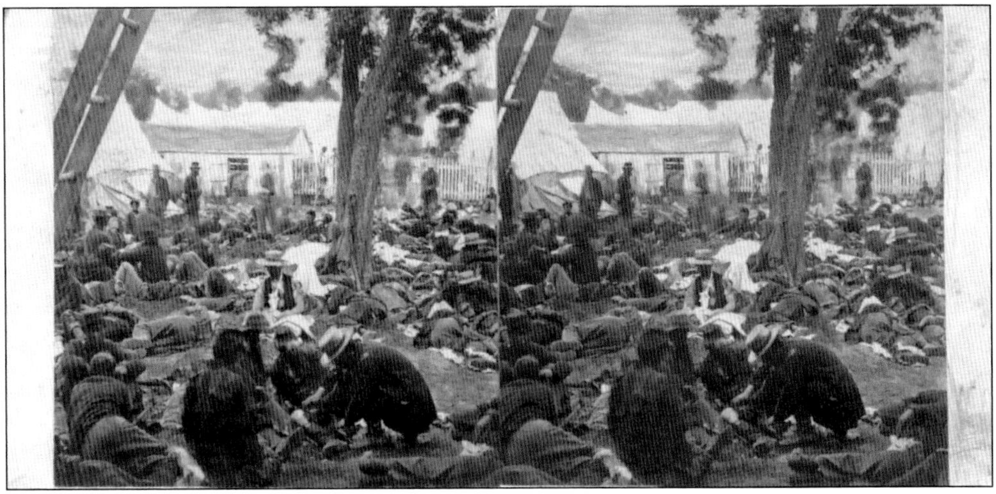

Both sides were shocked at the devastating effectiveness of rifle and cannon fire. Reports often described incoming volleys of enemy fire as sounding like rain, as the lead projectiles slammed into human flesh. The terror of seeing friends and family dying around them haunted combatants for the rest of their lives. Those who were not killed instantly often died agonizing deaths in field hospitals, such as this one, established following the Seven Days.

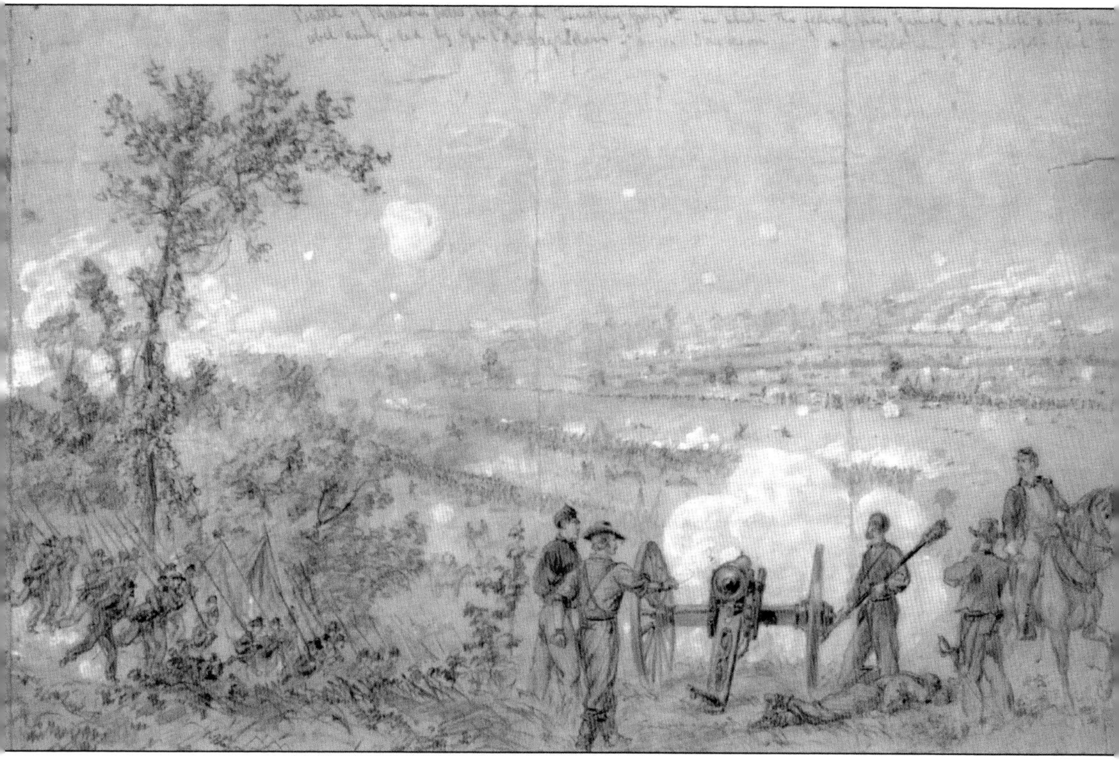

This artist's rendering of the Battle of Malvern Hill portrays Union artillery firing on the distant Confederate battle line. The bloody July 1 encounter resulted in fierce fighting and many dead and wounded. In the foreground is a Union Parrott rifle, which had an effective range of over one mile. Weapons used during the Civil War resembled those in the American Revolution, but only in appearance. Weapons of the Civil War were immensely more effective, and at significantly longer ranges, than their predecessors.

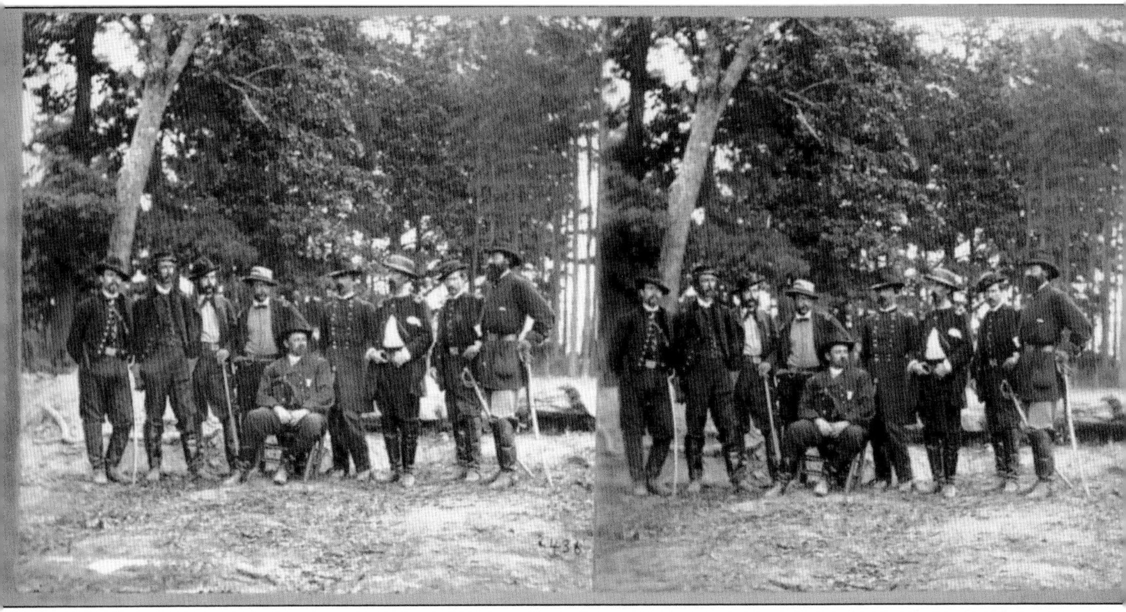

This fascinating photograph of Union general W.F. "Baldy" Smith and his cadre of officers was taken during the Seven Days. Smith, a controversial figure, received much praise for his gallantry during the campaign around Richmond. Note the wide array of uniforms worn by the officers. Many saw the Confederates as lacking general uniformity, but this image is evidence that the Federals also donned diverse attire.

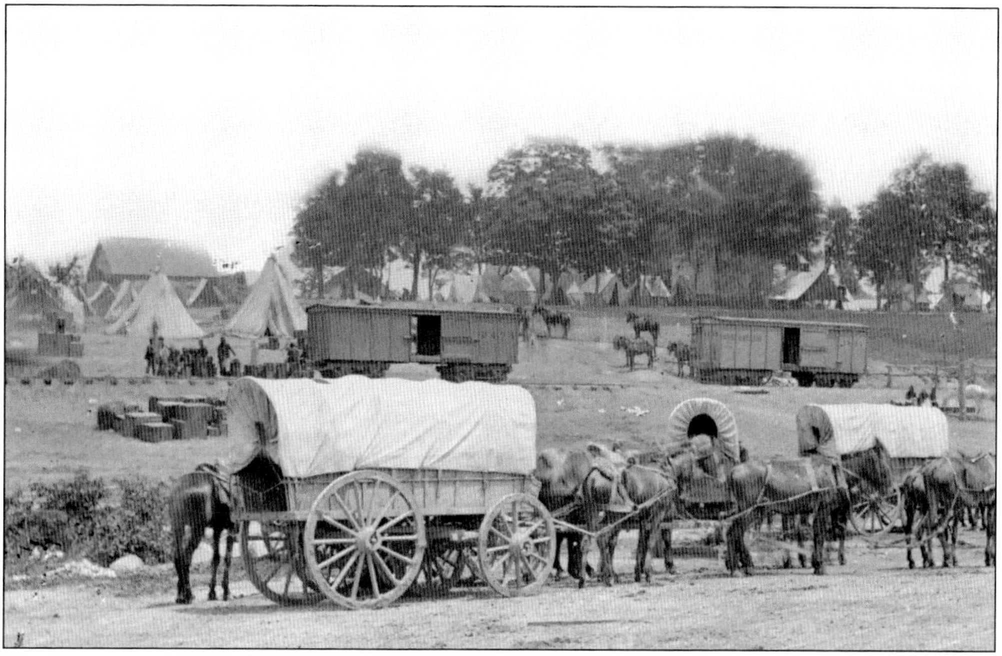

The large armies of the day often comprised tens of thousands of men who consumed a tremendous amount of food and ammunition. This necessitated that the armies on both sides transport food and supplies via wagon trains, some of which stretched for miles. Seen here are wagons at Gen. George McClellan's headquarters at Savage Station, Virginia.

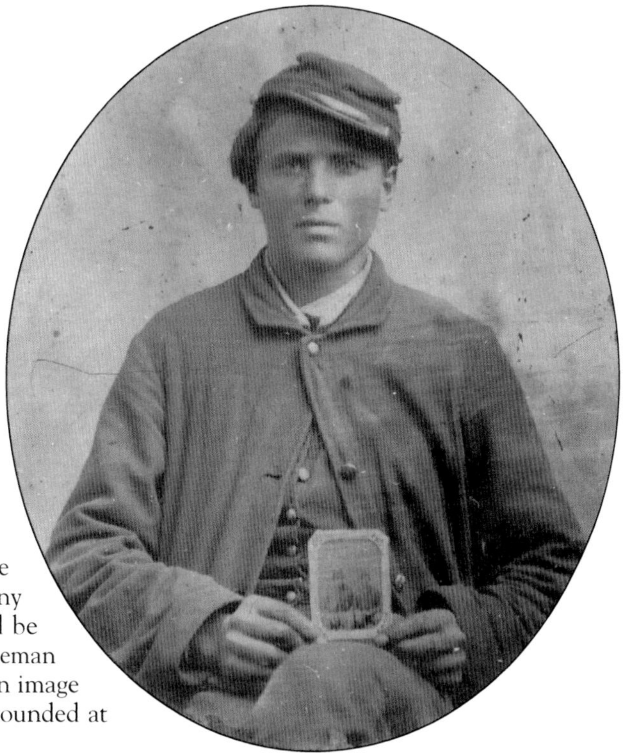

It was not uncommon for units in both Confederate and Union armies to have brothers fighting alongside each other. Often, brothers, caught up in nationalistic fervor, would enlist together and would be subsequently placed in the same regiment. Tragically, in many instances, these loved ones would be separated by death in battle. Here, Freeman Mason of the 17th Vermont holds an image of his brother, who was mortally wounded at Savage Station, Virginia, in 1862.

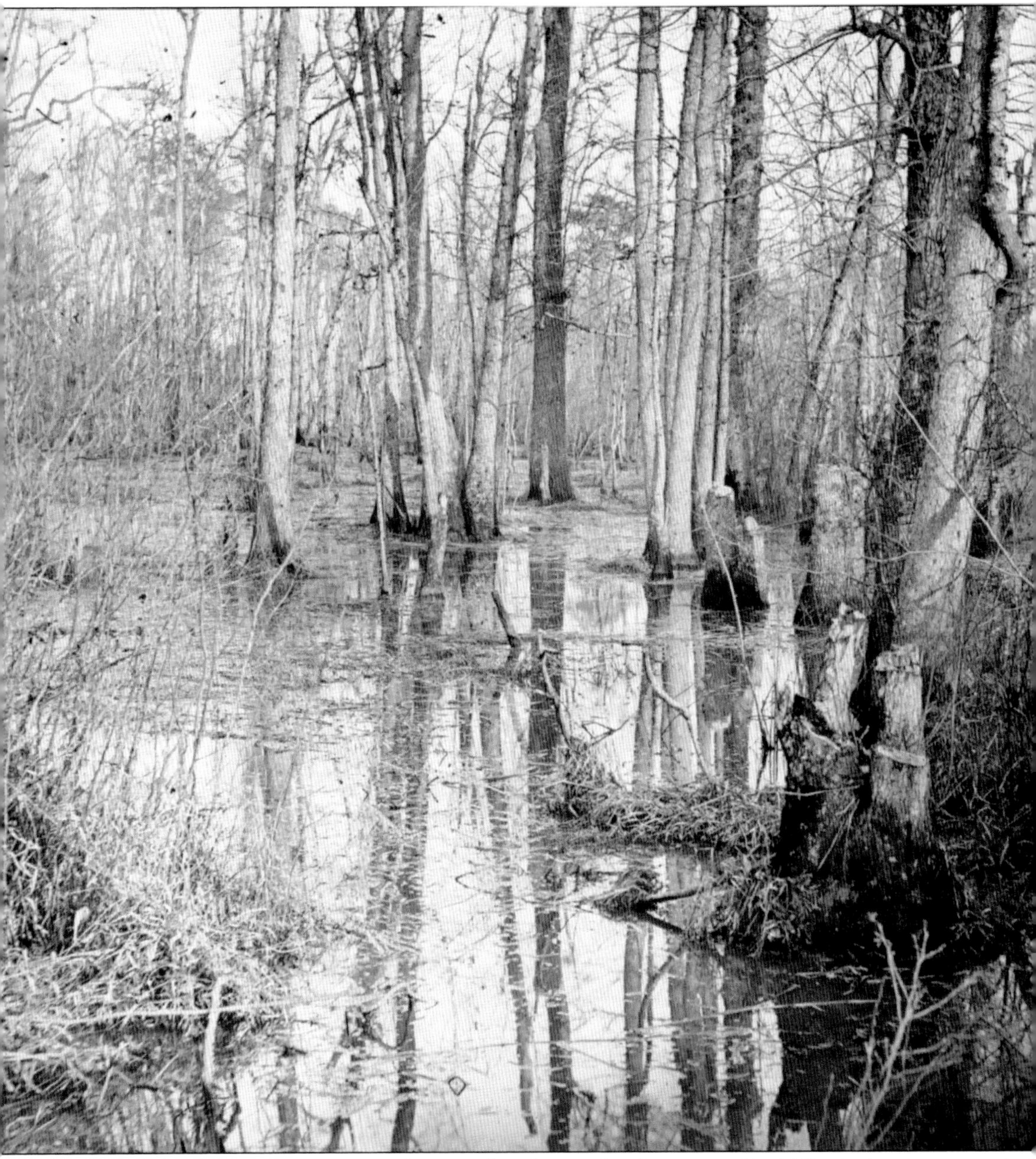

A modern misconception regarding combat during the American Civil War is that it occurred over sweeping plains, where both armies could maneuver into neat, Napoleonic-style rows. This, however, was rarely the case. On many occasions, combat transpired over the most treacherous topography and in the roughest of environments, as generals continually attempted to surprise or outmaneuver their opponents. The swampy location seen here was home to some of the fighting during the Seven Days.

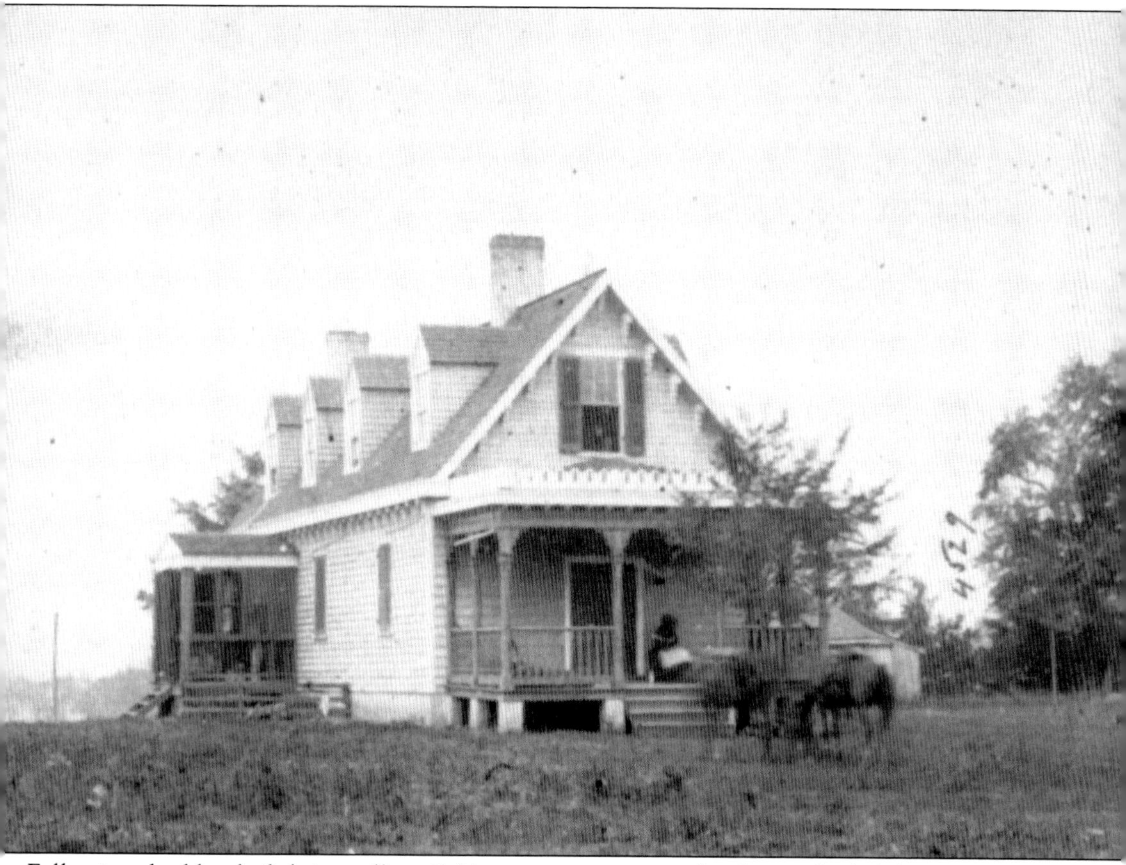

Following the bloody fighting, all available structures were utilized as makeshift hospitals in a desperate attempt to get the critically wounded out of the unbearable heat and elements. Unfortunately, these hospitals would quickly become overcrowded, as thousands of dying were funneled to these locations for treatment. Haxall's House (pictured) was used as a hospital after the clash at White Oak Swamp. One can only imagine the frantic and desperate attempts of doctors to save the lives of thousands of injured young men.

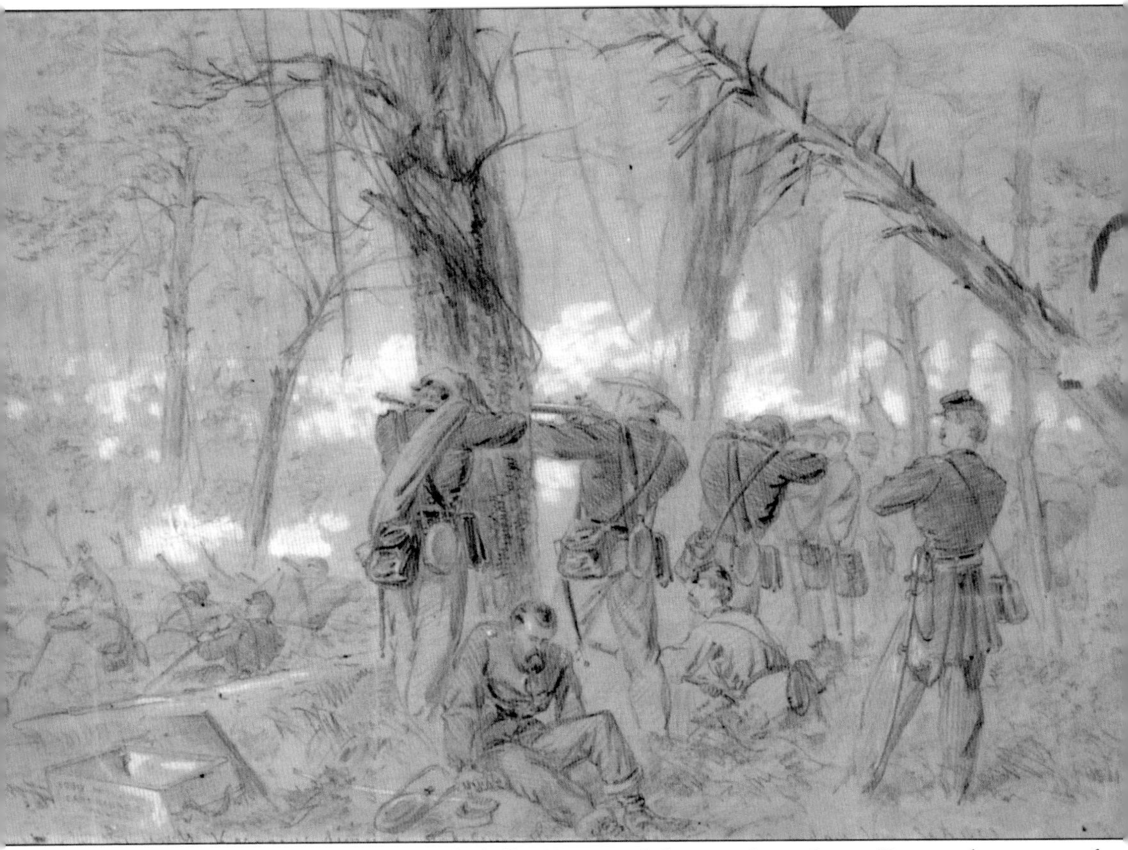

Here, troops under Union general Phillip Kearney fight in a dense forest. During the course of the fight, near Glendale, the smoke from the rifle fire became so thick that it was difficult to discern the enemy battle line. Reports from the clash indicate that one could only hear the cries of the wounded and dying through the fog of battle. Kearney led his troops quite well during the battle. He was killed a few months later by enemy fire at the Battle of Chantilly.

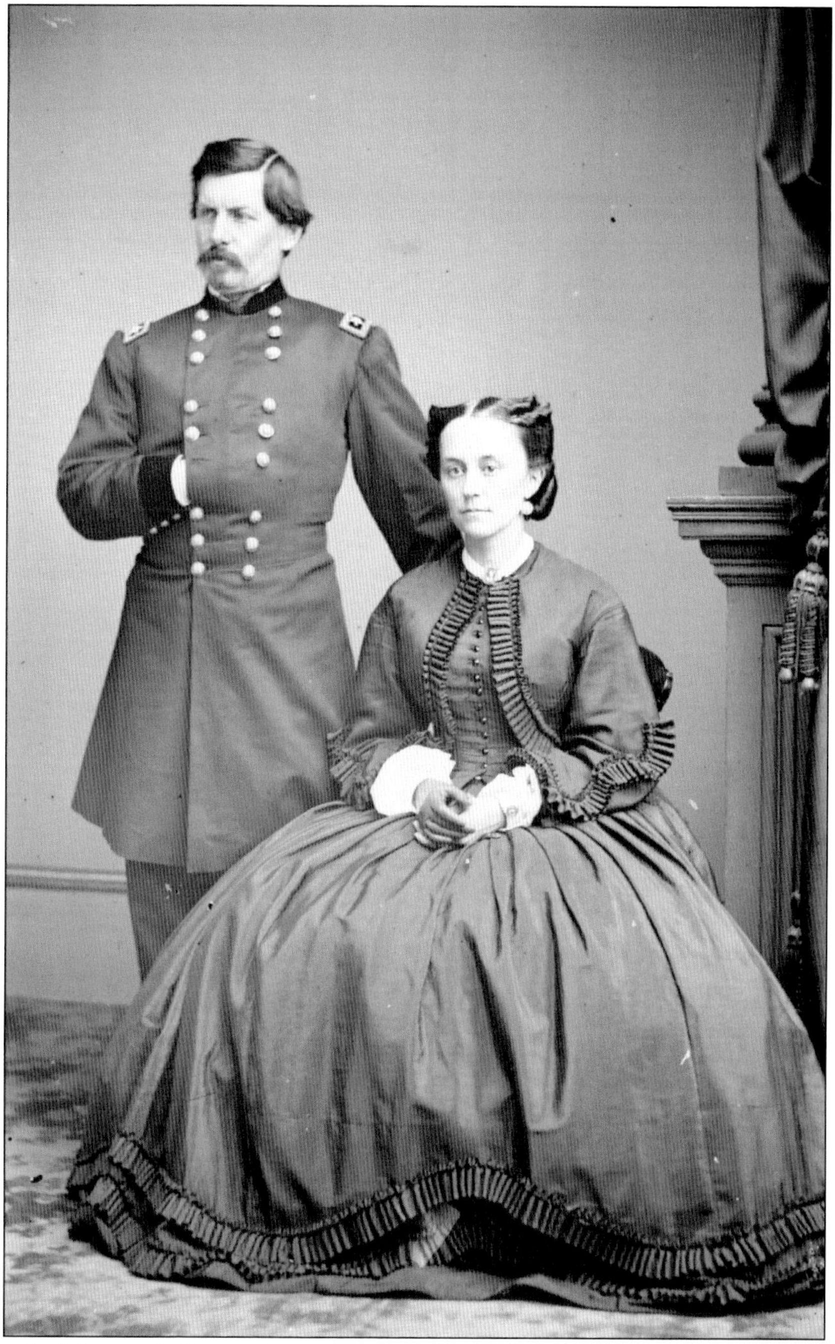

At the end of the costly Peninsula campaign, the Union military had little to show but heavy losses and a beleaguered army. President Lincoln had trusted George McClellan with command of an entire army to capture Richmond, but the general had been thwarted at every turn. McClellan had proven to be overly cautious, often missing crucial opportunities to strike at the Confederates. Although he failed in his campaign to capture Richmond, McClellan remained immensely popular in the Union. Like the great generals of antiquity, he eventually moved into the political arena.

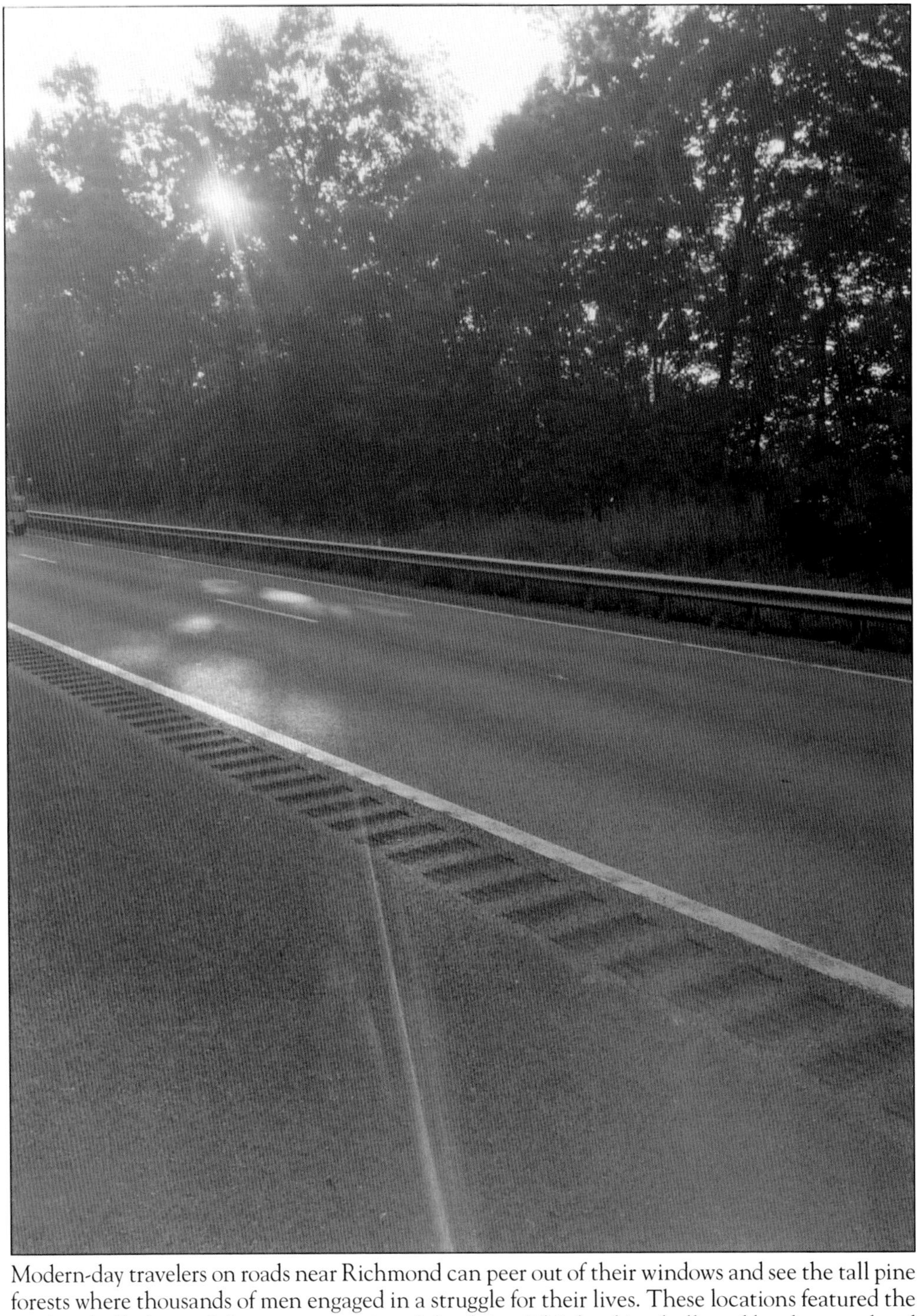

Modern-day travelers on roads near Richmond can peer out of their windows and see the tall pine forests where thousands of men engaged in a struggle for their lives. These locations featured the smoke of rifle fire and the agonizing cries of the dying. This land is a hallowed battleground and an integral part of the American story. (Author's collection.)

Although many consider Robert E. Lee to be almost synonymous with the Confederate military and its endeavors throughout the war, he was not, in fact, the supreme commander of forces in the field until after the Peninsula campaign. During the campaign, the Confederate army in Virginia was under the command of Gen. Joseph E. Johnston, but Lee soon assumed command when Johnston was wounded at the Battle of Seven Pines.

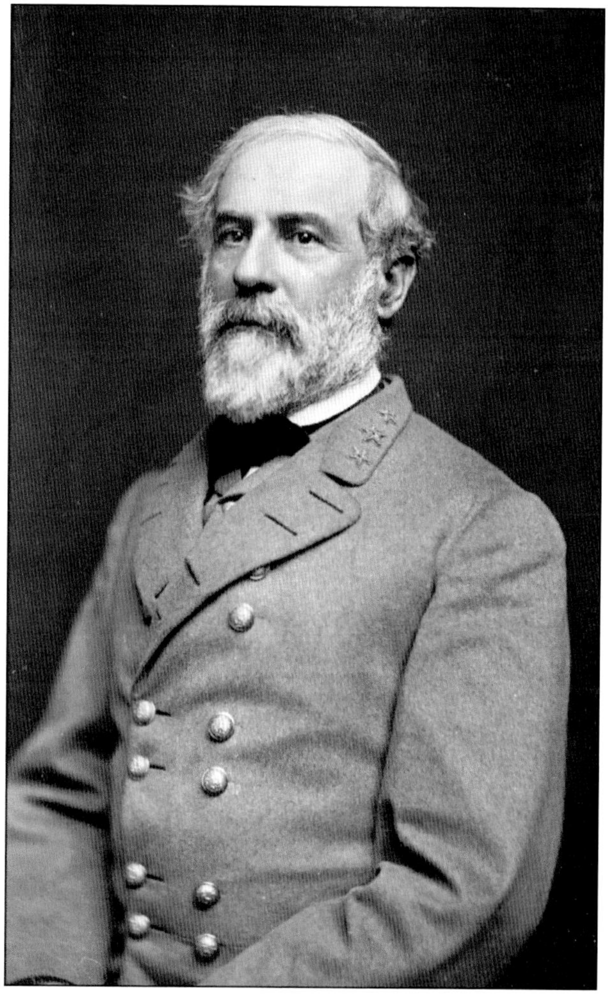

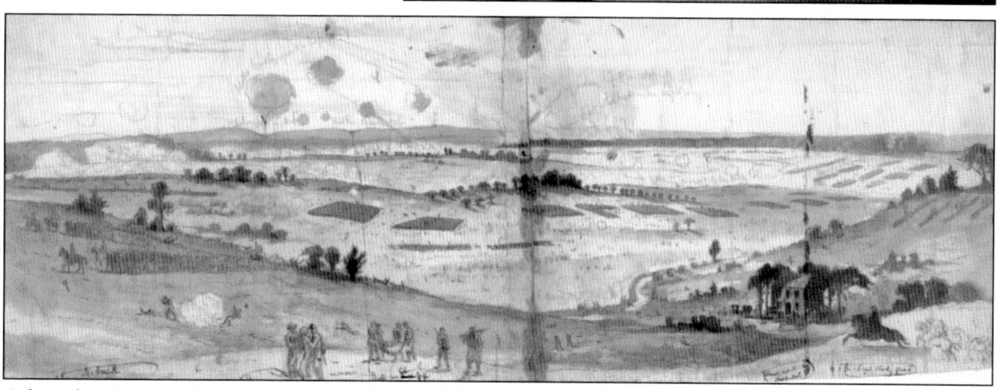

After the Peninsula campaign, the Federal army moved back toward Washington, and elements of the Confederate army worked their way north in pursuit. Often, roads and railways would force armies toward natural bottlenecks and junctions. Manassas was one such place. In late August 1862, both armies clashed on the same ground where they had fought the previous year at First Manassas. This is a battlefield sketch of the engagement around Manassas and Groveton, Virginia, during Second Manassas (Second Battle of Bull Run).

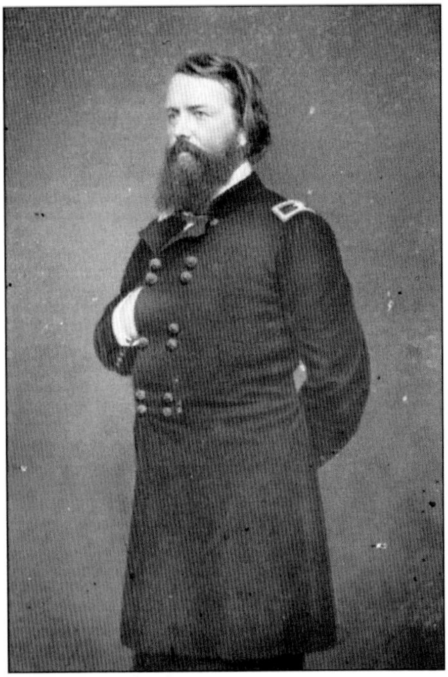

Following George McClellan's poor performance around Richmond, President Lincoln promptly replaced him with Gen. John Pope, who had performed reasonably well prior to being given command of an entire army. Lincoln hoped he would be able to defeat Lee's Confederates quickly and decisively. Although Pope was a competent commander, he proved to be no match for the military genius of Lee and was unable to thwart Lee's tactical prowess at the Battle of Second Manassas.

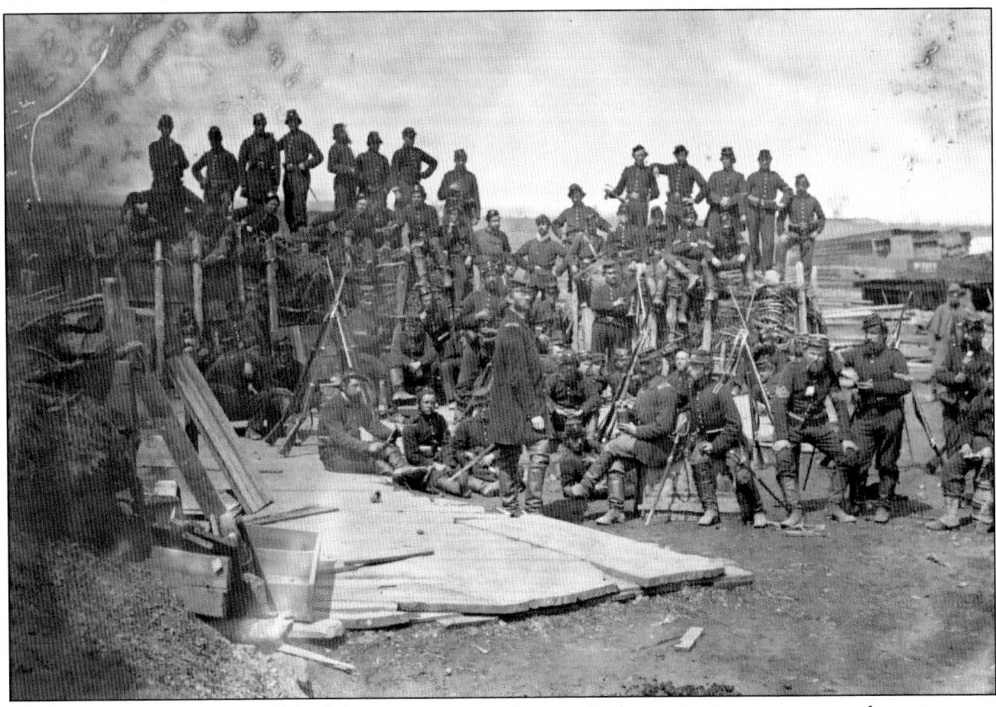

The war in Virginia exemplified the importance of numerical superiority; strategy and tactics were heavily dictated by the number of troops available for combat. This gave the Union a tremendous advantage throughout the war, as it could rely on its densely populated states to fill the ranks of its armies. Second Manassas was no exception to this numerical discrepancy, as John Pope's army drastically outnumbered Lee's troops. Pictured here are members of the 41st New York Infantry near Manassas, Virginia.

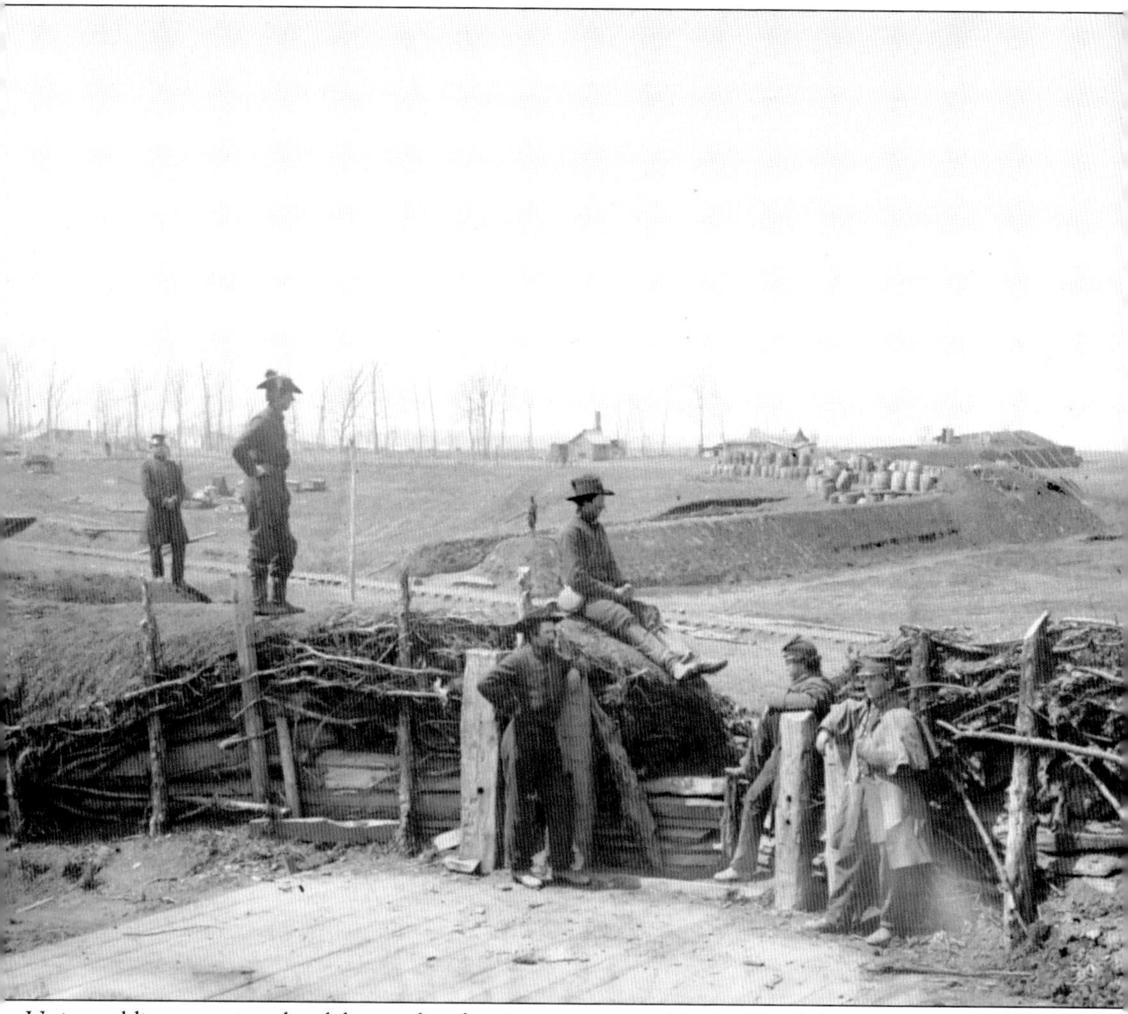

Union soldiers examine the elaborate fortifications constructed by the Confederates a year earlier at First Manassas. These well-constructed embankments more closely resemble a scene from World War I rather than a battlefield in the American Civil War, which is certainly a testament to the technical and military ingenuity of the time.

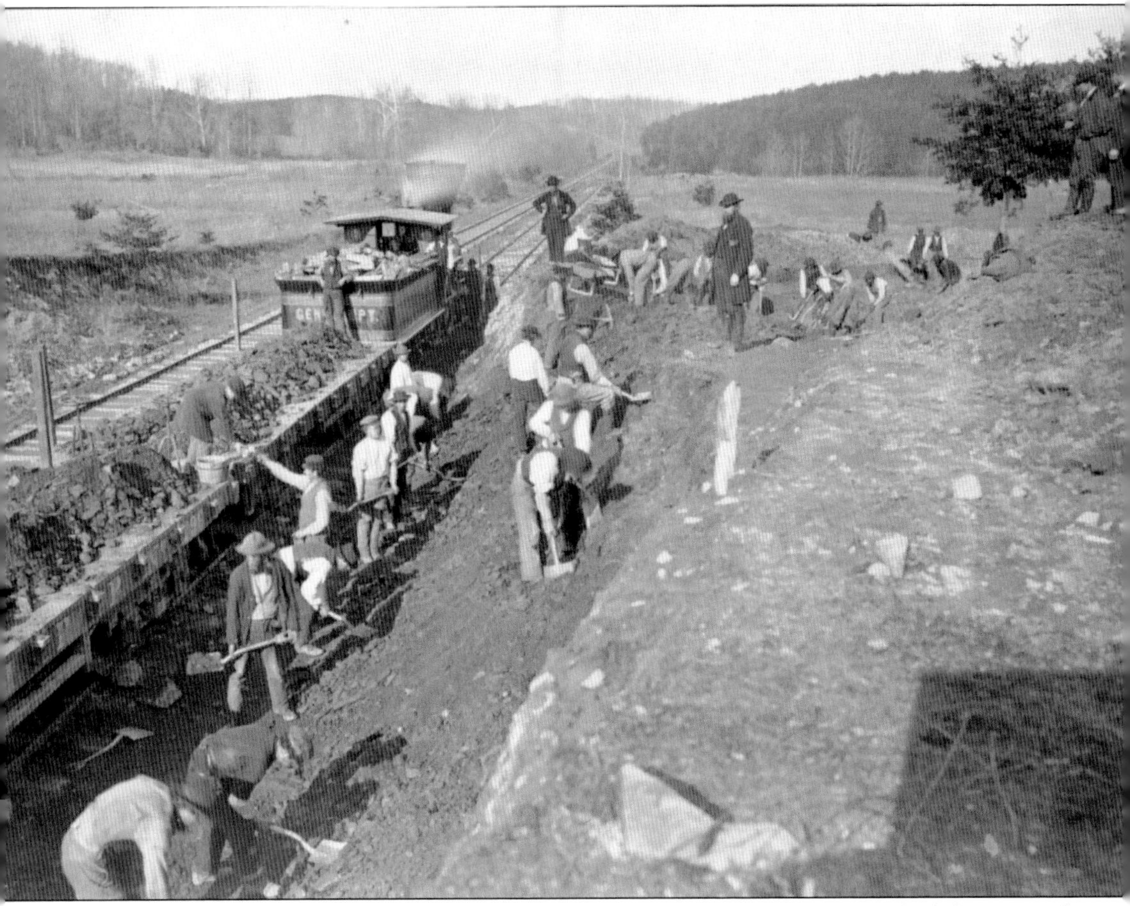

Not only were the Confederates outnumbered, but they suffered from supply deficiencies that inhibited their ability to challenge Pope's force. During the course of the fighting of Second Manassas, some Confederate units ran short on ammunition and took to throwing rocks from a nearby railroad cut, similar to the segment of track pictured here, at the advancing Union troops. This desperate measure demonstrates the tenacity with which many Southern units fought. Despite the profound shortfalls that militated against Lee's force, he was able to outsmart Pope and, in turn, won a decisive victory for the Confederates, much to the chagrin of Lincoln.

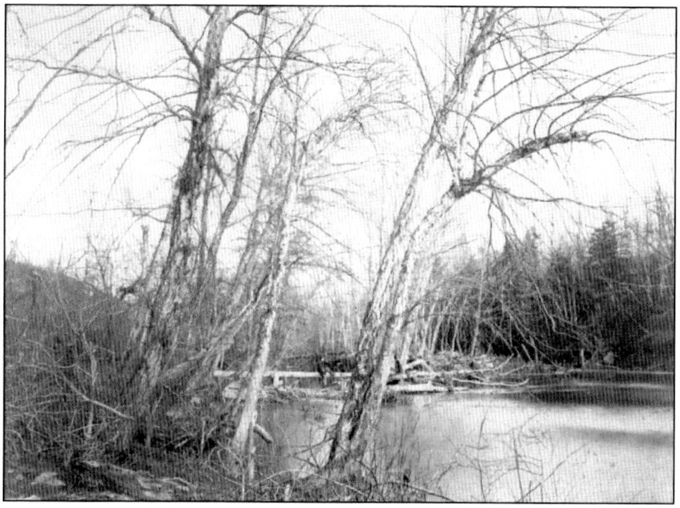

Many officers led from the front and aggressively managed their troops into battle. In late August 1862, near Centerville, Virginia, Brig. Gen. George W. Taylor's unit ran across a Confederate division and was involved in a violent clash near Bull Run. During the fighting, General Taylor was mortally wounded and died in Alexandria. Pictured here is the site of his fatal wounding.

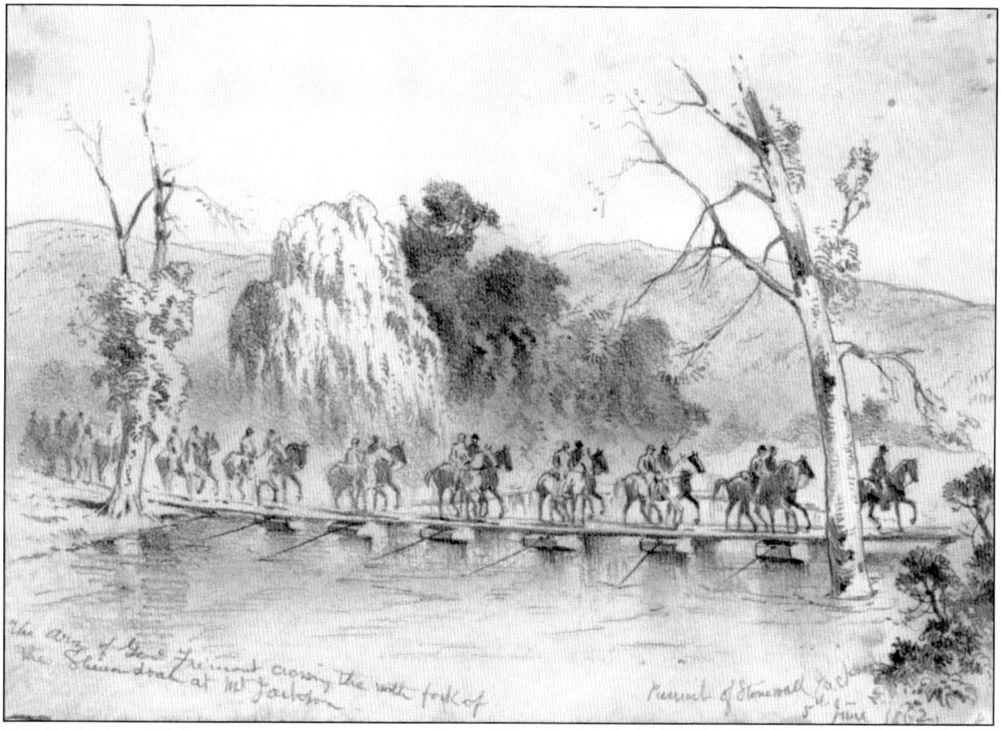

While Robert E. Lee was putting on an exposition in tactics and strategy in the eastern portion of the state, Gen. Thomas "Stonewall" Jackson was demonstrating the depth of his capabilities in the Shenandoah Valley. Jackson indelibly altered military doctrine for decades to come, demonstrating how a smaller force could achieve victory by rapidly moving to surprise the enemy, thus mitigating Confederate losses and wreaking havoc on Union operations. Jackson's tactics became world-renowned; the German Wehrmacht, prior to World War II, sent officers to the Shenandoah Valley to study Jackson's lightning-fast tactics. This is an artist's rendering of Union general John Frémont's forces attempting to catch Jackson's elusive army.

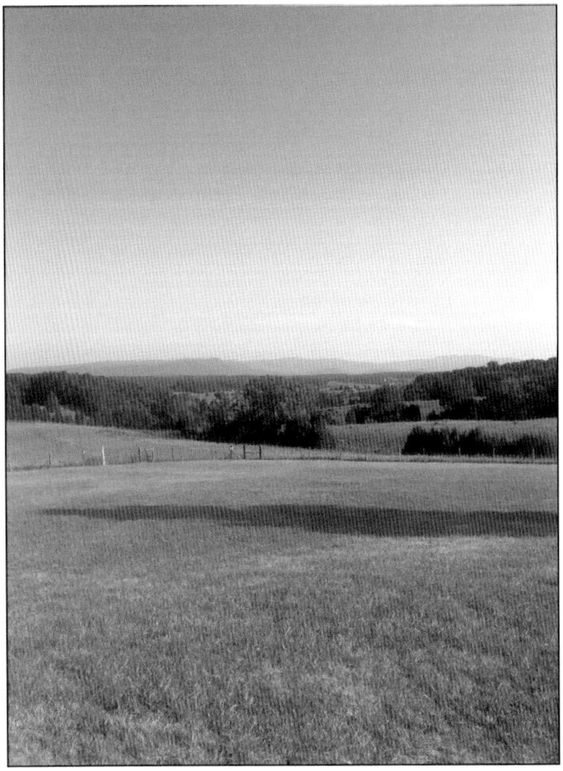

Today, much of the land on which countless clashes and skirmishes were fought has been obscured over time. Battlegrounds throughout the Shenandoah Valley and the rest of the state have become farms and neighborhoods. The locations of many clashes were not precisely recorded, and it is entirely possible that a current resident's property or neighborhood was the sight of troop movements or fighting. (Author's collection.)

While traveling up Interstate 81, through the Shenandoah Valley, drivers can imagine the surrounding bucolic scenery as, at one time, the highly contested ground and site of many of Gen. Thomas Jackson's greatest military achievements. What is now a serene highway was once a battleground where the fate of a nation was being determined. (Author's collection.)

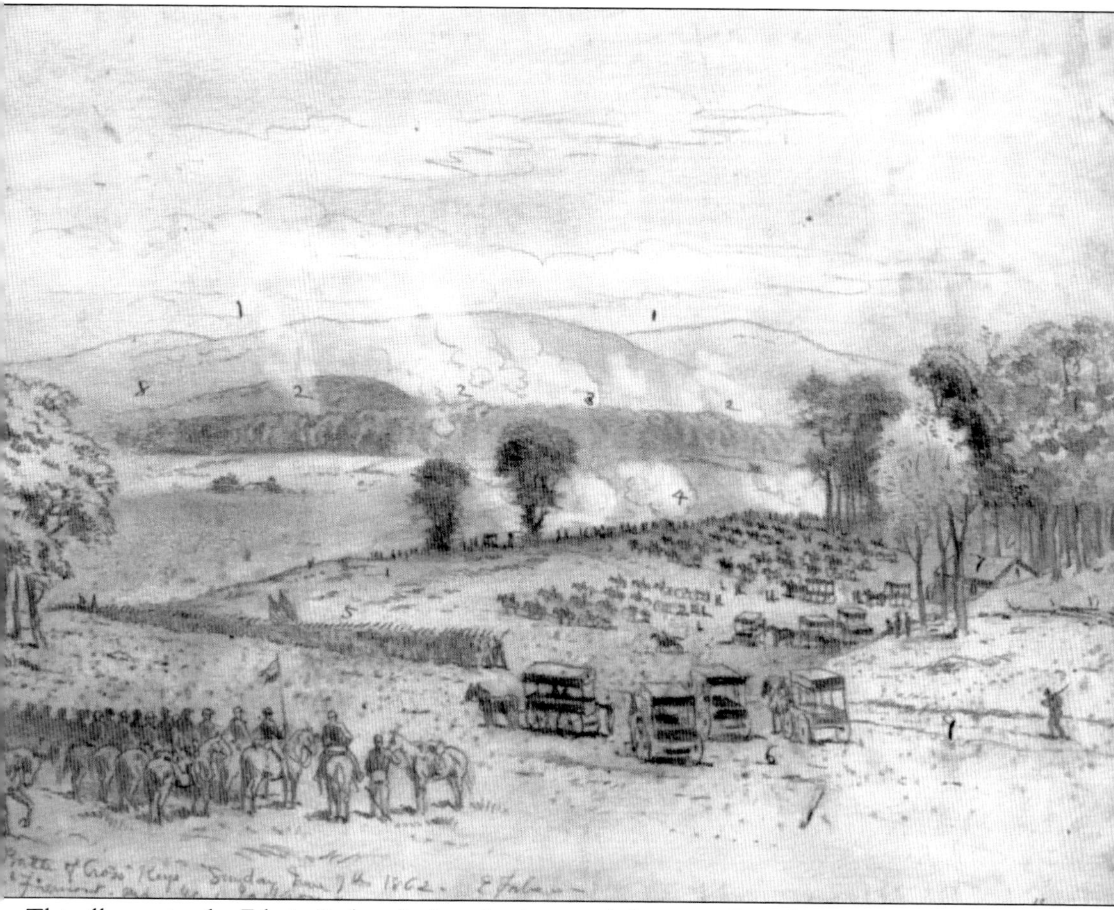

This illustration by Edwin Forbes depicts the intense fighting at Cross Keys, Virginia, where Jackson's diminutive force once again soundly defeated a larger Union contingent. This battle, one of the final clashes in Jackson's Shenandoah Valley campaign, set the stage for his elevation to greater responsibility in Lee's army.

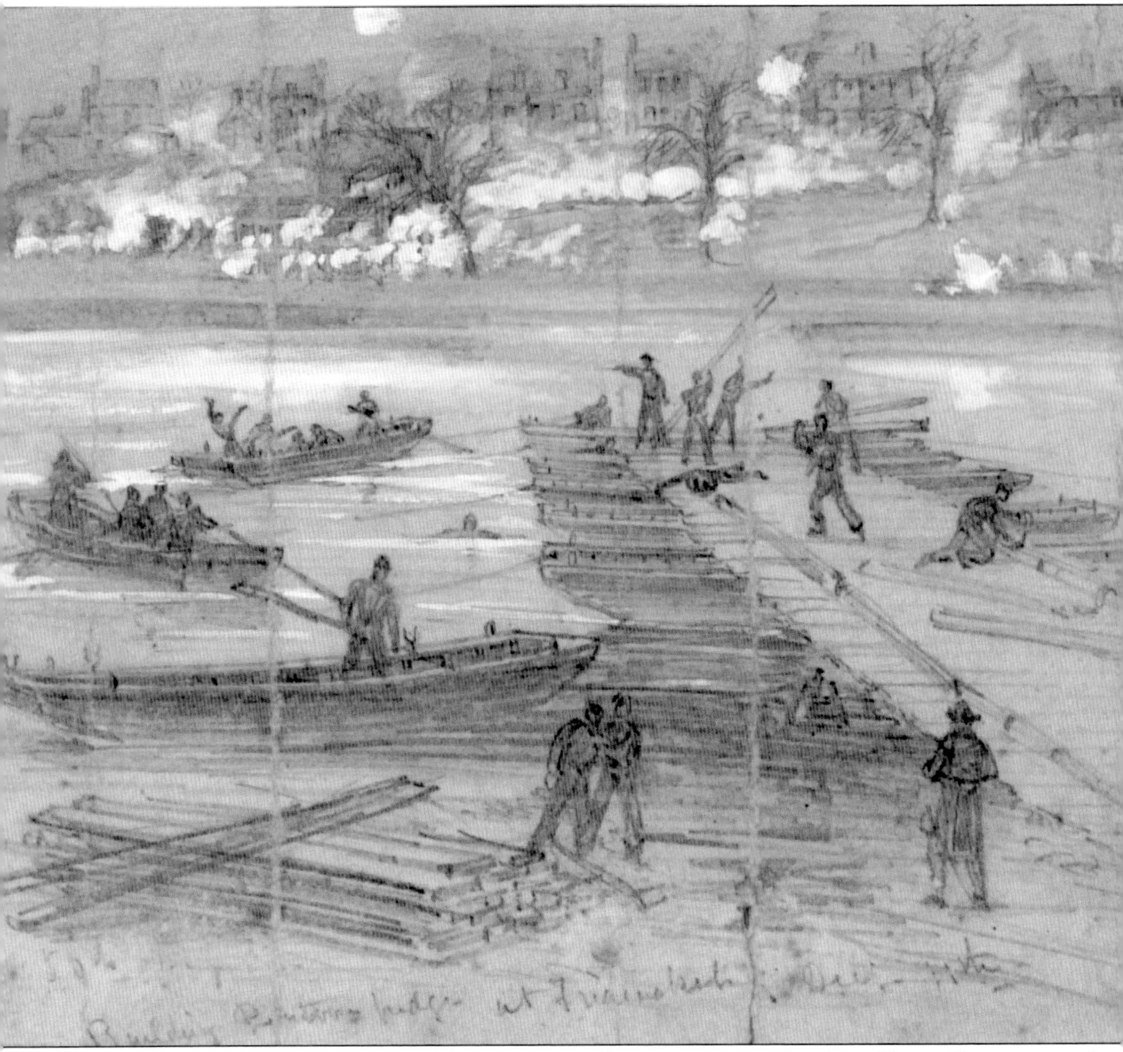

Following Pope's disastrous performance at Second Manassas, Lincoln relieved him of his command and placed Gen. Ambrose Burnside in charge of the Army of the Potomac. Burnside, known for his flamboyant facial hair, developed a bold strategy to strike Lee's army at Fredericksburg, Virginia. In order to do this, Burnside's troops would need to construct an elaborate pontoon bridge across the Rappahannock River to reach Lee on the other side. This is a sketch of the engineering feat during December 1862.

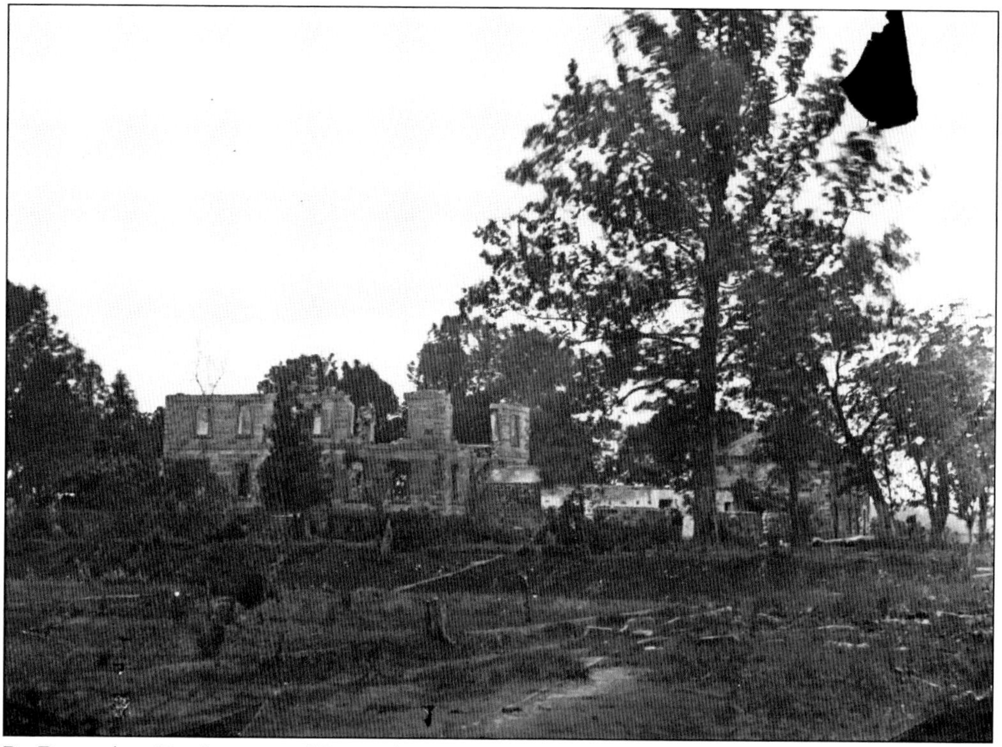

By December 12, elements of Burnside's army had crossed the Rappahannock River and were poised to push the Confederates from the town. However, the Confederates did not give ground easily, and a brutal street fight occurred. It was one of the most intense scenes of urban combat during the war. The fighting over the next few days destroyed many commercial and residential structures, like the Barnard House (pictured here).

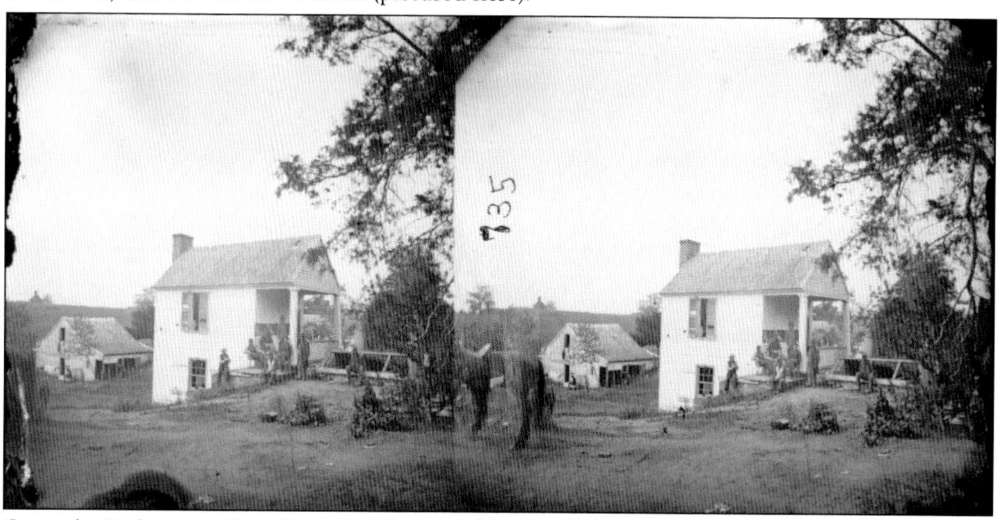

Once the Federals made it through the town of Fredericksburg, they came to the harsh realization that the Confederates, under Lee's directive, had positioned themselves atop an imposing ridge behind a stone wall. This Confederate position, atop Marye's Heights, was the focus of tremendous Union artillery fire. Although this structure remained standing, Marye's House, located nearby, suffered heavy damage during the course of the battle.

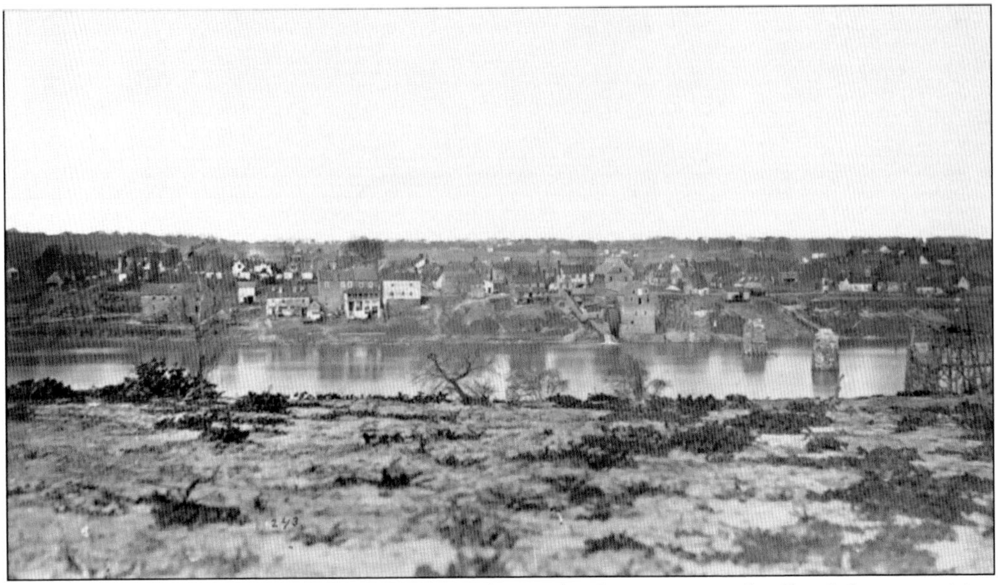

This view of Fredericksburg, with Marye's Heights in the distance, puts the Confederate position in perspective. Gen. Ambrose Burnside ordered numerous frontal assaults on the Confederate stronghold, only to suffer tremendous casualties. Many predominately Irish units suffered unconscionable losses as they attempted to breach the Confederate defenses. Following the brutal fighting that day, the Northern Lights appeared in the night sky as thousands lay dying. It is quite rare to see the phenomenon so far south, and it certainly added to the eerie scenes of carnage.

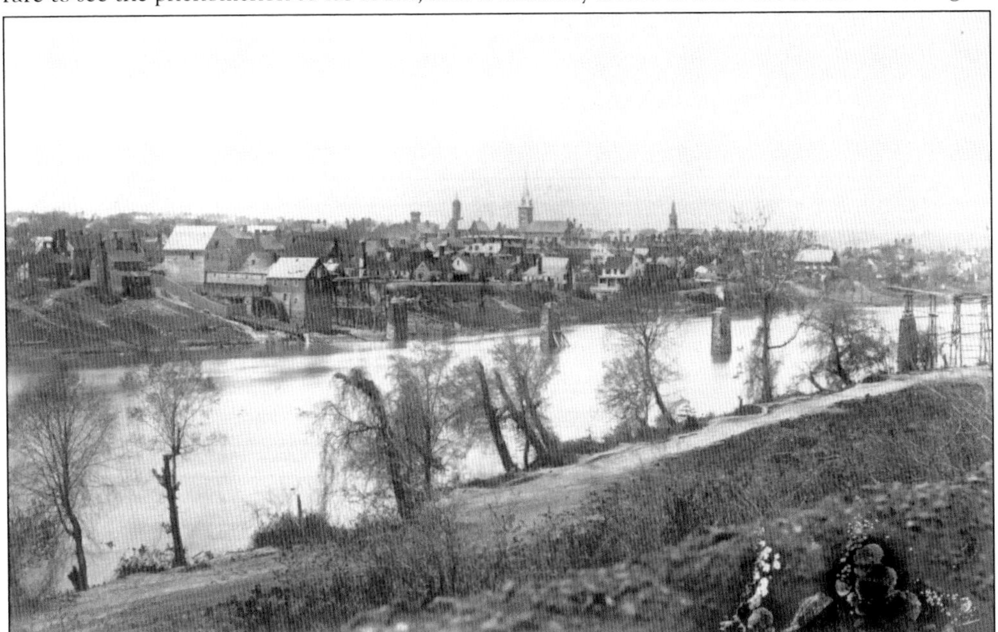

This photograph shows just how wide the Rappahannock River was near Fredericksburg and indicates how difficult it was for the Union to cross under heavy enemy fire. Following the battle, the town was significantly damaged, and many structures were not rebuilt for some time. By December 16, Burnside's devastated army retreated back across the river, thus concluding another failed Federal campaign.

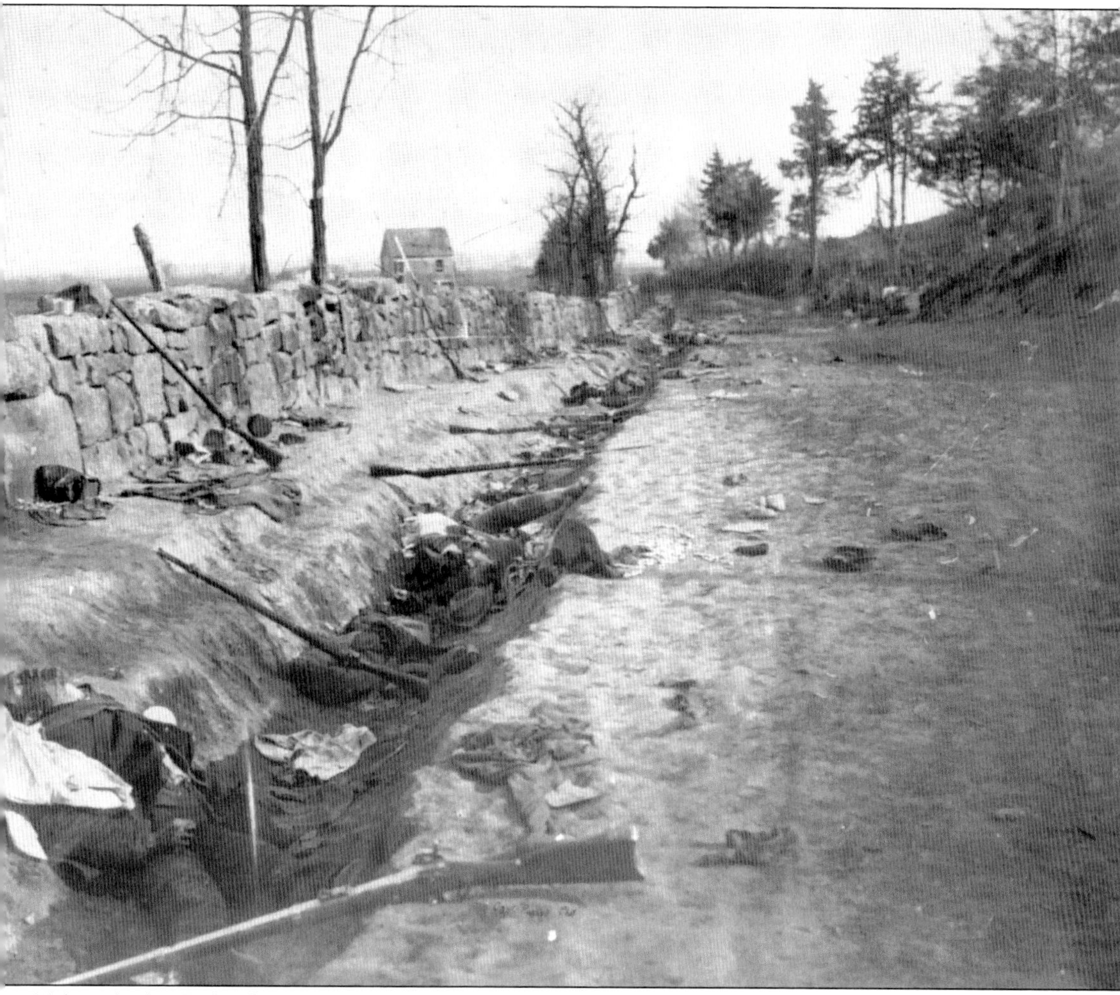

Although the Federals were soundly defeated, the Confederates suffered significant casualties as well. Pictured here are dead Confederates, probably from Gen. James Longstreet's corps, atop Marye's Heights. Note the tremendous amount of debris and accoutrements left behind. Such items are the prized finds of today's relic hunters and operators of metal detectors.

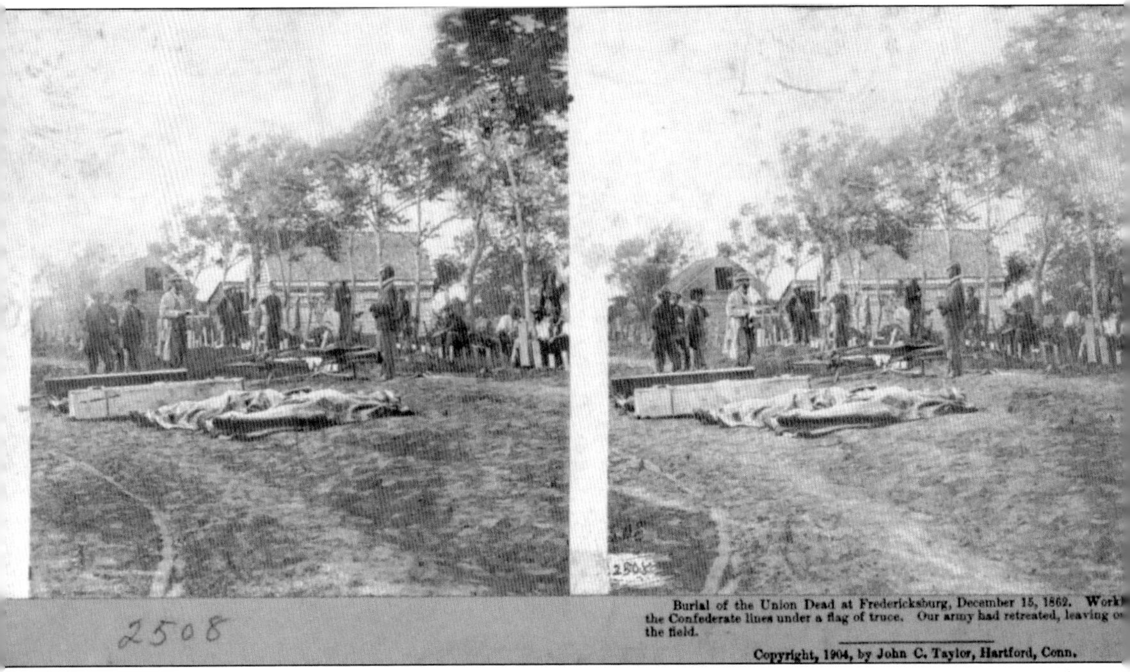

Here, Federal troops bury their fallen comrades, many of whom died during General Burnside's futile and costly attempts to take Marye's Heights. This Union defeat resonated deeply throughout the Northern states and severely injured morale for the Union war effort. Conversely, Confederates rejoiced in the news and lauded General Lee's now-famous Army of Northern Virginia.

Three

The Eyes of the World Are on Virginia

By 1863, both sides had lost their innocence, and the nation had become progressively more accustomed to the horrors of war. The previous year had ended with a resounding Union defeat that left Abraham Lincoln still searching for a general who was capable of defeating Robert E. Lee's vaunted army. The Confederates, however, had a very strong cadre of distinguished officers, including Robert E. Lee, Thomas "Stonewall" Jackson, and J.E.B. Stuart. This team of highly talented officers would work together to achieve great success over the next few months. Jackson had received critical acclaim for his performance in the Shenandoah Valley, and Lee sought to unite with Jackson to deliver a crushing blow to the Union army operating in Northern Virginia. Jackson's crowning moment came in April 1863, when he and Lee were poised to deliver a devastating attack on the Union army around Chancellorsville. Jackson devised an extraordinarily daring plan to divide the Confederate forces in order to crush the Union army camped there. As the Confederate army stepped off that fateful day, no one expected that the victory would come at such a high price. Jackson's plan was executed in flawless fashion; by the evening of the battle, Union troops were in headlong retreat. However, as the fighting came to a close, Jackson and his staff were mistaken by their own troops for Federal cavalry; following a hail of friendly fire, Jackson lay mortally wounded. The day lives on in infamy as a precise moment in time when the Confederacy lost a most capable officer. Despite the horrendous price of victory at Chancellorsville, Lee soldiered on and sought to bring about an expedient end to the war by achieving a victory north of the Mason-Dixon line. In the next few weeks, Lee prepared his army in Virginia to journey north, thus beginning what is now known as the infamous Gettysburg campaign. By the end of 1863, Lee's army had returned to Virginia, but the seeds of defeat had been sown, and the war was well on course to its eventual outcome.

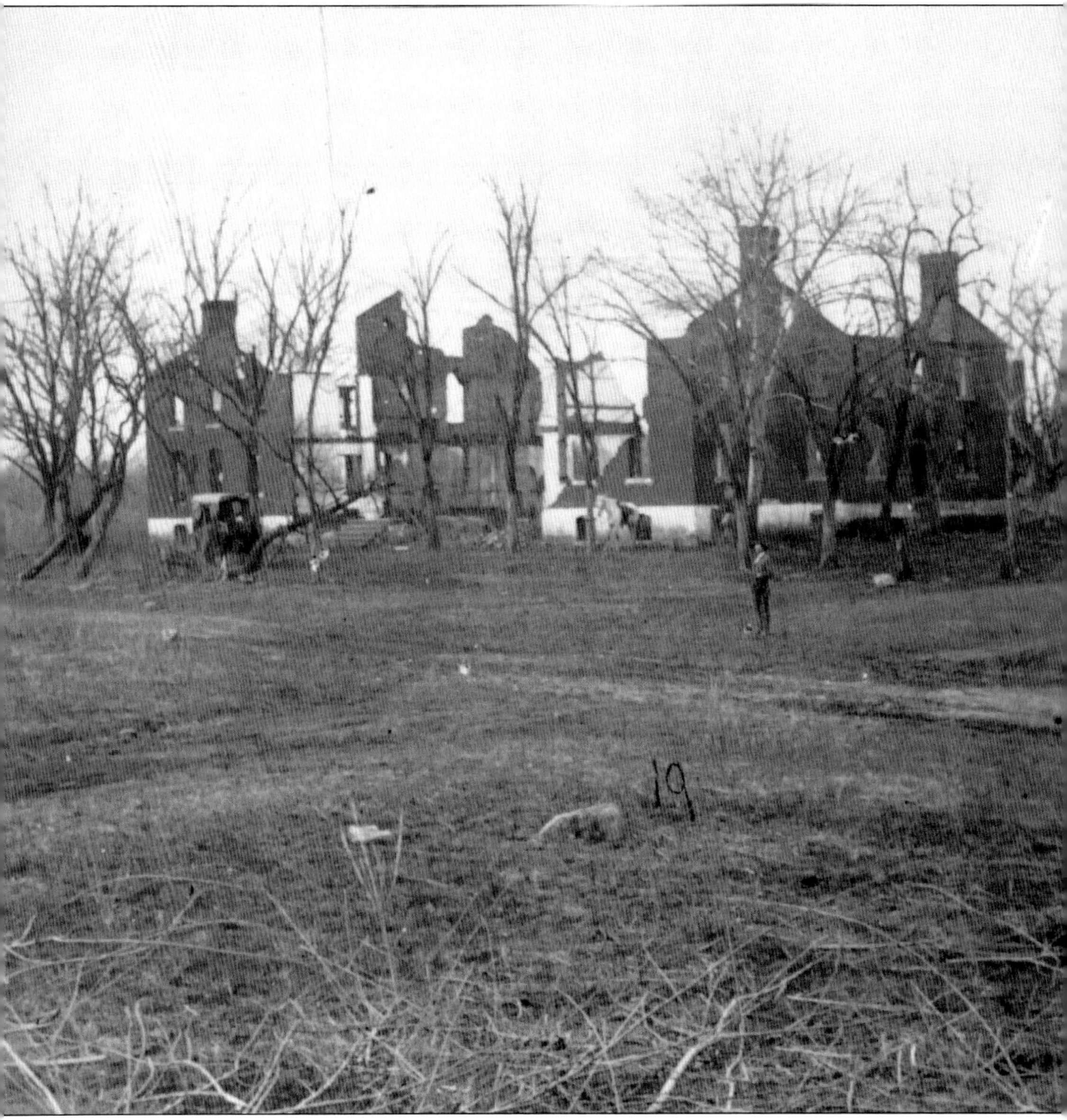

By 1863, the devastation in Virginia was far from over. As massive armies clashed in increasingly larger bloodbaths, the fighting could not help but touch all aspects of society. Many battles occurred over farmland; in most cases, local residences were destroyed or damaged. The Chancellorsville House (pictured) was no exception, as it was utterly destroyed during an engagement. Shown here are the only noncombustible remnants of the once-grand structure.

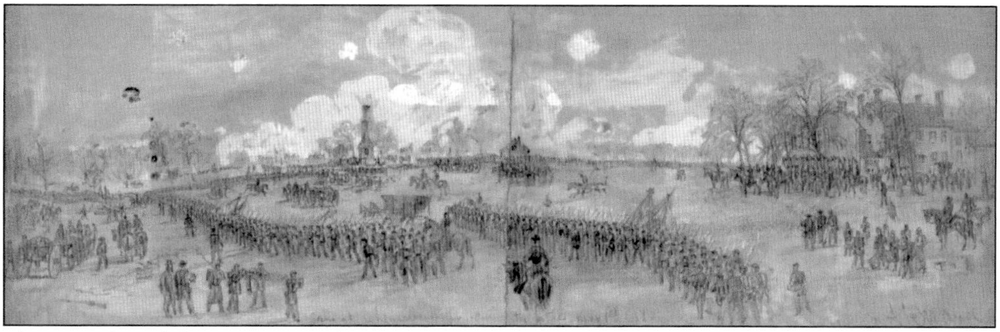

Photography of the time was still in its infancy and was not advanced enough to capture rapid movement. Still images were the dominant results of the era's photography. In order to augment the deficiencies inherent in the photographs of the time, battlefield artists were employed to capture the dynamic scenes of combat. This sketch depicts the opening phases of the Battle of Chancellorsville, which would be recorded as one of Lee's and Jackson's greatest achievements.

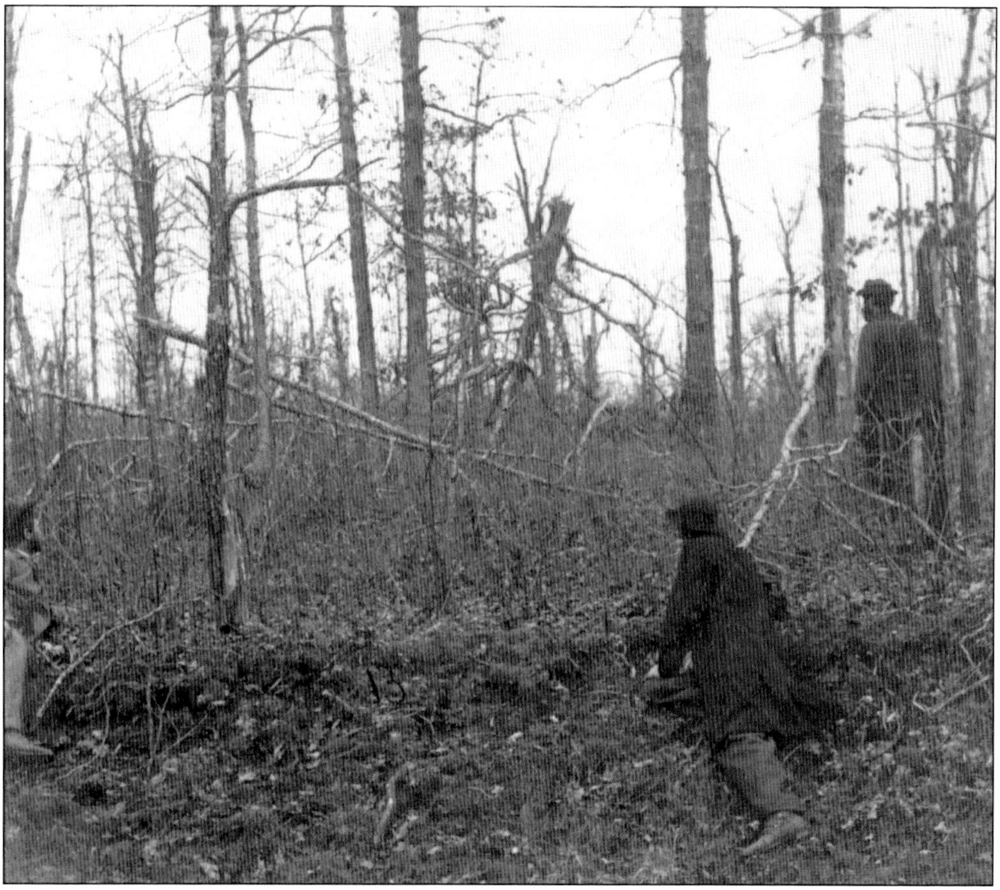

At Chancellorsville, the Confederates were significantly outnumbered, as they possessed approximately 60,000 men. The Federals, however, boasted over 120,000 troops at their disposal. Despite the numerical disparity, Lee and Jackson devised a strategy that would result in brutal combat. If executed perfectly, however, it would bring about victory. Shown here are shattered trees, the result of artillery shells. One can only guess at the number of rounds fired for this many trees to be damaged.

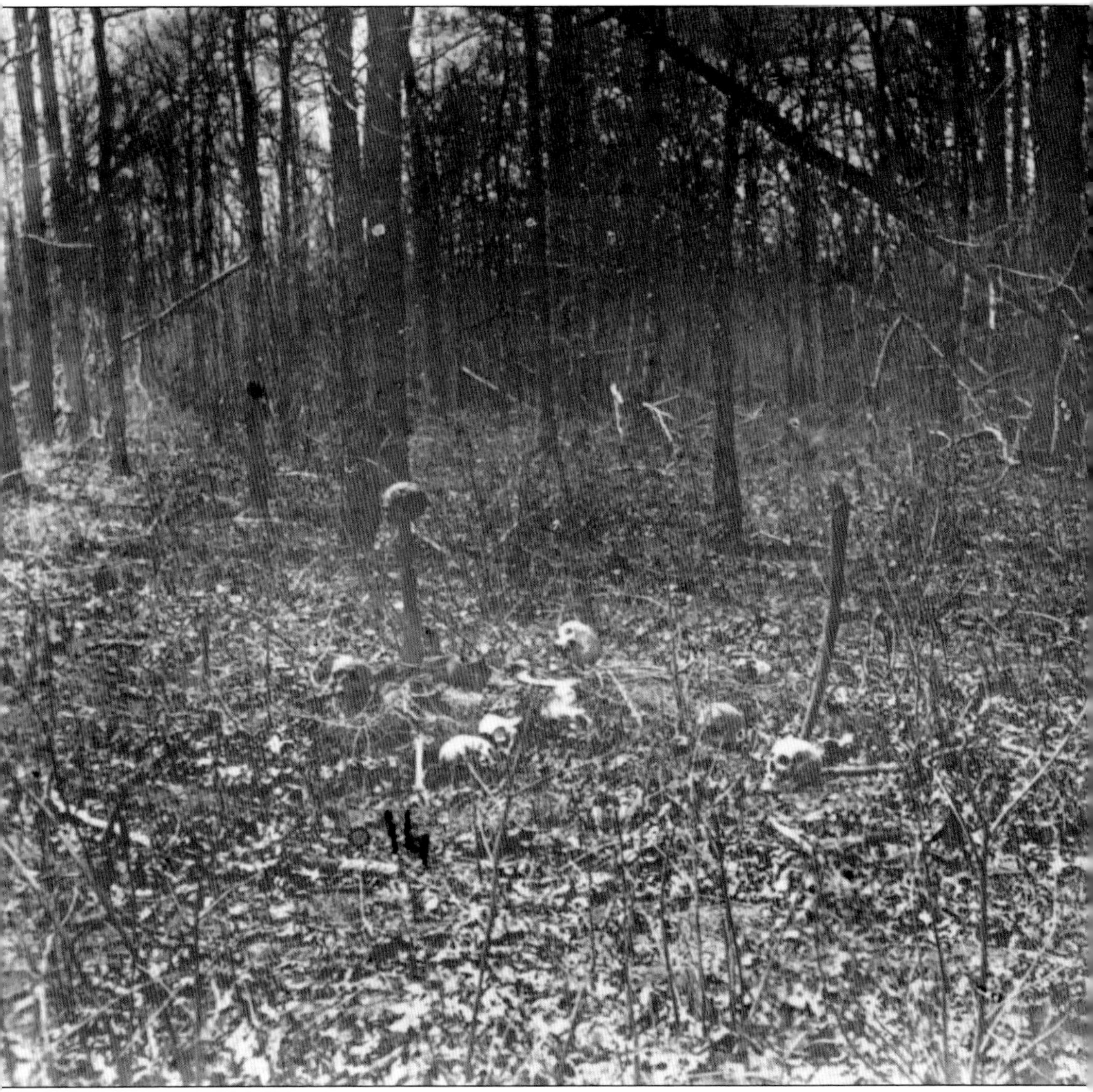

Fighting was so heavy along the Plank Road that there were too many bodies to be cleaned up, and many remained unburied until after the war. This sobering scene includes multiple skeletons of unknown provenance just off the Plank Road. It is likely that these men came from distant corners of the Union or Confederacy. They never made it home.

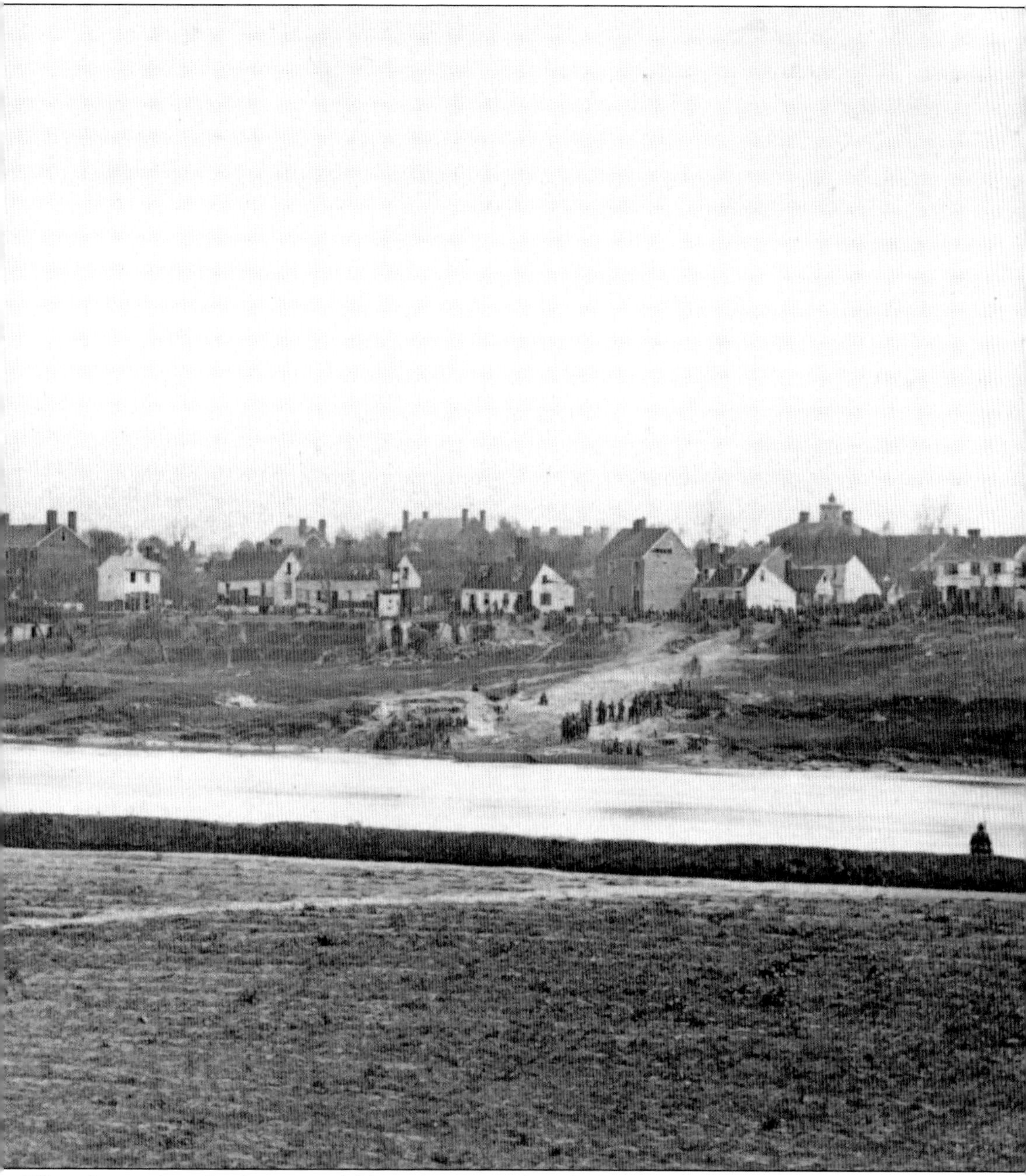

The advanced medical care available today was unheard of during the Civil War. Those that were fortunate enough to only be wounded would often receive limited treatment, as doctors did not have the time or resources to adequately aid most patients. Here, following the Battle of Chancellorsville, thousands of dying soldiers await transport across the Rappahannock River. Looking at the battlefield today, it is difficult to imagine thousands of wounded soldiers waiting to die in the stagnant Virginia heat.

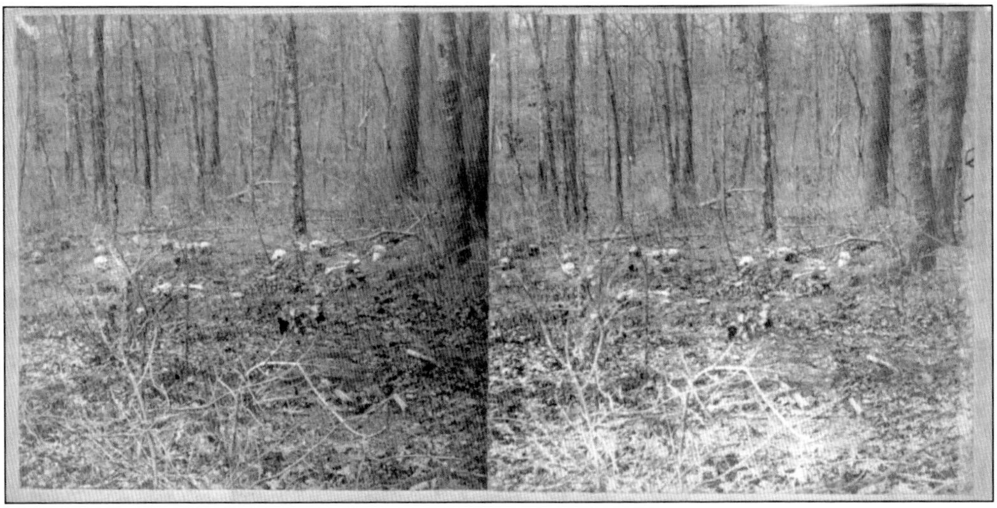

During the course of the Battle of Chancellorsville, Robert E. Lee split his already small force into two wings. In so doing, he surprised Gen. Joe Hooker's massive Union army. By the end of the day, Hooker's troops had been routed, and Lee had achieved another spectacular victory. By this time, newspapers were touting Lee's army as invincible, and citizens throughout the North were becoming dangerously disillusioned with the war effort. The battle took place over such a large swath of territory that many of the dead were not located for decades. Pictured here are the remains of a few of these unfortunate men.

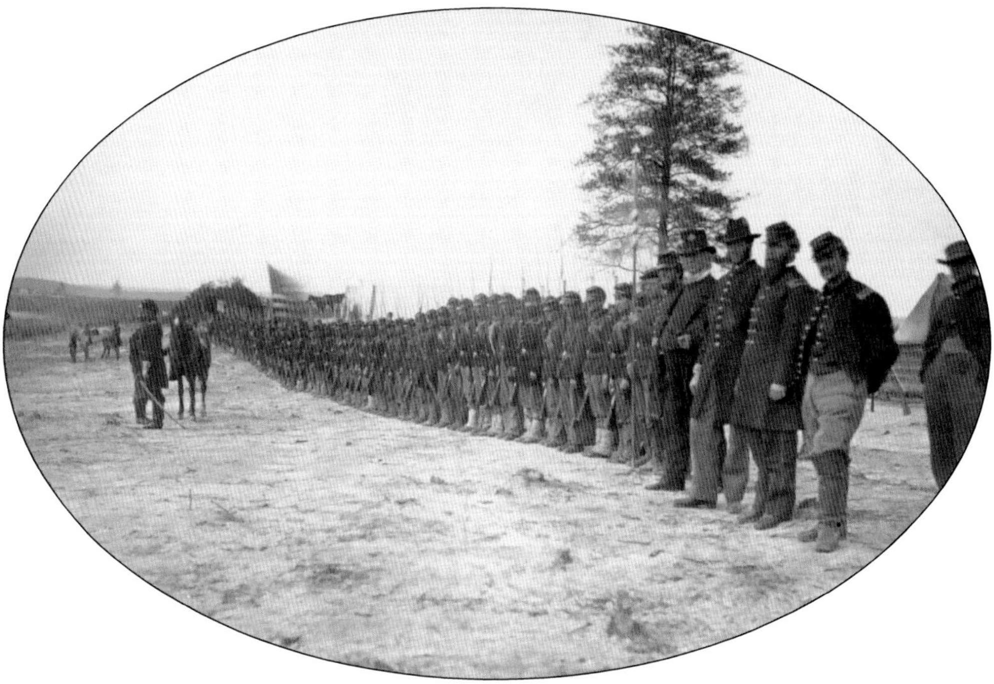

From the times of the Roman legions, soldiers have been accustomed to the adage "hurry up and wait." The Civil War was no exception. Here, members of the 110th Pennsylvania Regiment stand and wait. Unfortunately for these friends and neighbors who mustered together, they would probably also die together, as units were composed of people from close-knit communities. The 110th Pennsylvania was almost completely annihilated at Chancellorsville.

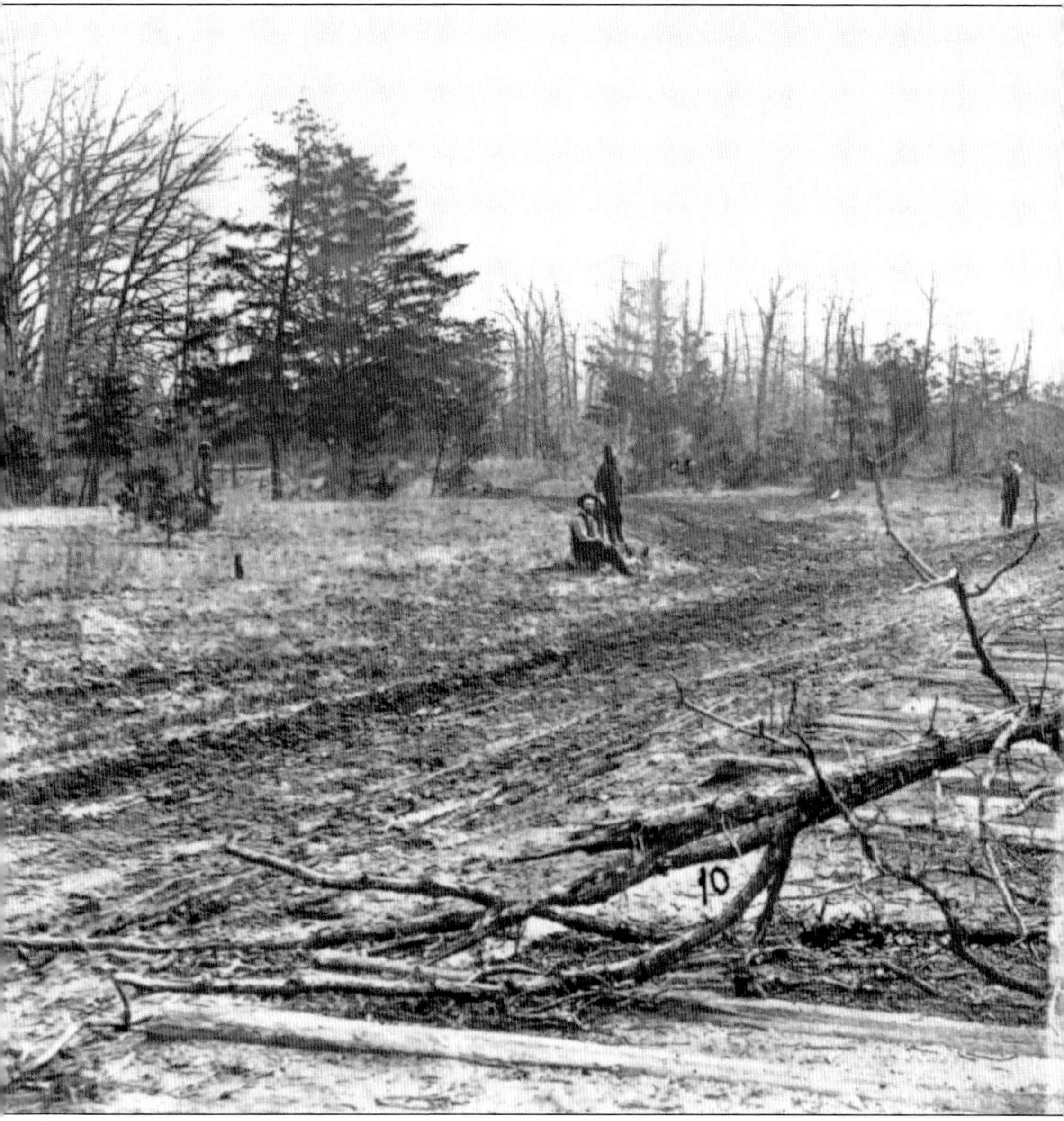

Although Lee and Jackson's plan to surprise Hooker worked impeccably, it came at a tremendously high cost. During the confusion of battle, which trailed into the night, a few Confederates mistook Gen. Thomas Jackson for a Union cavalry officer. They immediately fired on him, mortally wounding the general whom Lee affectionately referred to as his "right arm." The Confederates may have won the battle, but they lost a general whose skills would be sorely missed months later at Gettysburg. The area shown here is where the Confederates are believed to have mistakenly fired upon Jackson.

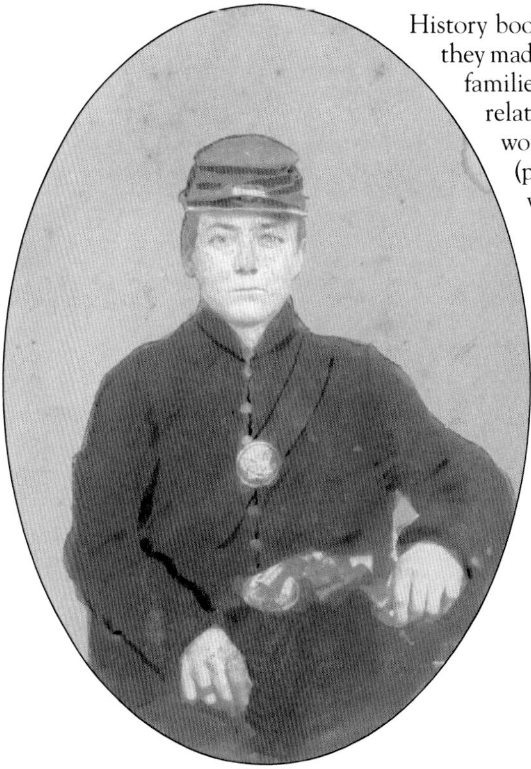

History books describe great generals and the decisions they made. Inevitably, such decisions indirectly affected families thousands of miles away, and in many cases, relatives would receive the news that their sons would not be returning home. Roswell Bishop (pictured) of the 123rd New York State Volunteers was killed in action at Chancellorsville. He is a reminder of the human toll such battles took on a delicate society.

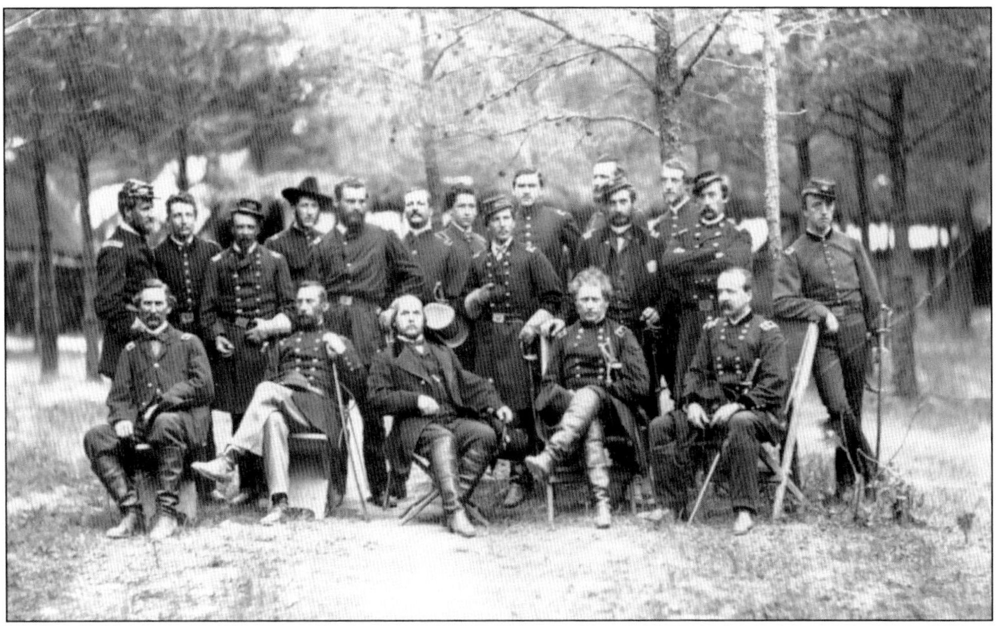

Despite all of their training, Gen. Joseph Hooker (seated, center) and his staff were completely outclassed by their Confederate counterparts. Here, General Hooker is surrounded by his cadre of distinguished officers. Many historians argue that, to this point in the war, the Confederates possessed a better officer corps than did the Union. Following the embarrassing defeat at Chancellorsville, Lincoln promptly replaced Hooker.

This man was the epitome of dash and classic military flamboyance. Thousands of young Southern men longed to serve in J.E.B. Stuart's cavalry units, as he was known for his strategic acumen and daring tactics. Following Stonewall Jackson's wounding, Lee temporarily placed Stuart in command of Jackson's troops.

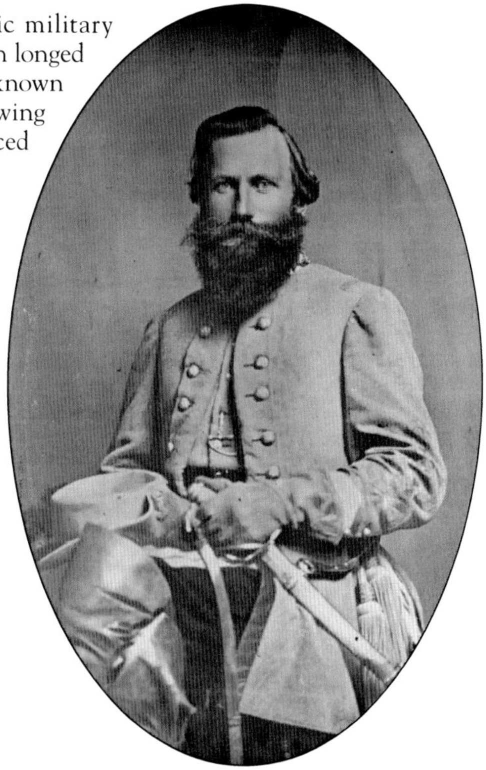

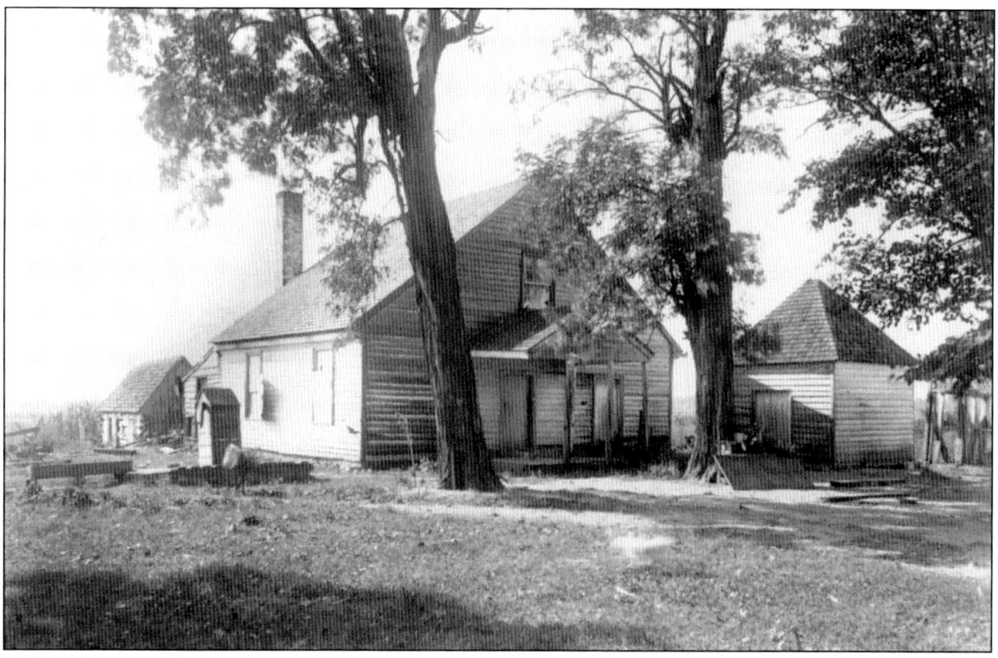

A few days after his crowning achievement, Gen. Thomas Jackson lay dying in this small house at Guinea Station, Virginia. On his death bed, Jackson was said to have been at peace and quoted scripture in his last hours. He mourned his separation in death from his wife, but he remained optimistic of a future after his departure.

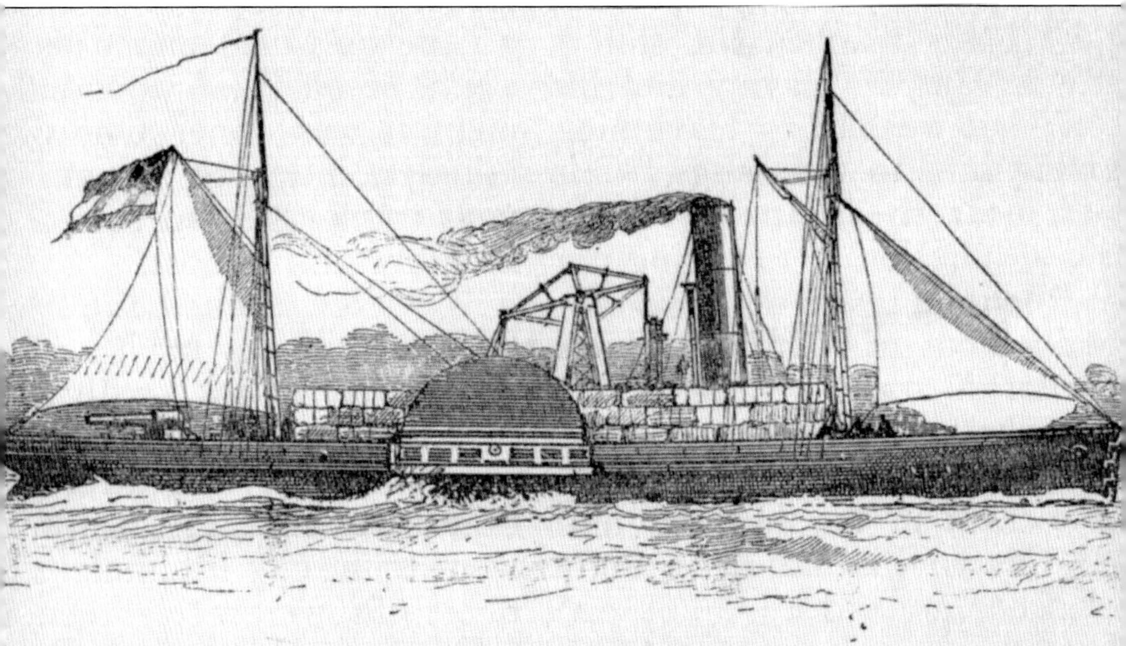

THE "STONEWALL JACKSON."

Even prior to his death, Stonewall Jackson had become a hero throughout the South and was immortalized in the hearts of adoring Southerners for decades to come. The Confederate navy went as far as to name a vessel (pictured) after him while he was still alive. Following his death, Jackson's popularity continued to rise. After the war, he came to represent the Lost Cause of the Confederacy. To this day, it is impossible to travel through the South without seeing his name emblazoned on street signs and monuments.

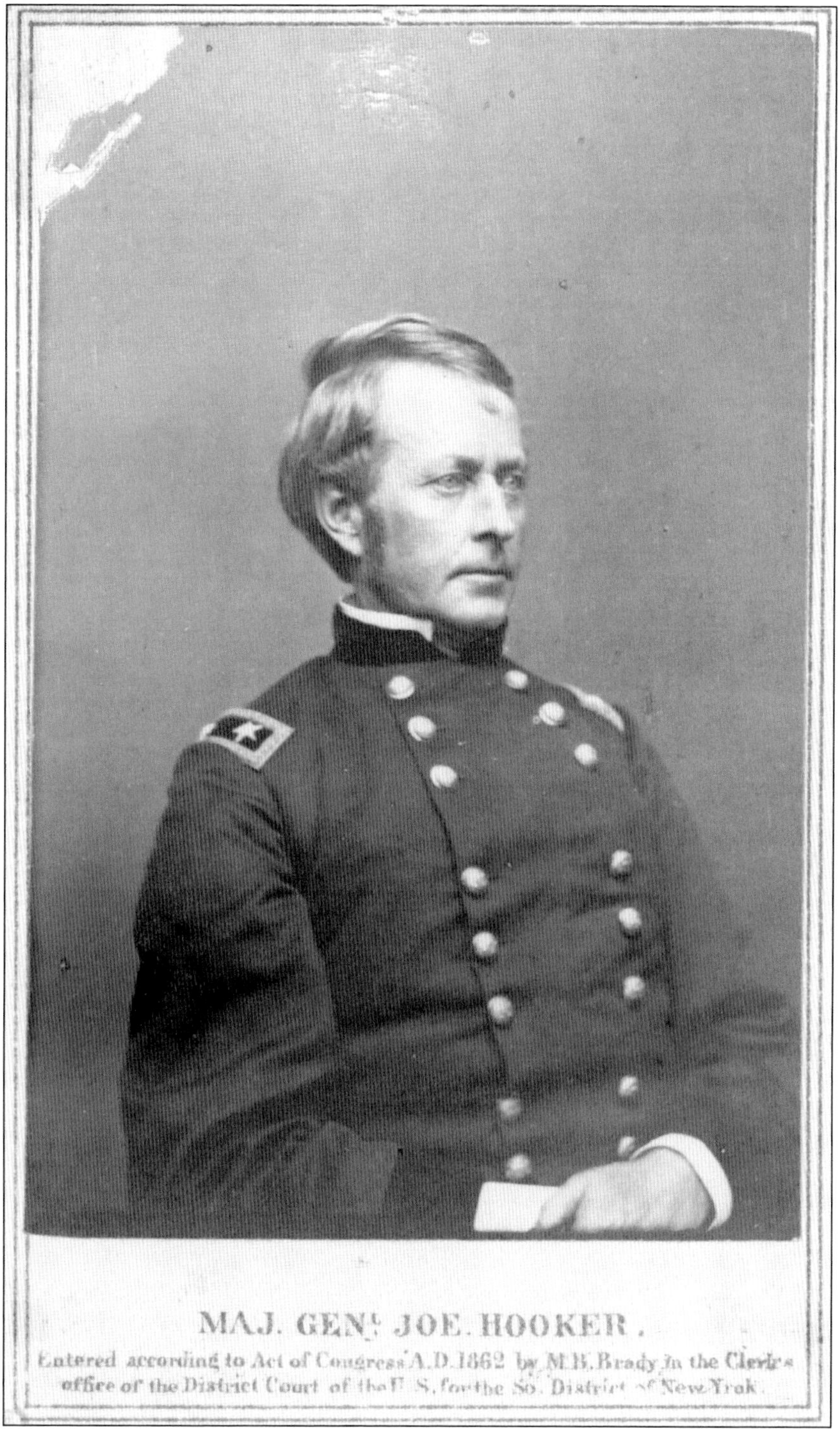

This photograph of Joe Hooker, showing his military bearing and fine uniform, cannot hide the fact that President Lincoln found him lacking in the aggressive qualities he was looking for in a general. Hooker was promptly replaced with George Meade. The North was beginning to get restless with underperforming generals.

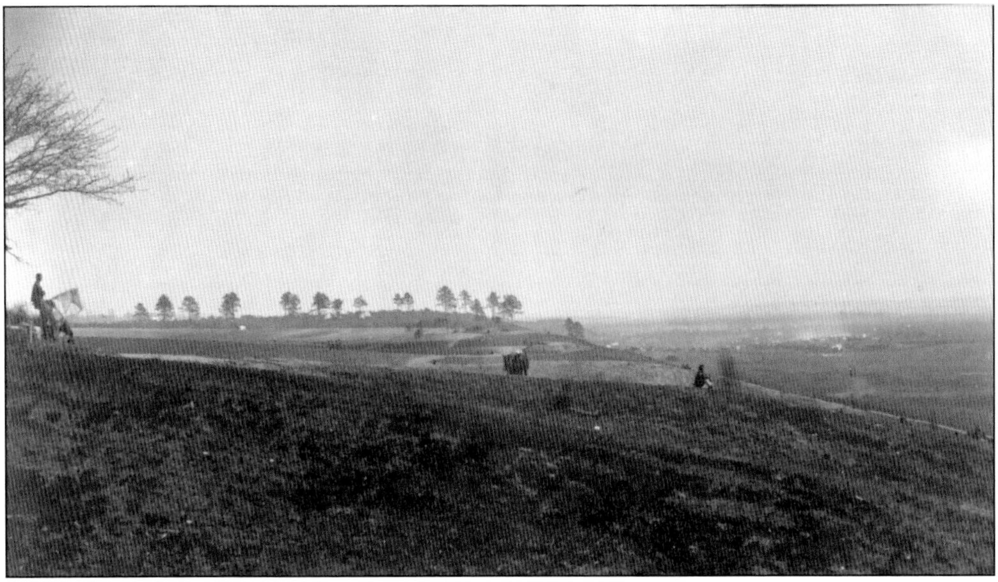

This eerie plain was the Union's equivalent to Gallipoli, as it was the site of immense carnage following a failed Union frontal assault. It is Marye's Heights, where the Confederates staved off repeated advances in 1862. Following the battle at Chancellorsville, a small Confederate force took up position here, only to be promptly expelled from their former stronghold.

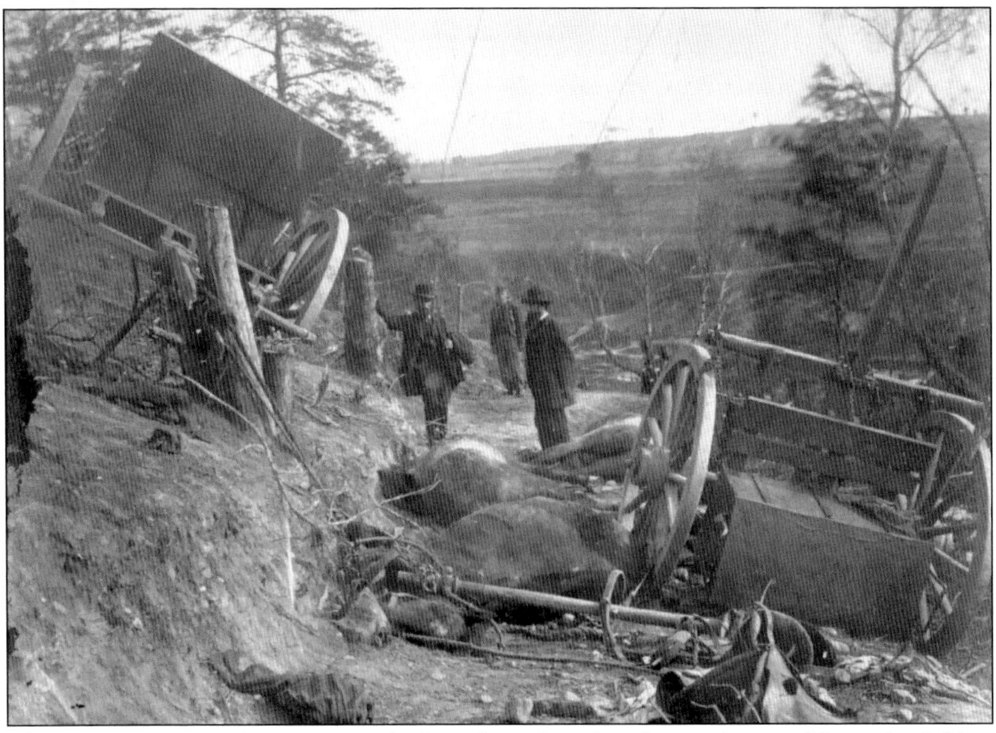

This gruesome scene demonstrates the brutality of combat during the war. Horses lay lifeless next to the Confederate caisson they were tasked with pulling after it exploded at Fredericksburg. Generals on both sides noted how the loss of animal life profoundly affected the morale of the men and troubled survivors of the conflict for years.

This jovial gentleman is Maj. Gen. John Sedgwick. He may be smiling because he led the successful Union advance at the Battle of Second Fredericksburg. Confederates had reoccupied the vaunted Marye's Heights, but they were pushed from their stronghold by Sedgwick's advance. Within a year, he would be dead.

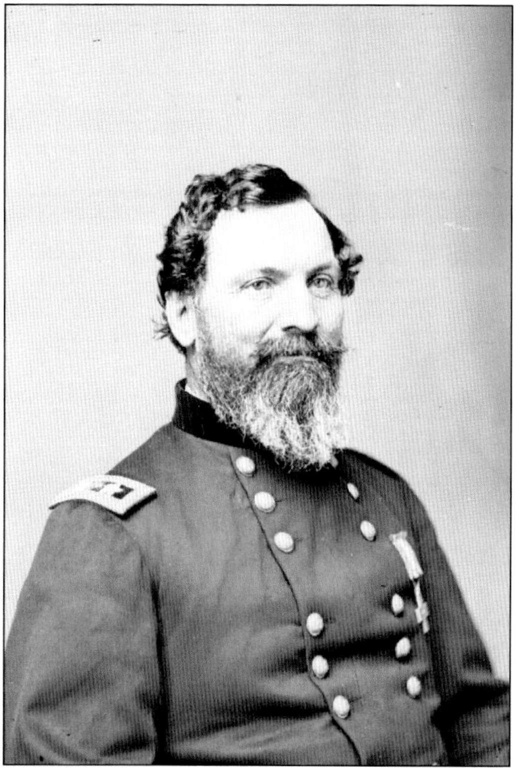

Only combat can forge the unique and special relationships that men find themselves in during times of great stress. Oliver Wendell Holmes described the bonding of men through the searing ordeal of martial combat with the timeless phrase, "We have shared the incommunicable experience of war." Here, General Sedgwick (center) and his staff take a break from the rigors of command to pose for a photographer.

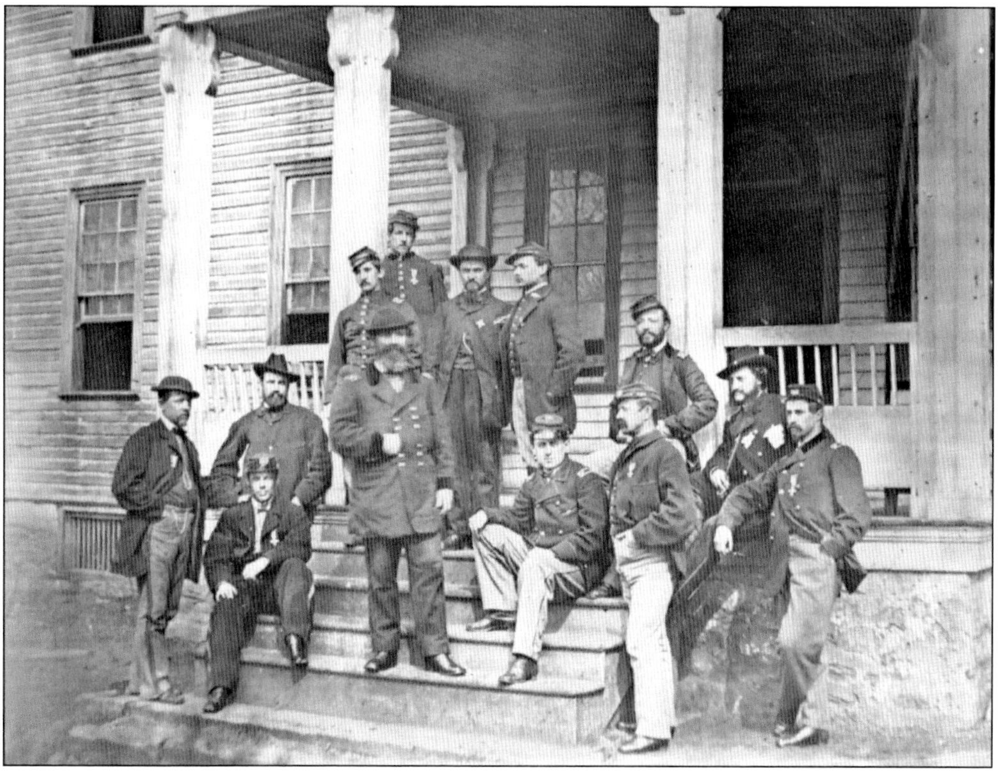

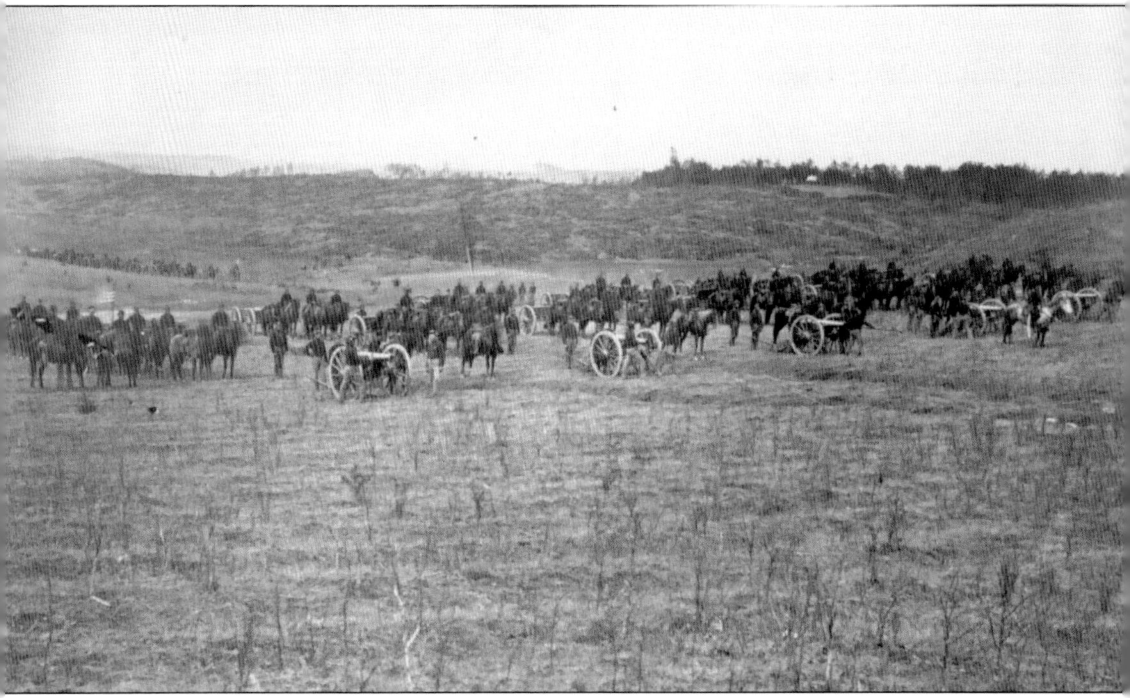

This Union artillery battery is ready for action. At a moment's notice, it was capable of firing multiple three-inch projectiles at distances exceeding one mile. The resources of the industrial North made such artillery units commonplace, while the predominantly agrarian South struggled to supply its own artillery. These disparities increased as the war continued.

Col. John Singleton Mosby, "The Gray Ghost," jauntily poses for a photographer. Mosby pioneered guerilla warfare, terrorizing and raiding rear-echelon Union troops throughout Northern Virginia. On the night of March 8, 1863, he performed one of his most daring feats at Fairfax Courthouse, abducting Brig. Gen. Edwin Stoughton from his bed. Following the war, the former Confederate went on to become the US consul to Hong Kong under his former adversary, Pres. Ulysses S. Grant.

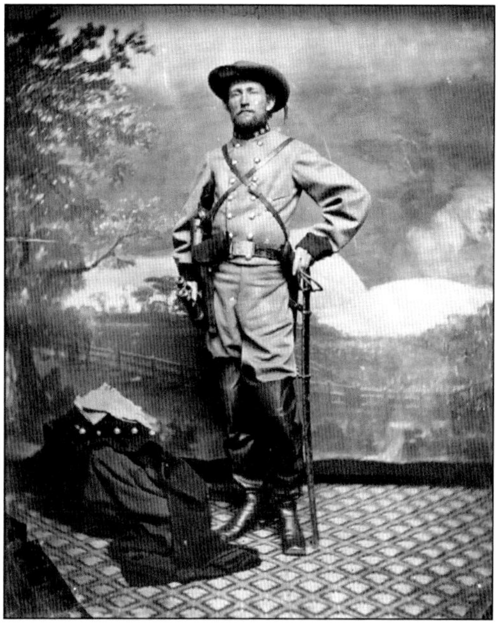

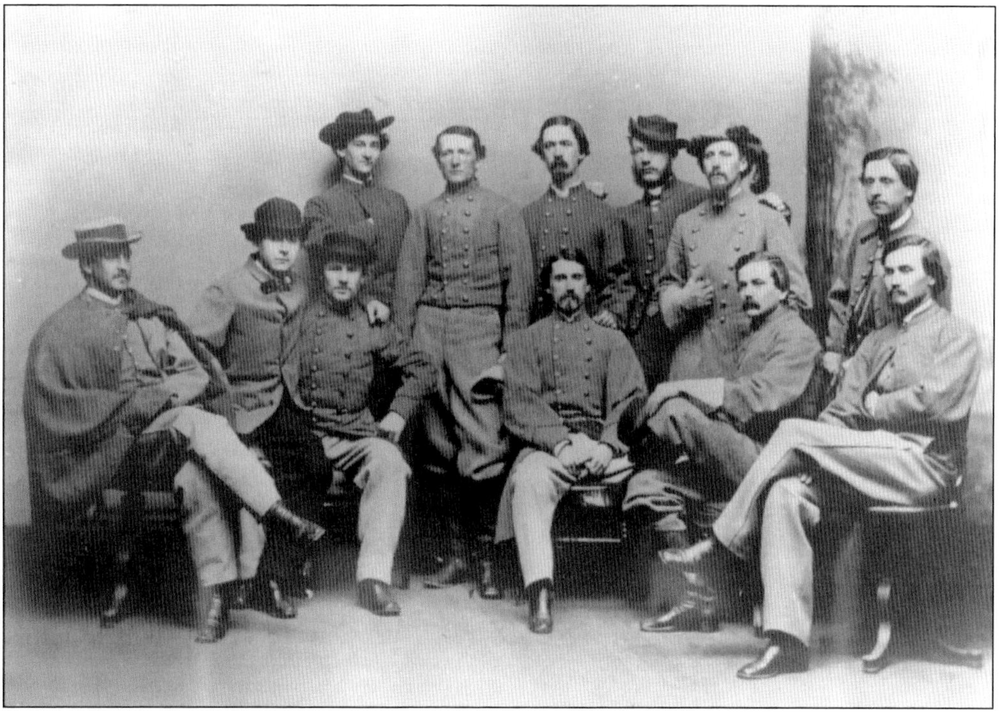

Something between a gang of pirates and a highly disciplined military unit is how many Union soldiers described Colonel Mosby's infamous raiders. Here, a few members of his unit pose in rakish fashion. These men were proud of their role in the Confederate war effort and certainly enjoyed the spoils of war. Following the war, John Mosby became close friends with the Patton family and would spend countless hours "playing war" with a young boy named George S. Patton. The boy would grow up to become one of the greatest generals in American history, following his achievements in World War II.

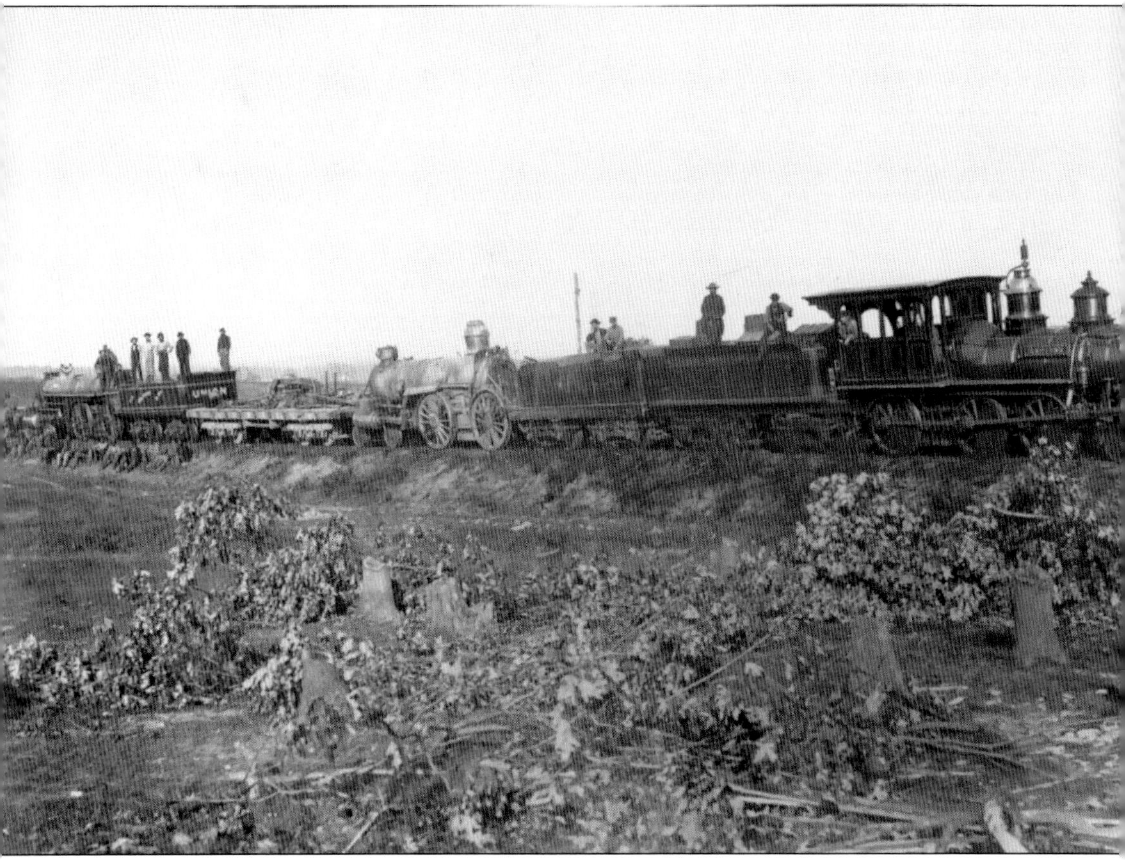

This timeless photograph could have just as easily been snapped in Ukraine during the German occupation of the Soviet Union. For decades, armies have been plagued with protecting their interior rail lines. European partisans did well to study Colonel Mosby's groundbreaking techniques. Here, Confederate partisans have successfully derailed a locomotive, temporarily paralyzing Federal shipments.

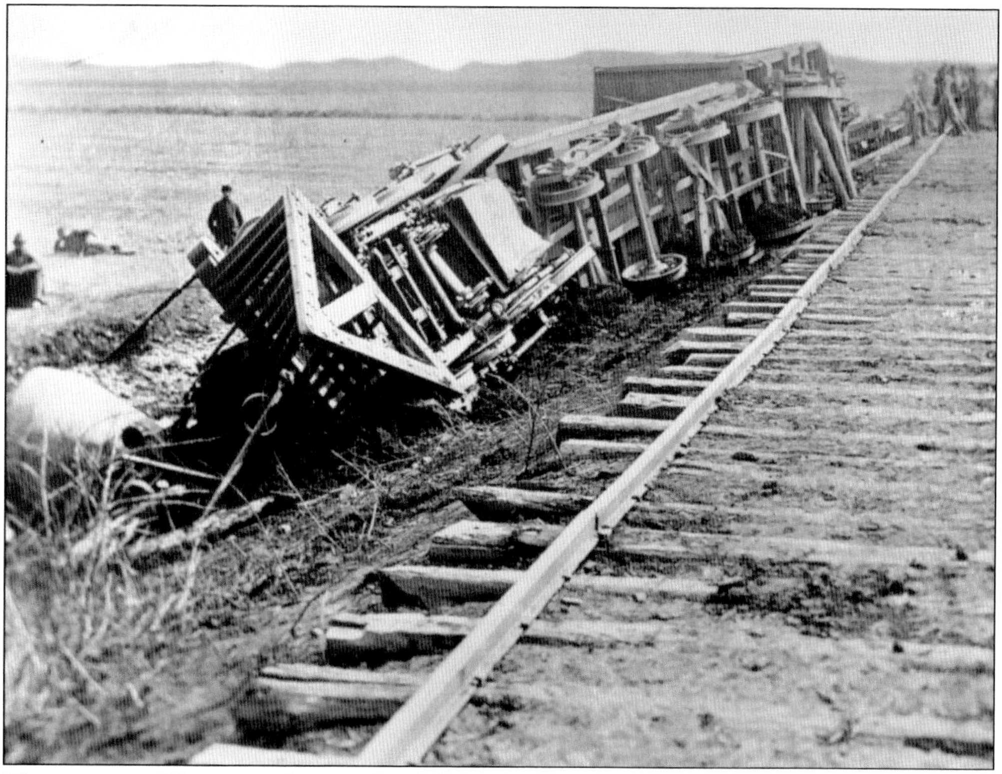

The menace of Union conductors, Confederate rangers became a constant thorn in the side of Federal operations in the northern portion of Virginia. Despite the efforts of men like Mosby, the Union juggernaut could not be stopped. By 1863, the Union military industrial machine had far outpaced that of the Confederates, and no amount of partisan activity could impede it.

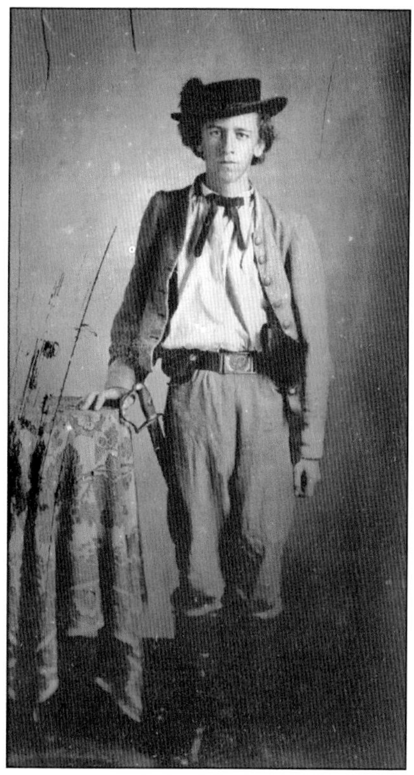

An 1860s Robin Hood, John Singleton Mosby became a legend across Virginia as stories of his merry band of raiders took newspaper headlines by storm. Young, bright-eyed boys from across Loudoun and Fauquier Counties rushed to join Mosby's ranks. Here, Pvt. Lucien Love of Mosby's Rangers does not appear much older than many high school students. He no doubt enjoyed the opportunity to engage in state-sanctioned mischief.

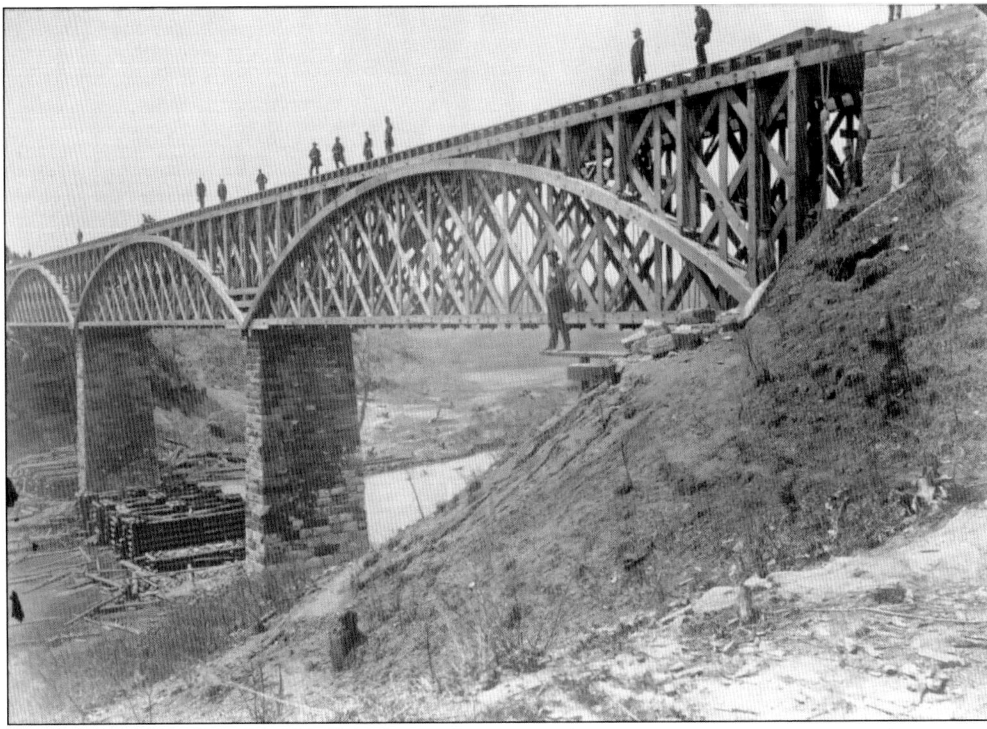

Bridges and other pieces of infrastructure, targets of partisan operations, required constant protection in order to keep the Union's supplies flowing to the armies in the field. The construction of bridges involved great amounts of time and resources. Their destruction severely disrupted the movement of goods, thus inhibiting Federal operations.

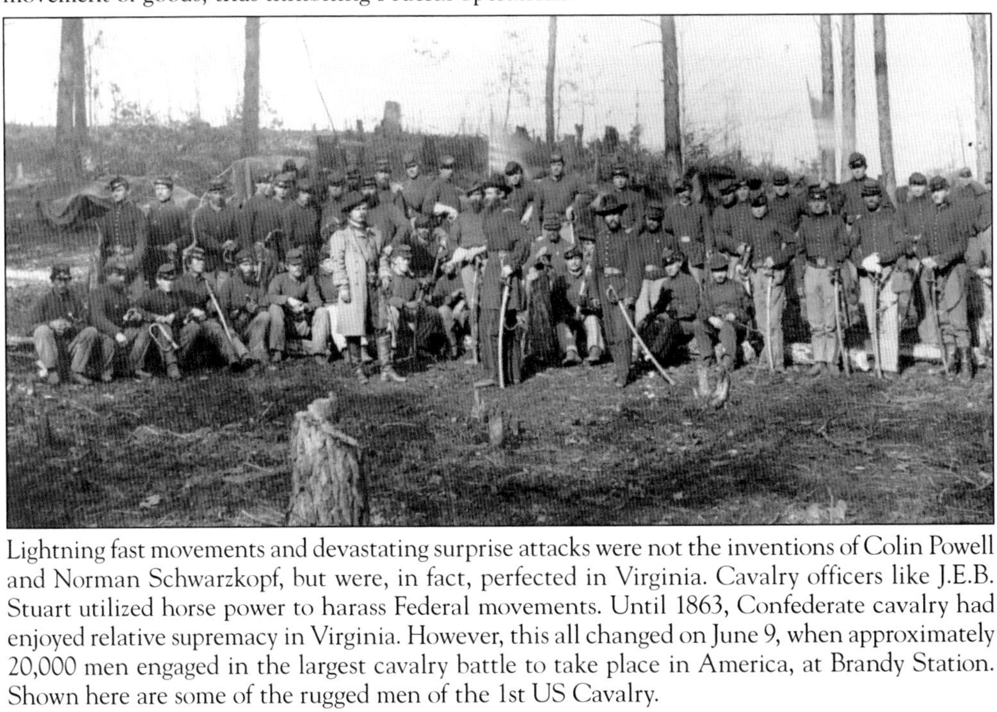

Lightning fast movements and devastating surprise attacks were not the inventions of Colin Powell and Norman Schwarzkopf, but were, in fact, perfected in Virginia. Cavalry officers like J.E.B. Stuart utilized horse power to harass Federal movements. Until 1863, Confederate cavalry had enjoyed relative supremacy in Virginia. However, this all changed on June 9, when approximately 20,000 men engaged in the largest cavalry battle to take place in America, at Brandy Station. Shown here are some of the rugged men of the 1st US Cavalry.

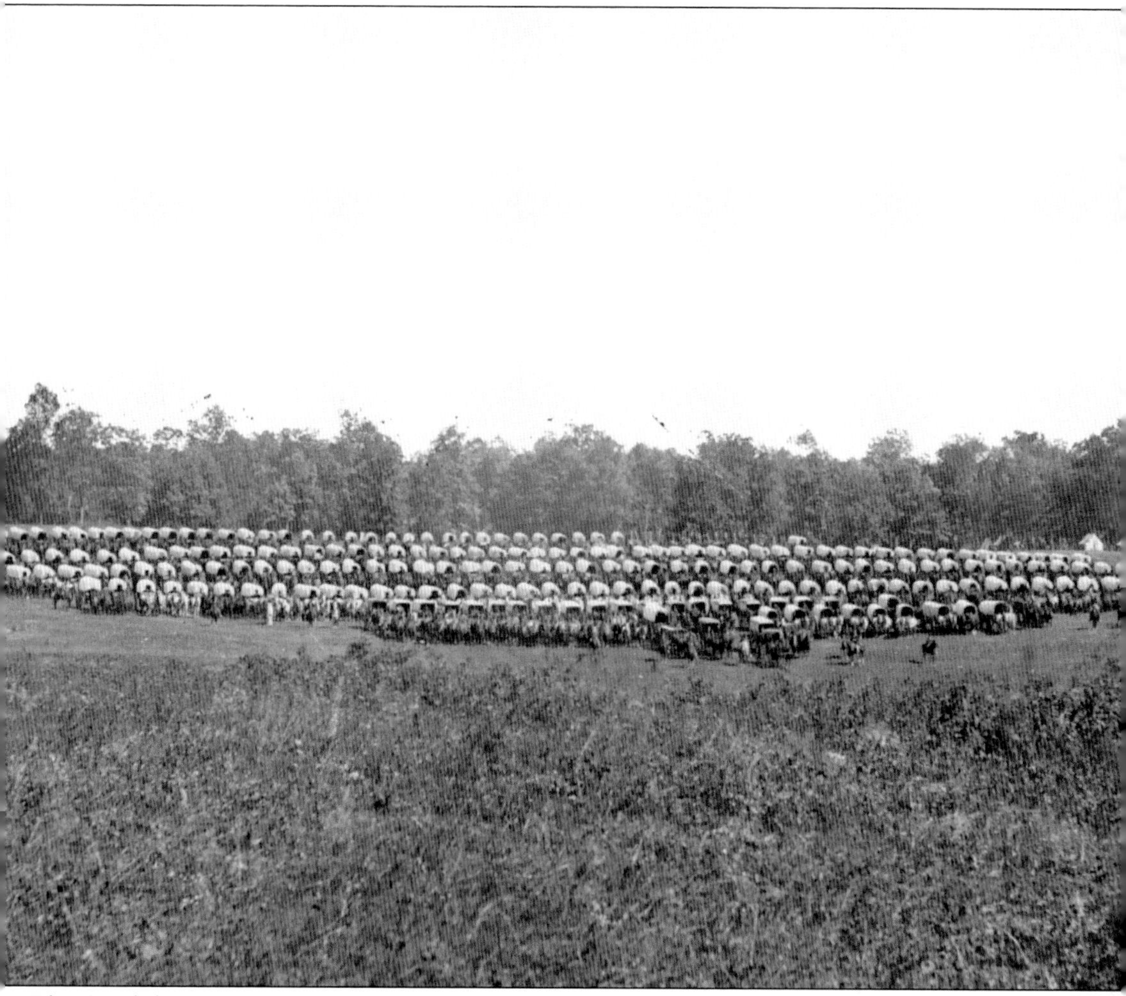

The Confederate cavalry suffered a tremendous defeat at Brandy Station, from which it never entirely recovered. The Confederates could not afford to lose valuable horse flesh, and they became progressively disadvantaged as the war raged on. The victory was a much-needed morale boost for the beleaguered Union. Shown here is a fleet of wagons that carried necessary supplies to the massive cavalry units of the day.

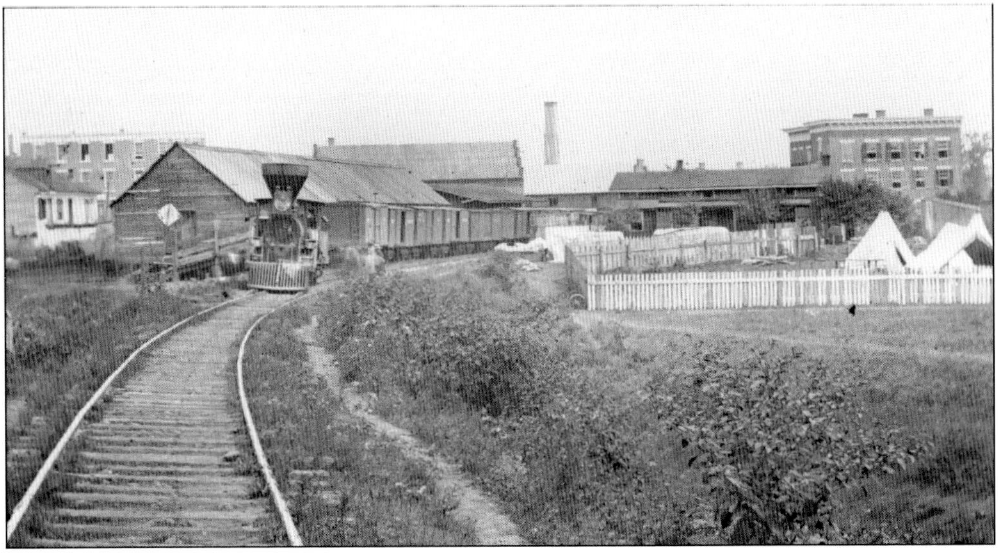

Time has been the foe of caesars and khans throughout the ages. Robert E. Lee was acutely aware that the Confederacy was running out of time. The South lacked men and material to compete with the North, and Lee recognized that the Confederates needed to act fast. He hoped to achieve a victory in a Northern state to break the Union's will to continue the war. To stage this campaign, Lee organized portions of his army at Culpeper, Virginia.

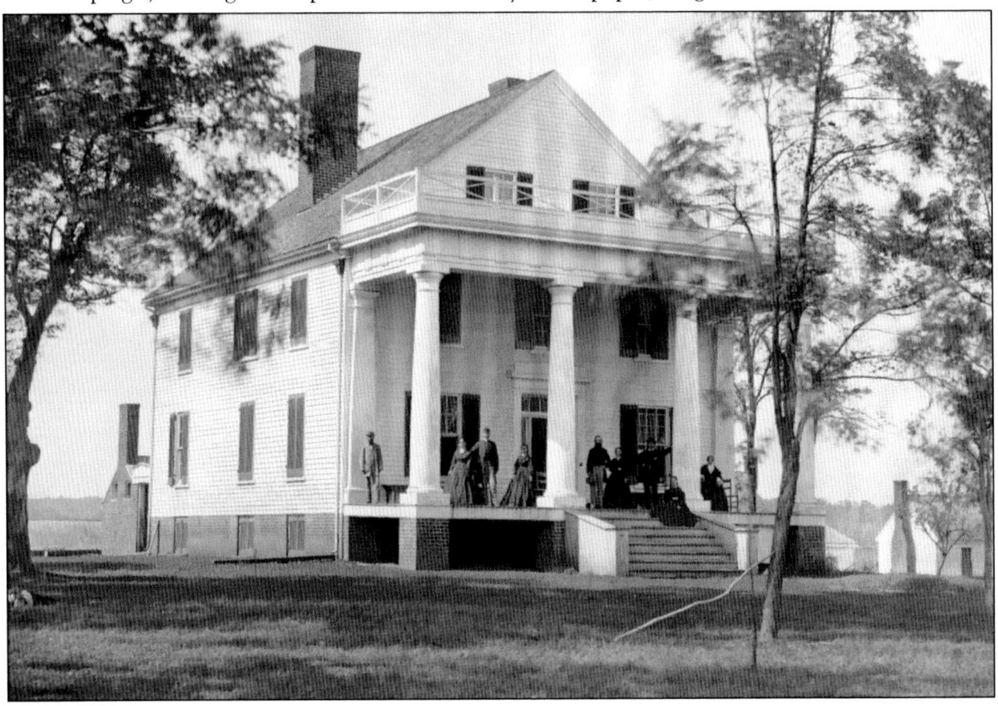

For many Southern regiments, Culpeper was the birthplace of the Gettysburg campaign. Numerous Confederate units had passed through the region multiple times during the war. A peculiarity of the region was Botts House, owned by an ardent Unionist. Despite his pro-Union proclivities, Confederates showed the stubborn owner the utmost respect, embodying the military decorum that had been drilled into them at West Point.

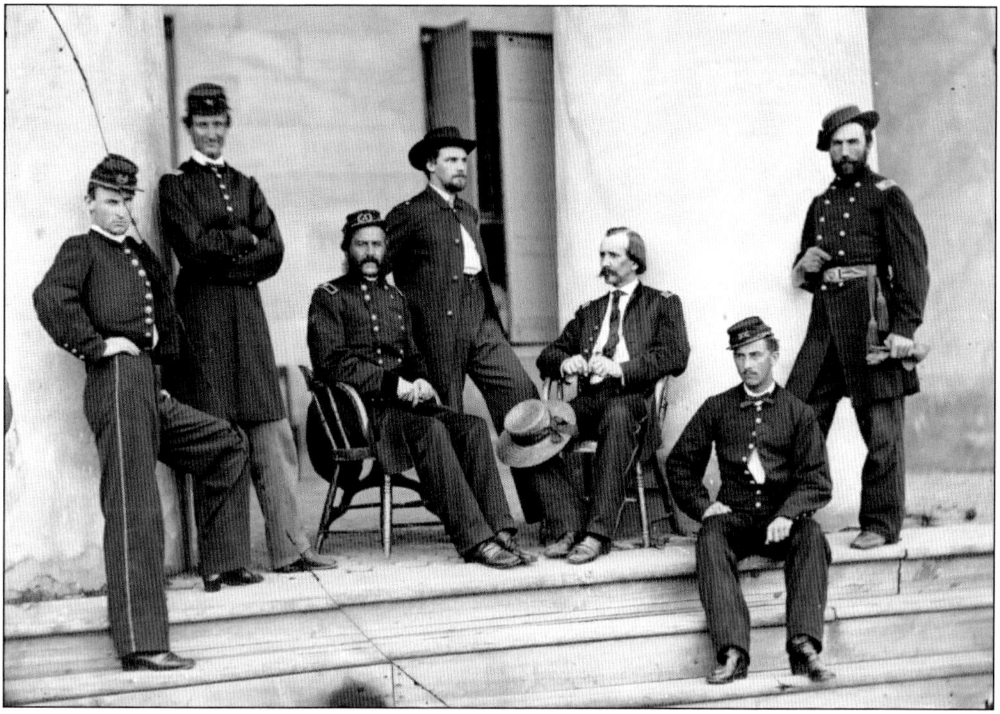

For millennia, poking about the lion's den has been an irresistible treat for soldiers. The 1860s was no exception. Here, a few Union soldiers pose on the porch of a gorgeous home. The house provided a nice backdrop for the photograph, but its importance came from the fact that it was owned by Gen. Robert E. Lee. After the outbreak of the war, Lee was forced to leave his home to the invading Federals.

Robert E. Lee's home at Arlington became an increasingly popular destination for occupying Union officers to pose for photographs. Here, Gen. Samuel P. Heintzelman (standing, upper right) and his staff gather on the front steps of Lee's home. Numerous general officers had their images captured on Lee's old grounds.

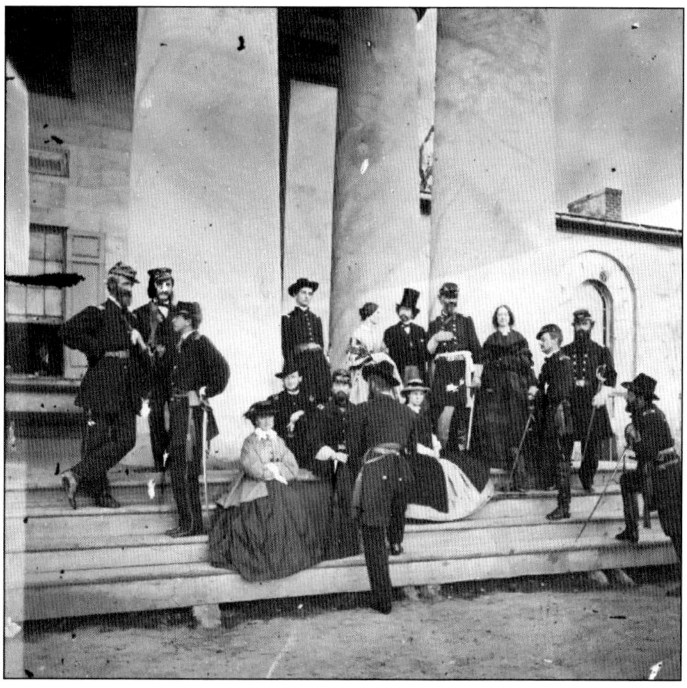

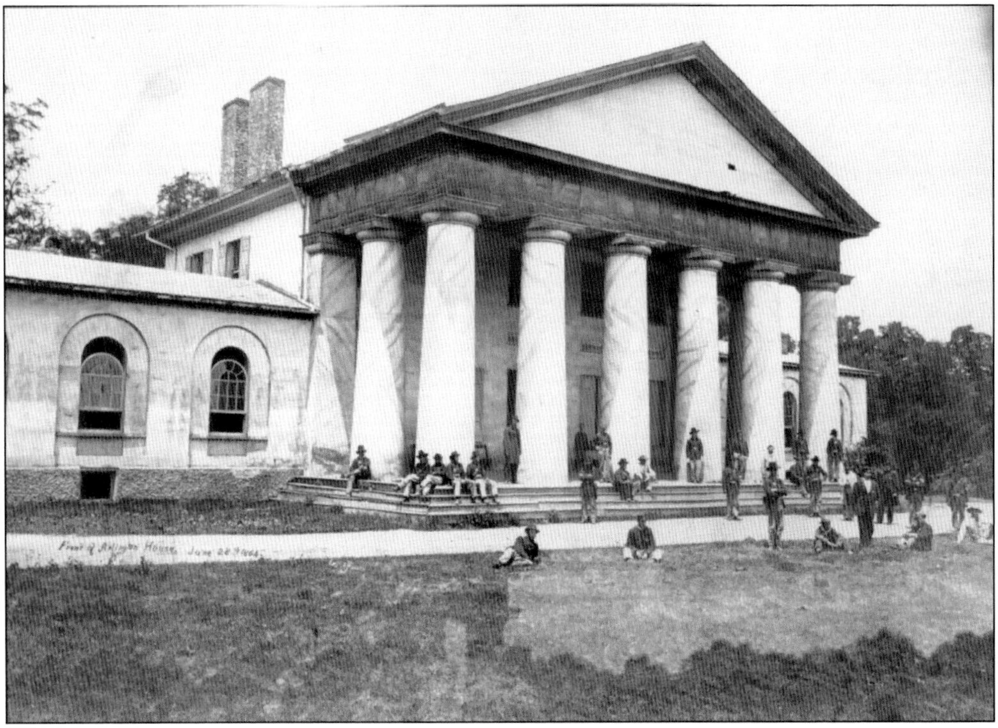

Robert E. Lee's home was built by Martha Washington's grandson. When Lee married George Washington's great-granddaughter, he inherited the home. Lee spent a portion of his youth in Alexandria and was the son of the ninth governor of Virginia. Following Lee's return from West Point, he took up residence at Arlington, only to leave it for good at the onset of the war.

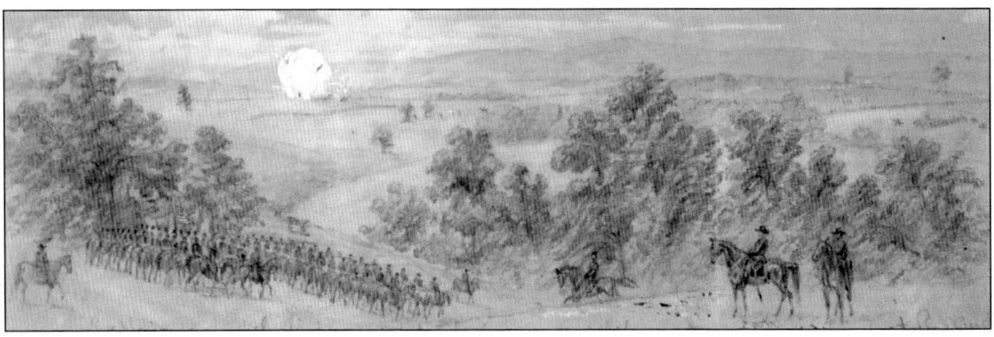

Dangerous work hardly describes the life of artillerymen during the Civil War. During nerve-wracking artillery duels, limbers containing massive amounts of gunpowder would often explode, killing all life within the blast radius. Illustrated here is one such scene following a battle near Middleburg, Virginia. Although no large-scale battle transpired here, it is interesting to note that many towns along modern-day Route 50 saw military action during the war.

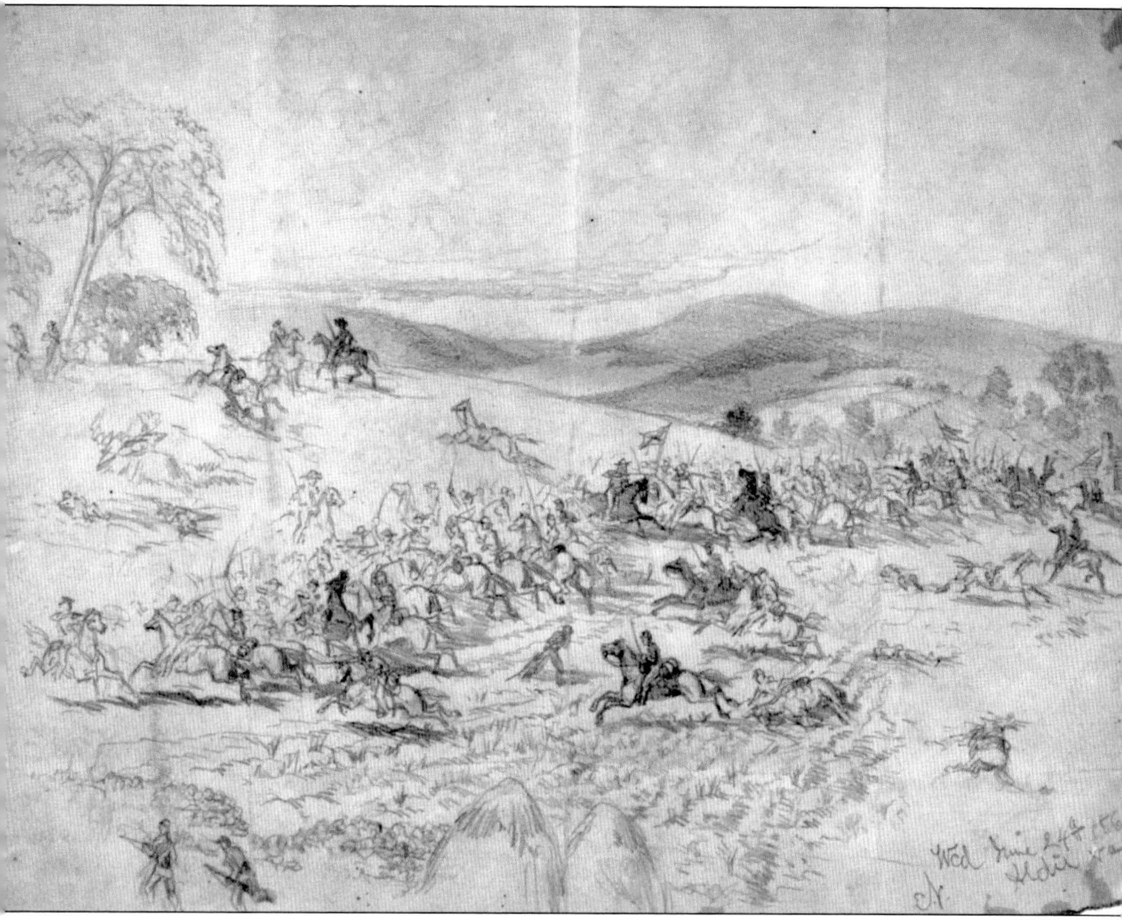

This sketch depicts the fierce clash at Aldie, Virginia. Looking at the serene town today, it is difficult to imagine such a dramatic battle taking place there. In late June 1863, J.E.B. Stuart's cavalry clashed with Union units on their way to Gettysburg. Typically, these cavalry engagements were violent but brief.

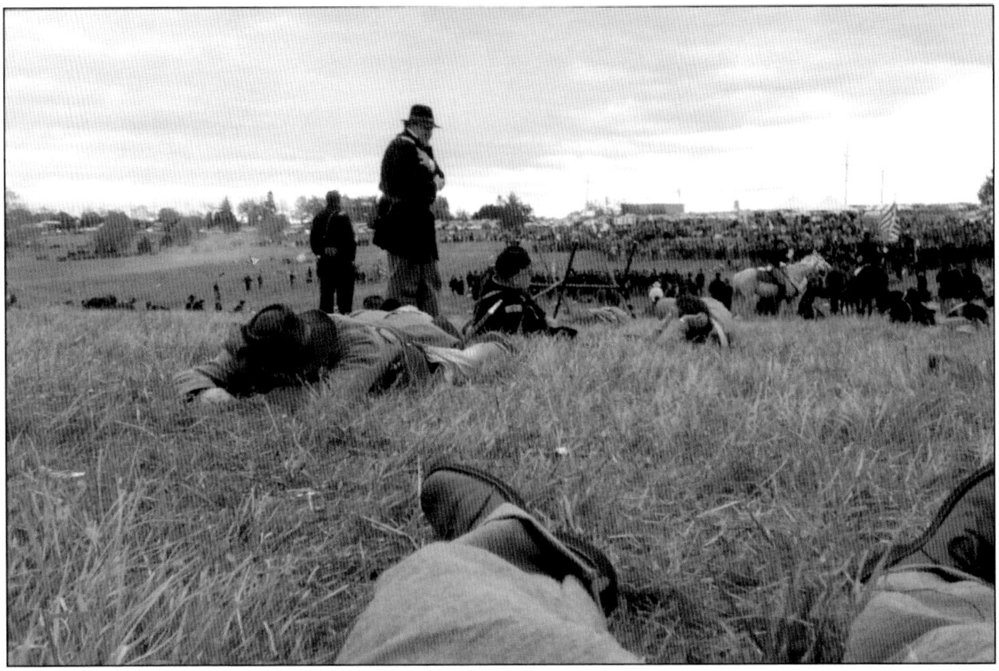

Today, many historians pay homage to those who fell during the war by attempting to re-create battles and events. Due to Virginia's prominent role in the conflict, many of these reenactments occur within 100 miles of the nation's capitol. Here, reenactors depict the horrors of battle. Although scenes like this are not capable of doing the real conflict justice, they are valuable in engaging future generations in remembering the war. (Courtesy of Hannah Berge.)

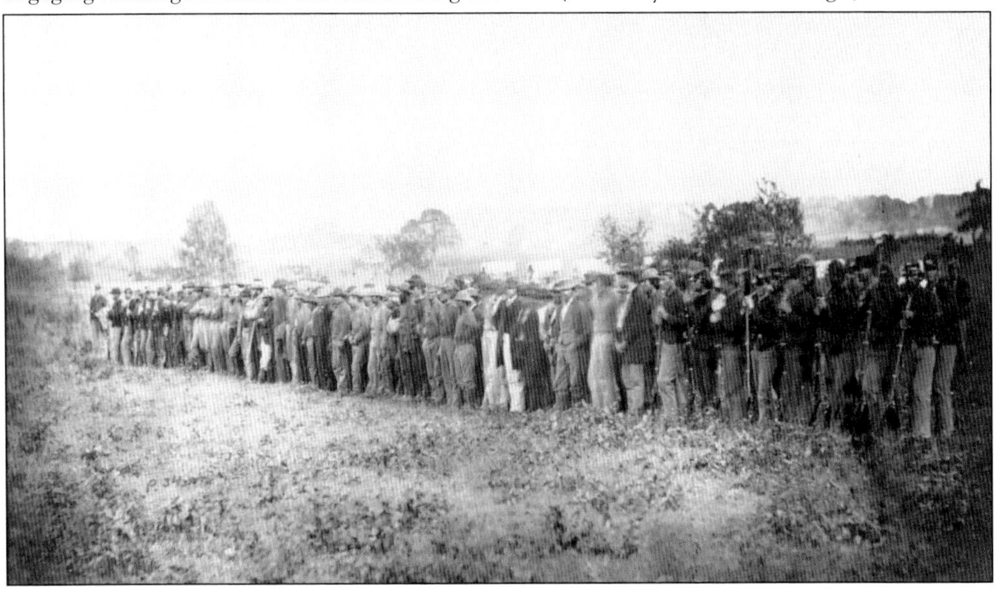

Shown here are ragged Confederates captured near Aldie, Virginia. The rough appearance of these men starkly contrasts their well-outfitted Union counterparts. For these unkempt men, their horrors are just beginning. They are on their way to a Union prisoner-of-war camp. Thousands of Confederates died in prison camps, as they were crowded within poor conditions, wrought with disease and infections.

Four

THE SEEDS OF DEFEAT

The commonwealth saw significant action in 1864, as Lincoln finally found his general. Ulysses S. Grant used his superior numbers to force Robert E. Lee into a defensive position around Richmond and Petersburg, as Southern troops desperately attempted to retain control of the Confederate municipality. Lee's smaller army was surrounded and in dire need of relief. In order to alleviate the pressure on the besieged army, Lee dispatched one of his loyal lieutenants, Jubal Anderson Early, to disrupt Union operations in the Shenandoah Valley and draw some of Grant's force away from the Confederate capitol. Early's campaign began with much success. He then shocked the Union as he pierced into Maryland and eventually assaulted one of the fortifications at Washington, DC. This daring Confederate foray sparked harsh criticism from Northern newspapers, which, in turn, spurred Lincoln to dispatch a competent general to quell Early's rambunctious maneuvering. By the fall of 1864, Phillip Sheridan had arrived in the Shenandoah Valley and successfully annihilated Early's force, thus eliminating Lee's hopes of diluting the Union siege around Richmond. In 1864, other characters arose, such as John Singleton Mosby and his partisan rangers, which became the topic of newspaper headlines in both nations as he performed daring raids against the Federal army and occupied counties in the northern portion of Virginia. Despite these operations, the Confederate fate had been sealed, and defeat appeared increasingly eminent.

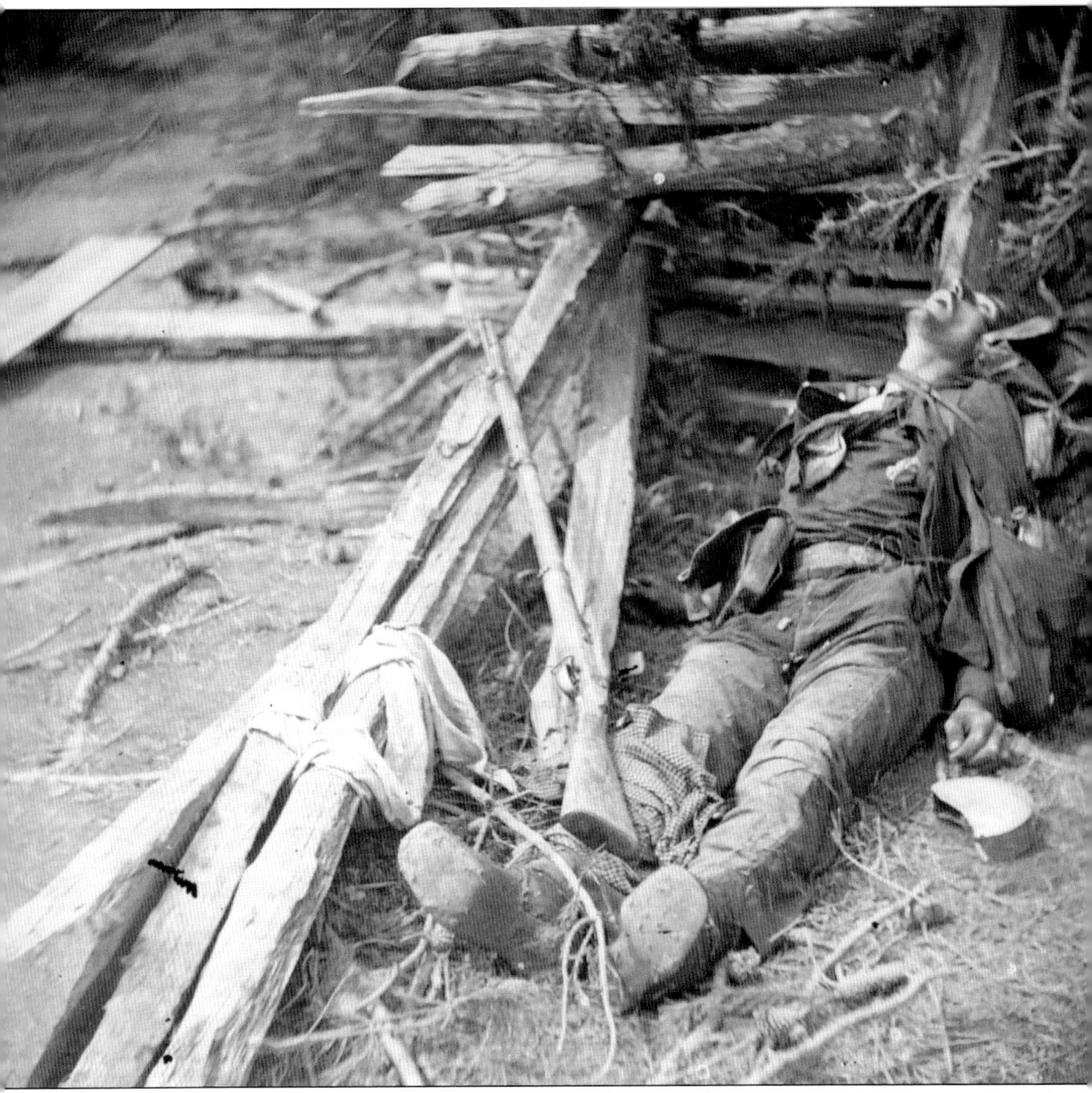

After months of embarrassing defeats at the hands of Southern troops, Lincoln went through multiple generals in his search for an officer who could match Robert E. Lee's military abilities. Despite the Union's advantages in both men and production, it had been unable to destroy Lee's army. However, by 1864, Lincoln had found his man when he promoted Ulysses S. Grant to command of Union military operations. The Confederates immediately felt the effects of Grant's bloody tactical style, and casualties on both sides skyrocketed. Shown here is a dead Confederate infantryman near Spotsylvania, Virginia.

General Grant was a rough, hardened soldier who embodied the word "grit." He had fought hard in the Western theater of the war and brought his tough attitude east. Grant immediately garnered respect from his troops and possessed a talent for selecting competent officers for promotion. Grant was responsible for men like Sherman, Sheridan, and Custer being utilized to their fullest capacities.

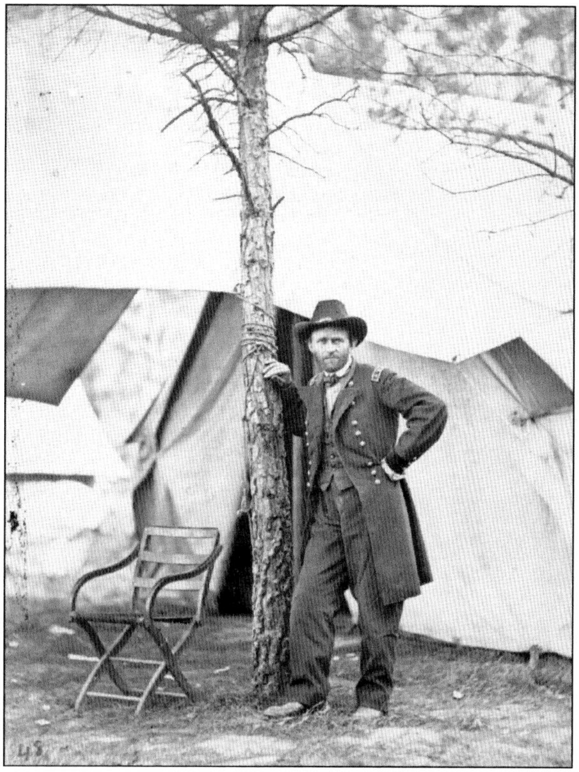

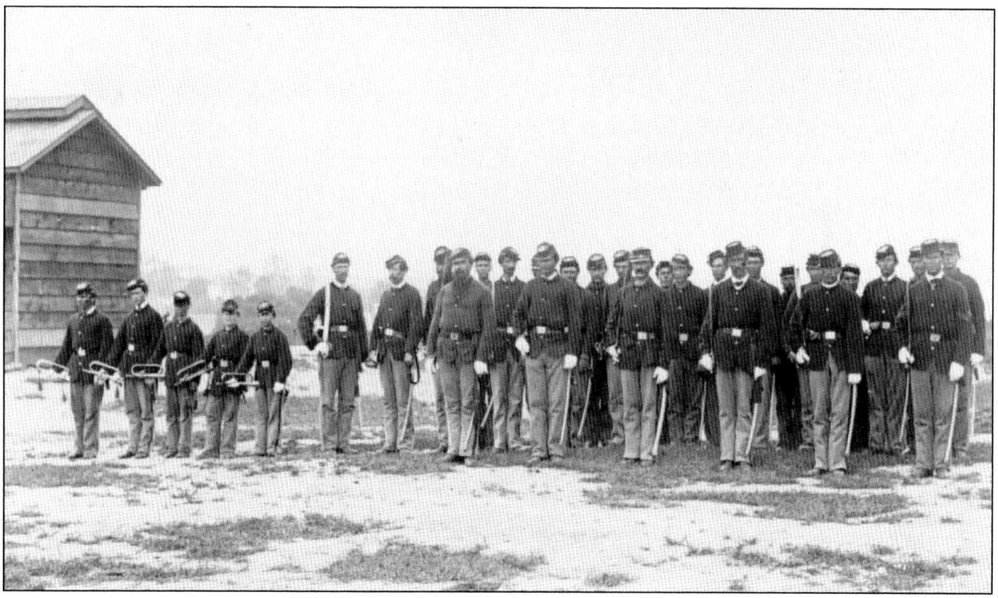

Grant had the ability to discern talent in his subordinates and possessed strategic foresight. But he was not the most garish or flamboyant general. He often wore very plain uniforms lacking the conventional adornments of an officer of his rank. Furthermore, he was said to have drank and smoked profusely. Nonetheless, he was good at his job, and Lincoln was willing to overlook Grant's peculiarities for the sake of his immense talent. Here, a contingent of Grant's cavalry escort gathers near City Point, Virginia.

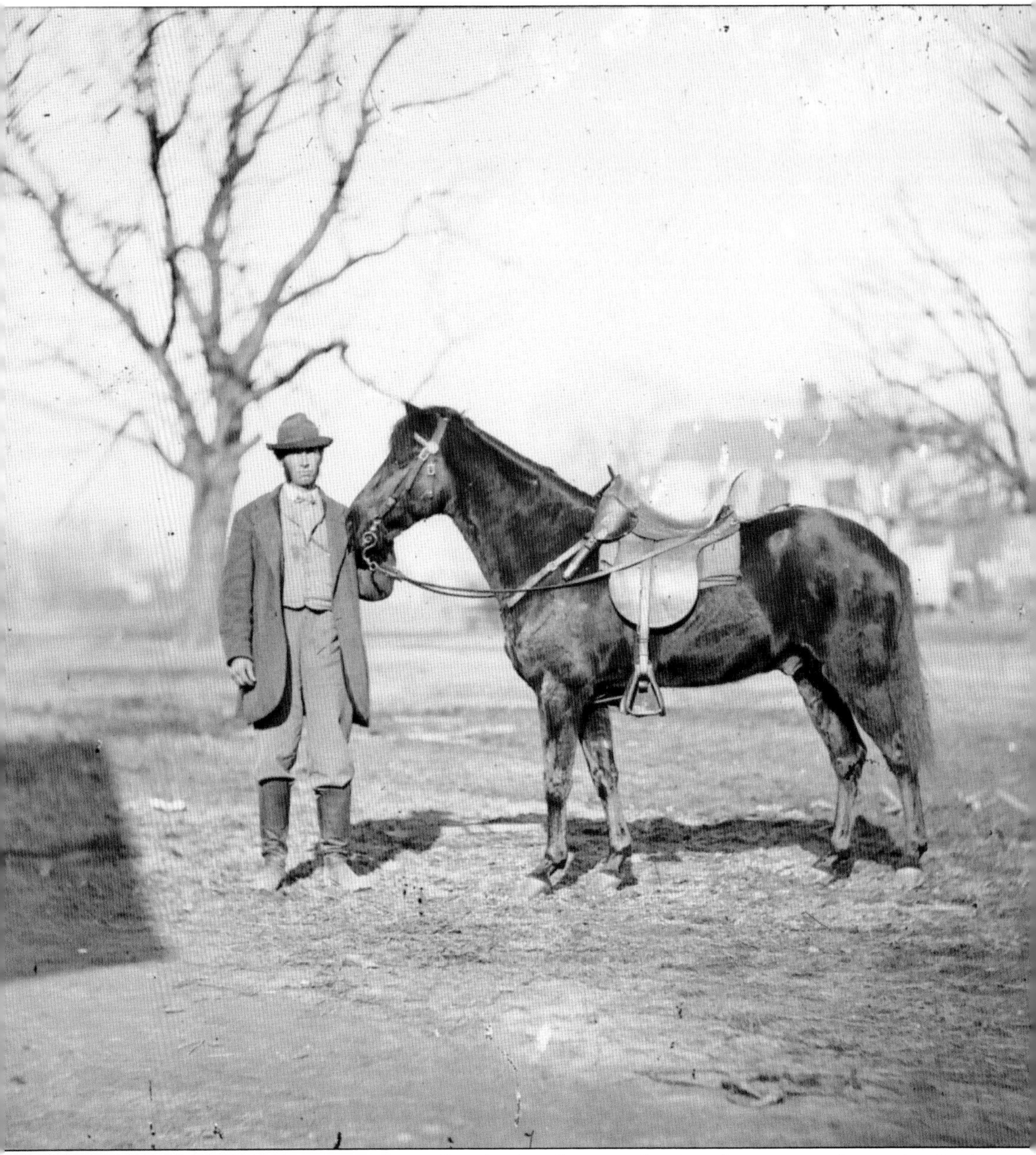

Although the war was a gruesome affair, both officers and enlisted troops tried to make the best of their situations. Humor was one method of coping, and even generals such as Grant would join in the fun. Seen here is Grant's horse, Jeff Davis, named after the Confederate president. Ulysses S. Grant's down-to-earth demeanor won the hearts of his men, many of who became loyal supporters during his postwar political career.

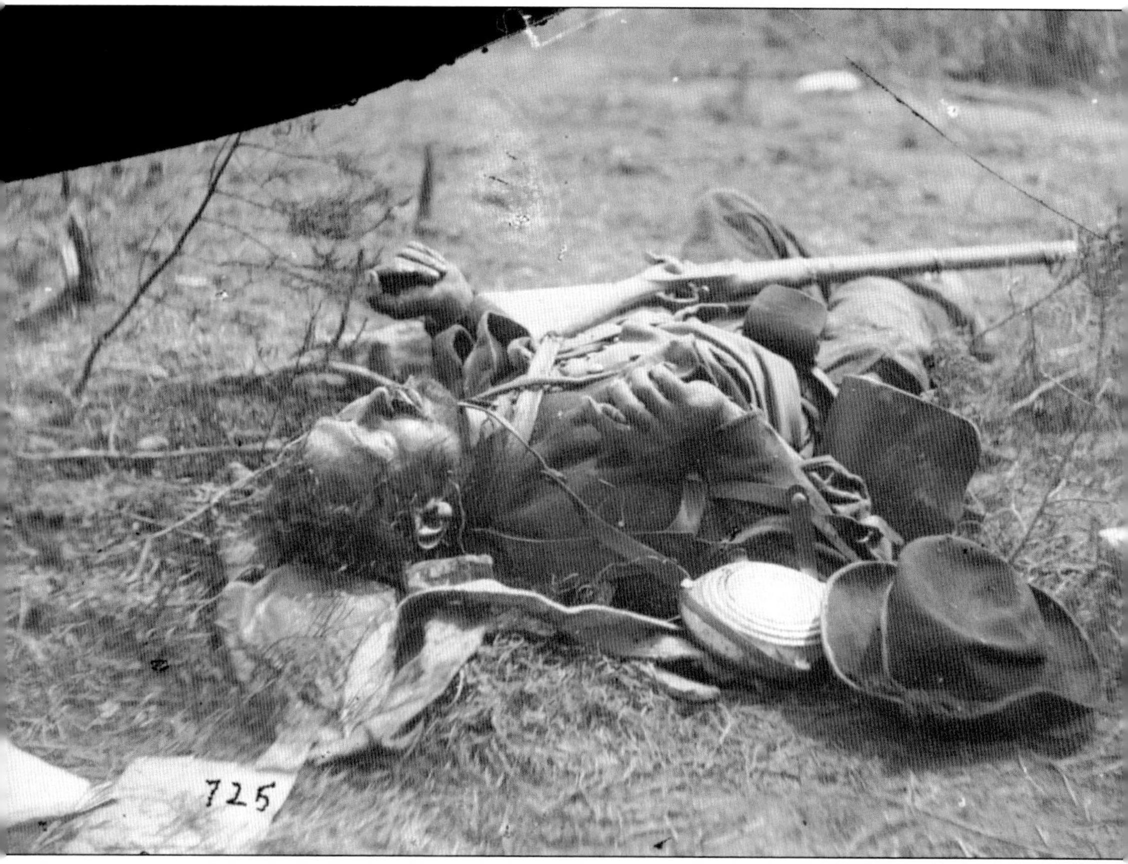

Grant recognized that he had at his disposal plenty of troops with which to assault Lee's position north of Richmond, and the Union general did so in violent fashion. In early May 1864, Grant initiated a series of attacks that would leave thousands dead and countless others wounded. This photograph shows the aftermath of the violent carnage that ensued.

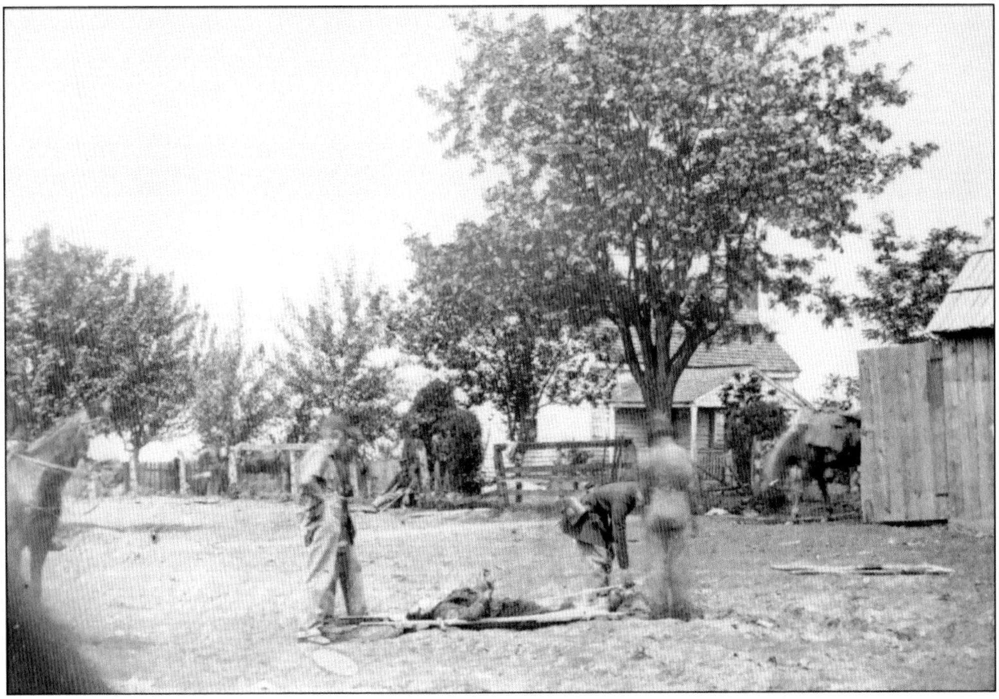

This photograph shows the site of Confederate general Richard Ewell's assault on Grant's position in early May. It was the scene of horrendous fighting. Over the coming weeks, Grant brought to bear the Union's superior manpower as he initiated countless assaults on Lee with seeming disregard of the high casualties. Many Confederate officers claimed that the fighting in May 1864 was some of the most brutal they had encountered.

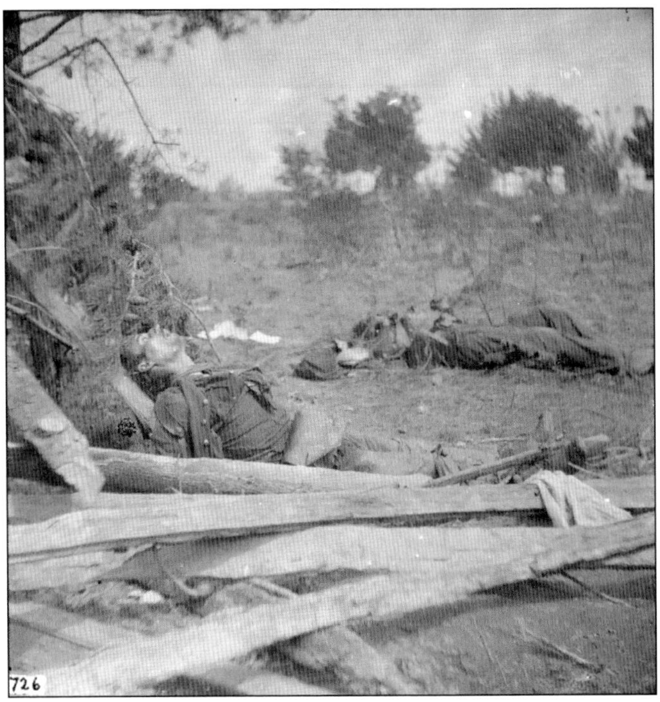

Ulysses S. Grant employed a strategy of relentless contact with the enemy. Prior to Grant's arrival in Virginia, Union officers would often discontinue combat after the sun set or following significant casualties. General Grant, however, pushed his army to the limit. Throughout May 1864, the two armies fought almost constantly. The combat was more akin to the ferocity experienced at Tarawa or Iwo Jima in World War II than to popular perceptions of Civil War battles.

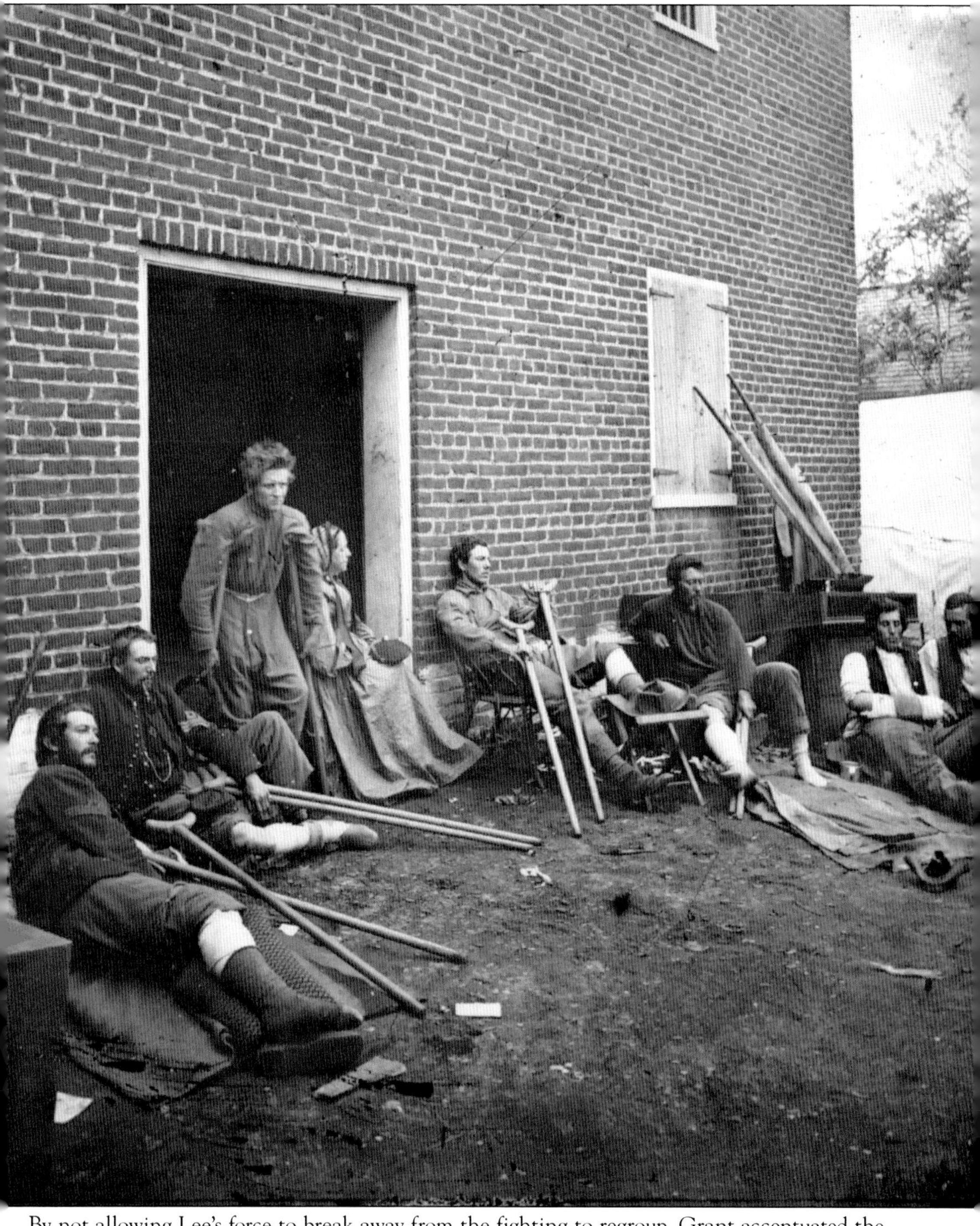

By not allowing Lee's force to break away from the fighting to regroup, Grant accentuated the Confederate deficiencies in manpower. Lee's army could not afford to lose valuable men, and Grant's bloody tactics were most felt by the smaller Confederate force. The Federals had men to spare. Even among the Union ranks, Grant's tactical style was criticized as barbaric; many Union troops referred to him as "the butcher."

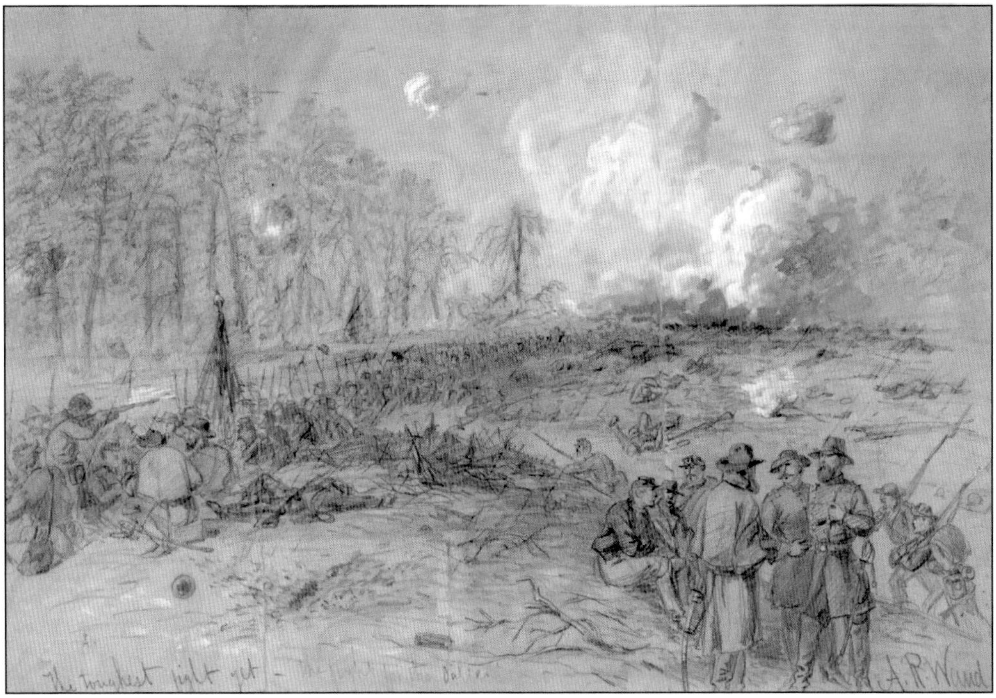

As Grant pushed Lee closer to Richmond, both armies entered a region referred to as The Wilderness. Here, the ground is rough and wooded, and this forced battle lines to closely approach one another before firing. After a few volleys, it was not uncommon for fierce hand-to-hand combat to ensue, involving terrifying bayonet charges and soldiers bludgeoning one another with the stocks of their rifles.

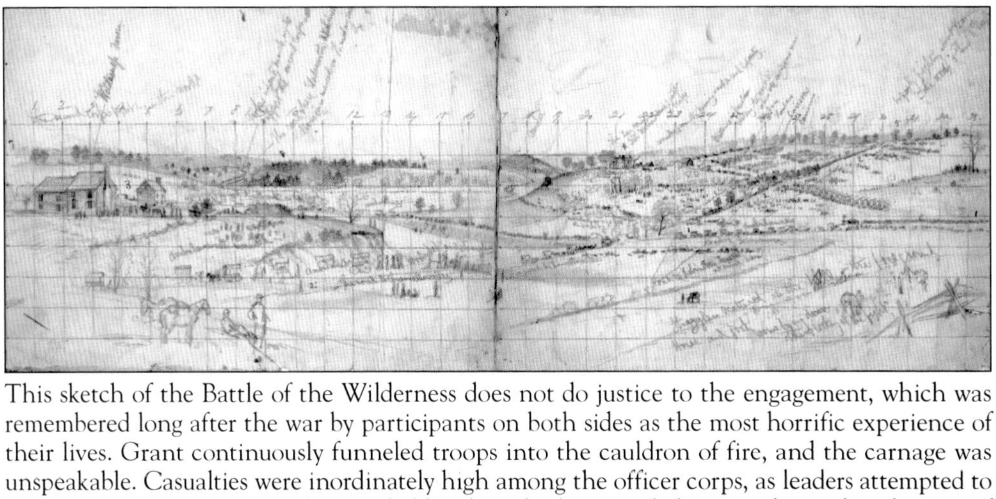

This sketch of the Battle of the Wilderness does not do justice to the engagement, which was remembered long after the war by participants on both sides as the most horrific experience of their lives. Grant continuously funneled troops into the cauldron of fire, and the carnage was unspeakable. Casualties were inordinately high among the officer corps, as leaders attempted to manage their battle lines in the tangled brush and subsequently became the preferred target of enemy fire.

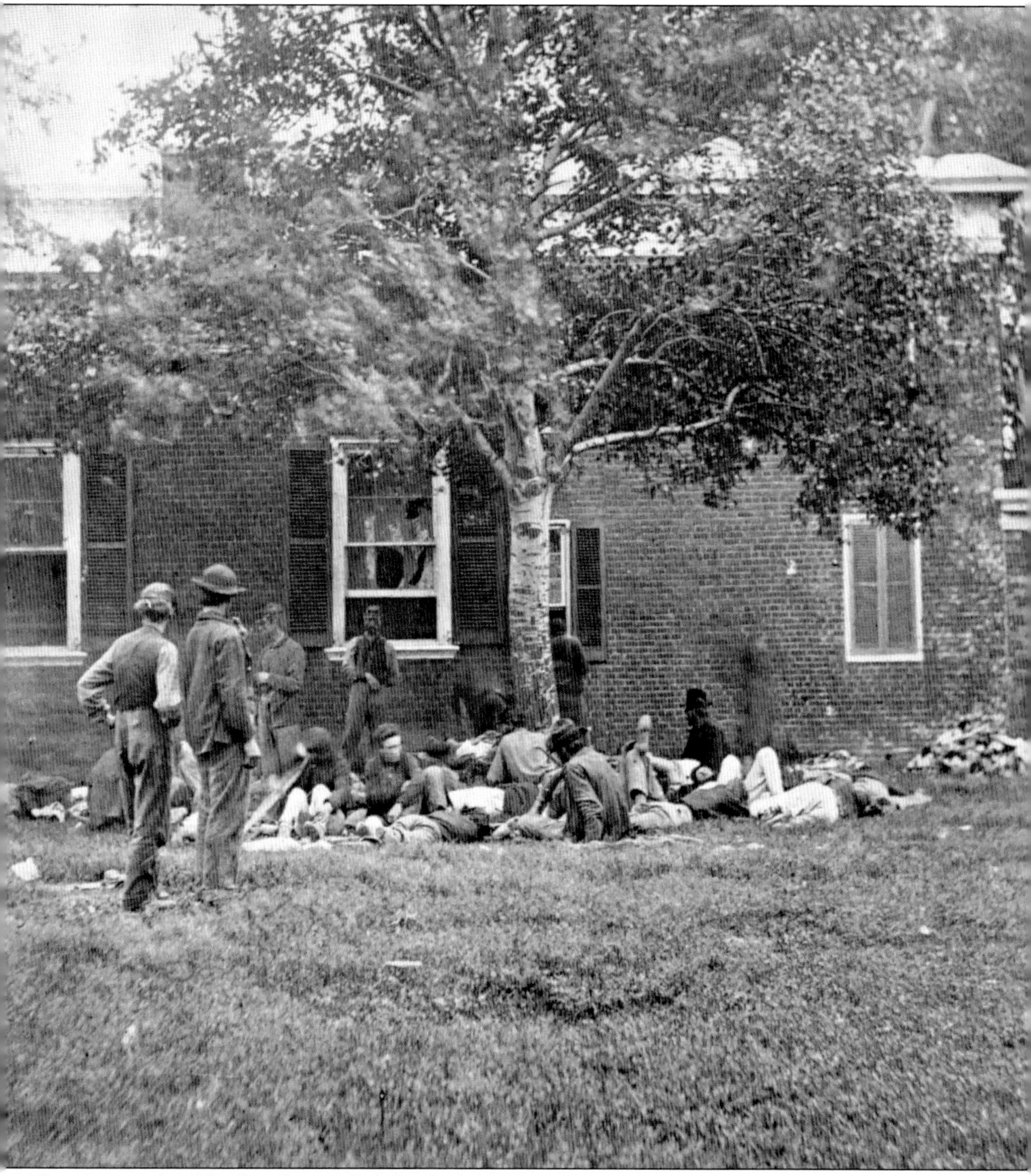

The thousands of dead and wounded shocked the nation. As the campaign to reach Richmond raged on, bodies poured into Union depots, like this one at Fredericksburg, for transport north. Although the human cost was extremely high, General Grant stayed on the offensive, relentlessly engaging Lee's ever-shrinking force. Although many historians argue that Lee was one of the most talented generals in American history, Grant knew how to accentuate his advantages, and his nerves of steel allowed him to maintain pressure on Lee for weeks.

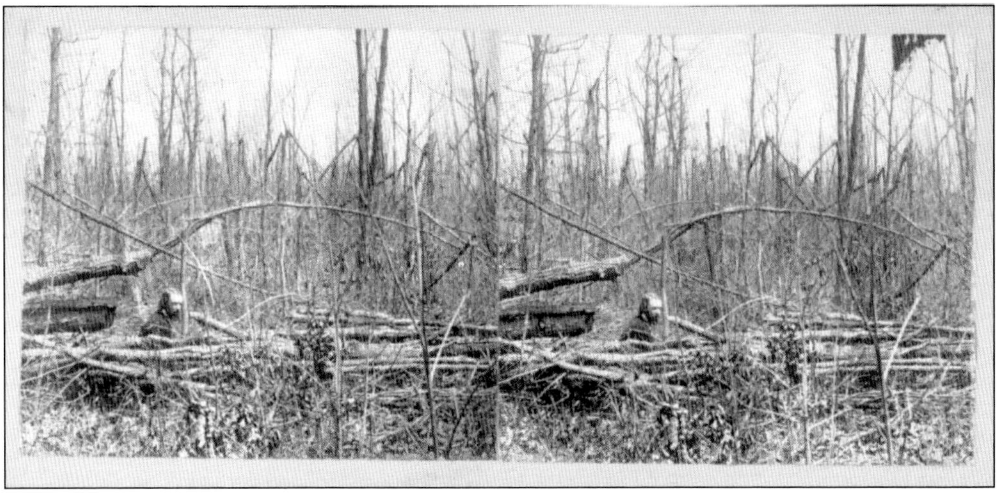

Fighting took on a modernistic feel when both sides began to heavily employ breastworks and elaborate trench systems to prevent exposure to enemy fire. This photograph offers a striking depiction of the dense woods at The Wilderness. The rough conditions made tending to wounds nearly impossible; even the smallest of injuries often resulted in death due to infection. Seen here are some of Grant's trench works, created in early May.

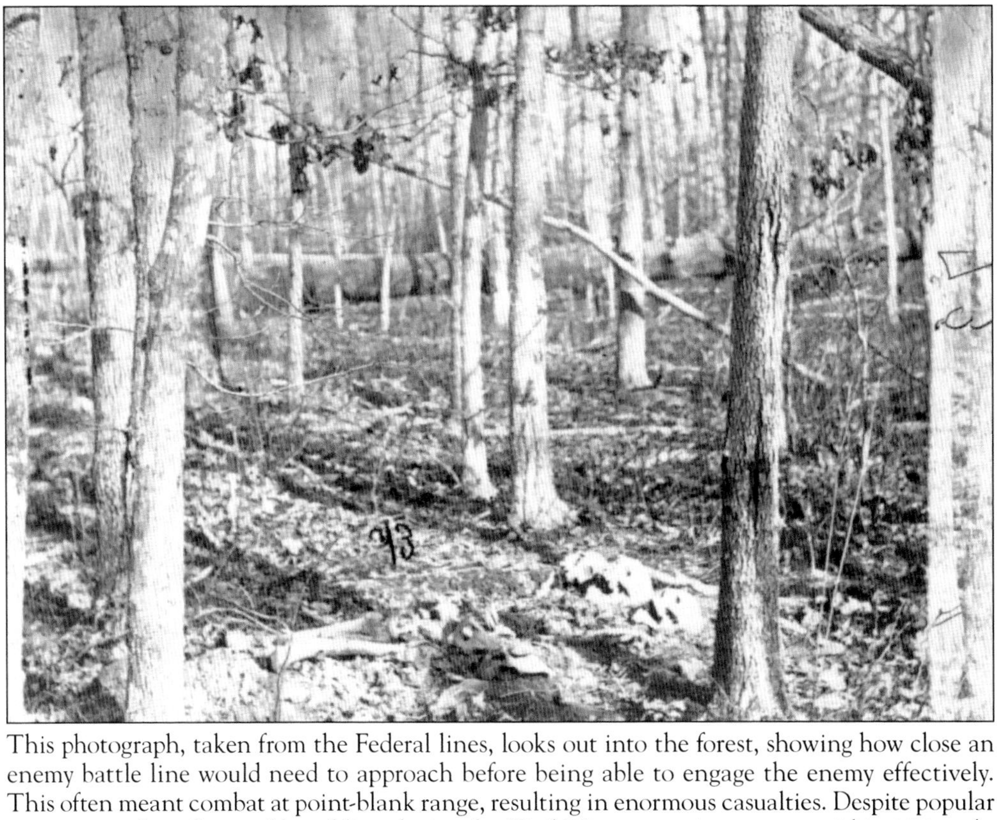

This photograph, taken from the Federal lines, looks out into the forest, showing how close an enemy battle line would need to approach before being able to engage the enemy effectively. This often meant combat at point-blank range, resulting in enormous casualties. Despite popular conception, the rifles used by soldiers during the Civil War were quite accurate within 100 yards. This photograph conveys the sense of dread Federal troops felt when a Confederate battle line approached, howling its eerie "Rebel yell."

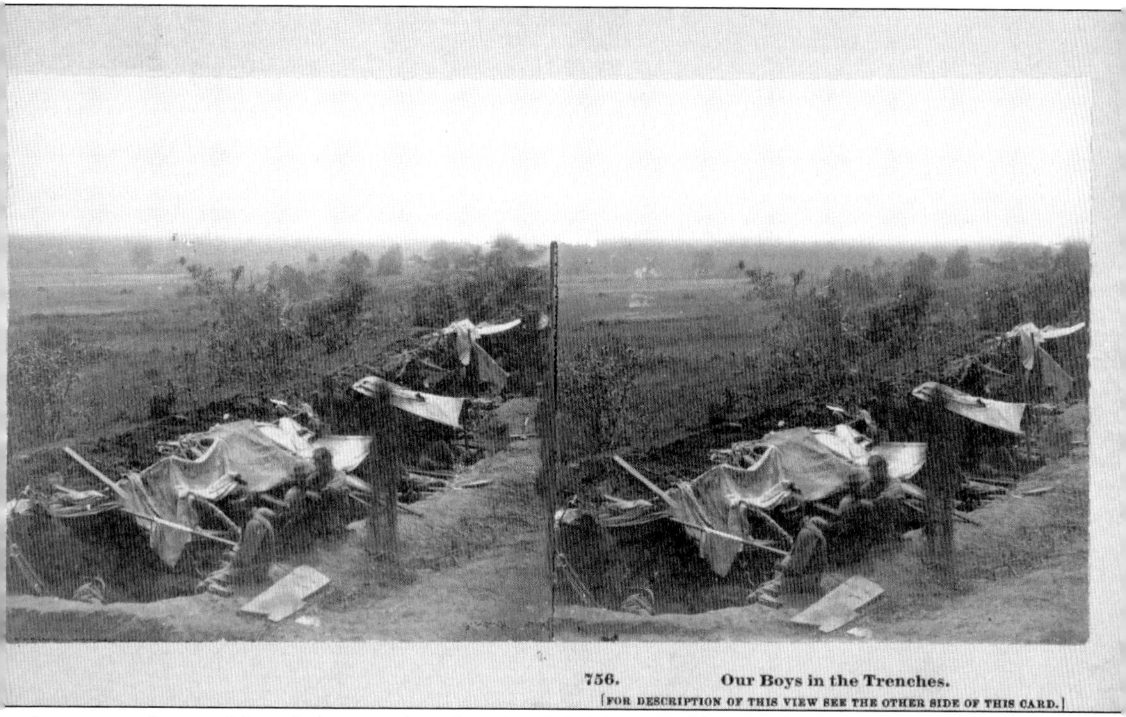

In a scene that could easily be mistaken for a battlefield in World War I, battle-hardened Union troops are stationed in a muddy trench just north of Richmond. By this point in the war, most units from both the Union and Confederacy were veterans of many battles and were good at their jobs. Gone were the days where a bayonet charge would send the opposing line fleeing. Instead, hardened soldiers welcomed combat and were prepared to have their lives snuffed out on the order of their beloved generals.

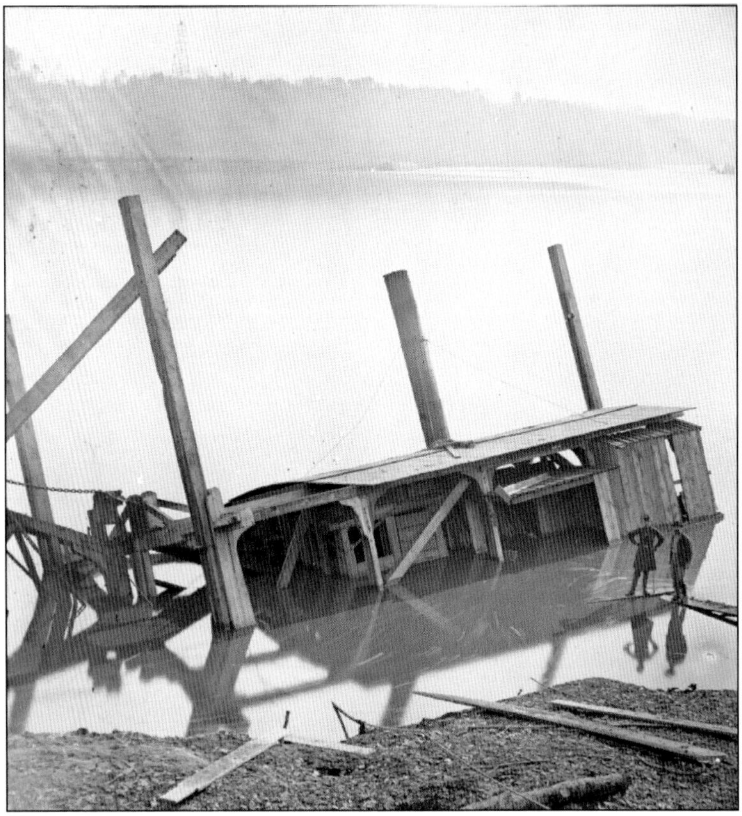

War brings about the strangest of scenes. This Union dredging boat was struck by a Confederate artillery round. Although the Union had achieved relative supremacy on the water, the Confederates still challenged Federal naval presence when possible. Often, weaker, smaller vessels such as this one would be targeted. The Confederates tried anything to disrupt the Union military juggernaut.

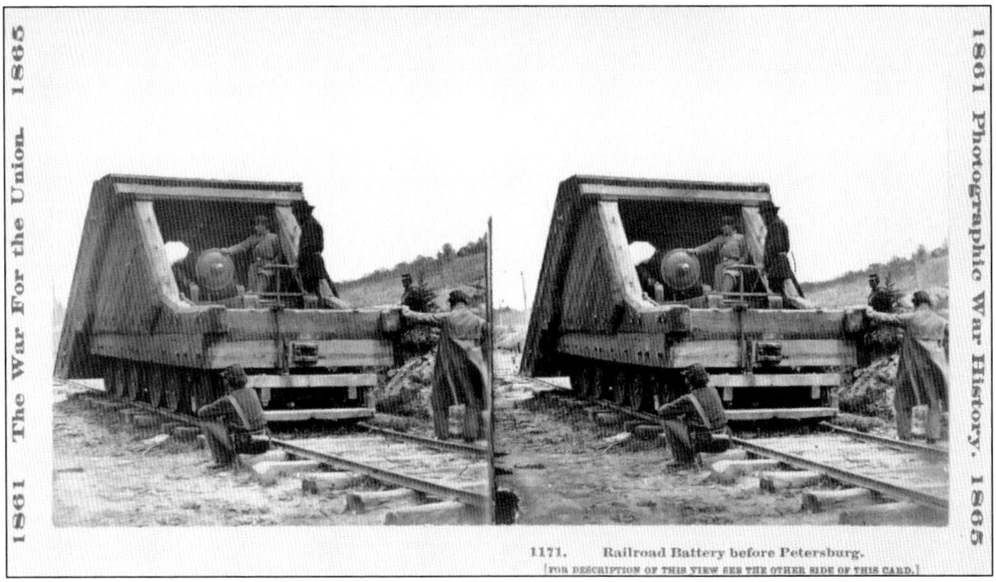

After weeks of horrific fighting, the Union had pushed Lee's shattered army into defensive works around Petersburg and Richmond. The already weakened Confederates were now starving and running low on supplies, yet they continued to resist the ever-tightening noose of Grant's army. Grant, exceptionally good at sieges, brought in unique weapons, such as this rail-mounted mortar, to bomb the dying Confederates into submission.

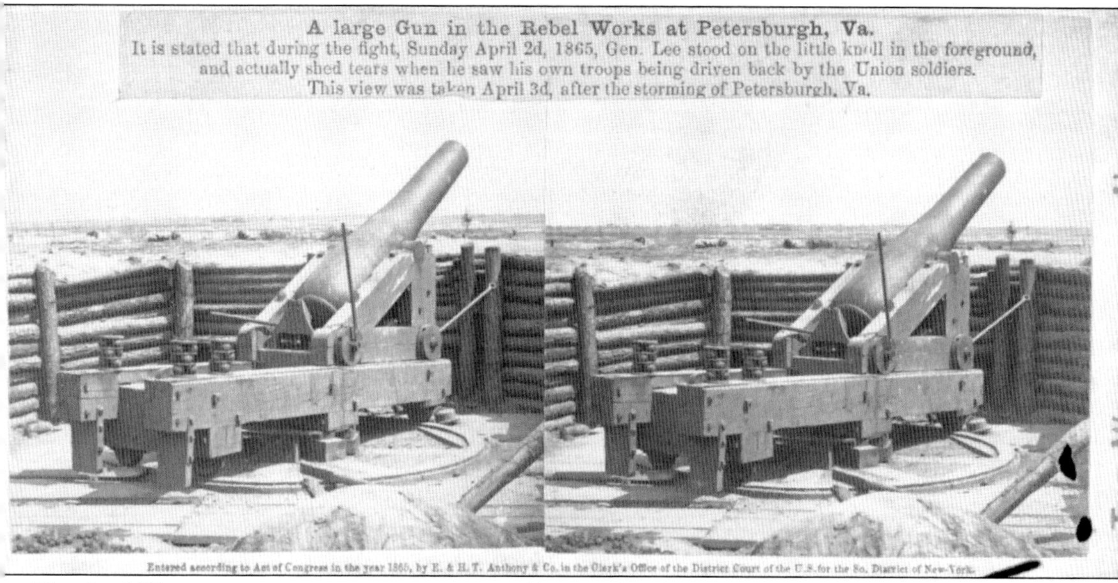

The Civil War saw massive improvements in artillery, and both Confederate and Union foundries attempted to create more powerful weapons. This massive artillery piece could decimate targets hundreds of yards away. Any Union advance on Confederate trenches would need to endure the carnage that artillery pieces such as this could generate—that is, if they had ammunition to fire. The Confederates lacked the industrial might to supply its armies in the field; in many instances, these cannons lay silent, awaiting ammunition.

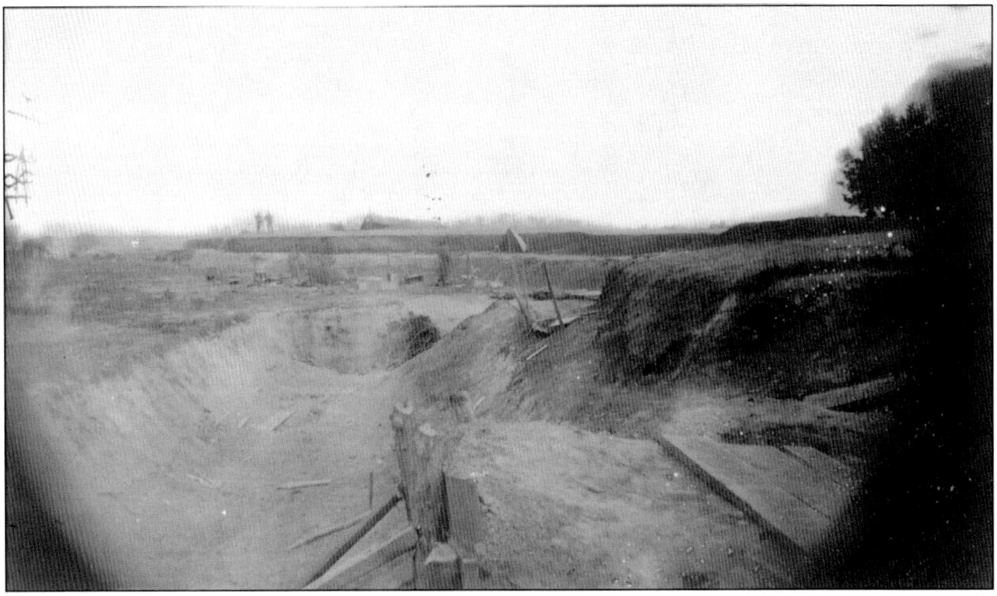

A few feet of dirt would make all the difference in the world to a veteran soldier accustomed to little cover on the open battlefield. Entrenchments like this were a welcome change that dramatically increased the life expectancy of the troops within them. These captured Confederate trenches were overrun by the Union 18th Corps in late June 1864.

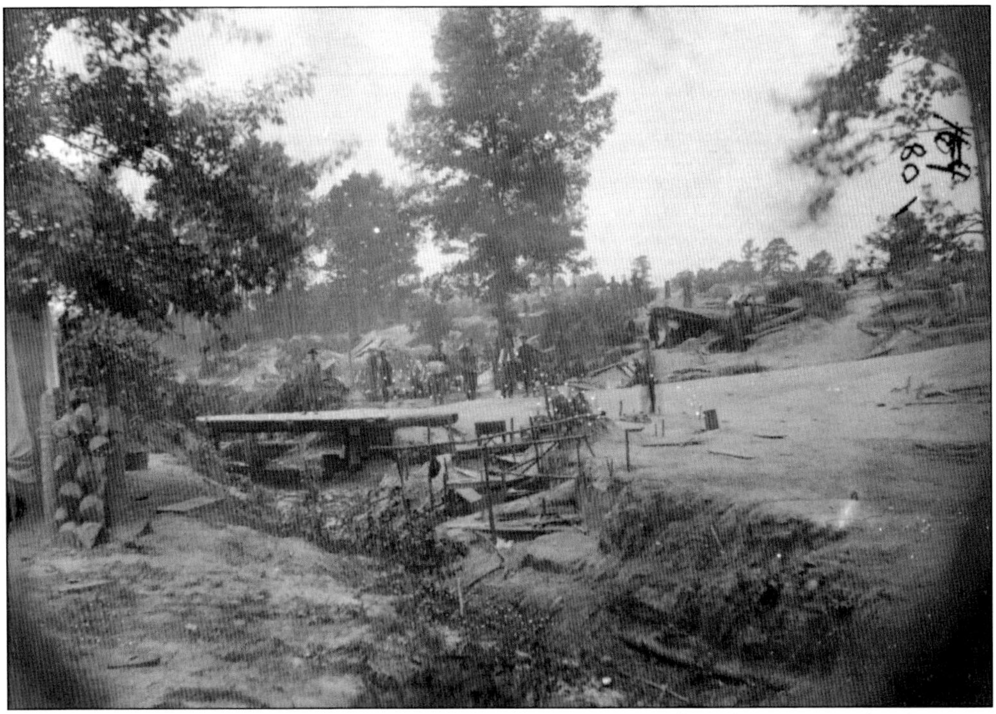

As both sides employed increasingly more mortars and similar artillery devices, trenches began to evolve into more secure emplacements. The action around Petersburg and Richmond saw the early development of modern-day bunkers, designed to protect critical staff members from incoming artillery. Here are a few such shelters, integrated into the Union line.

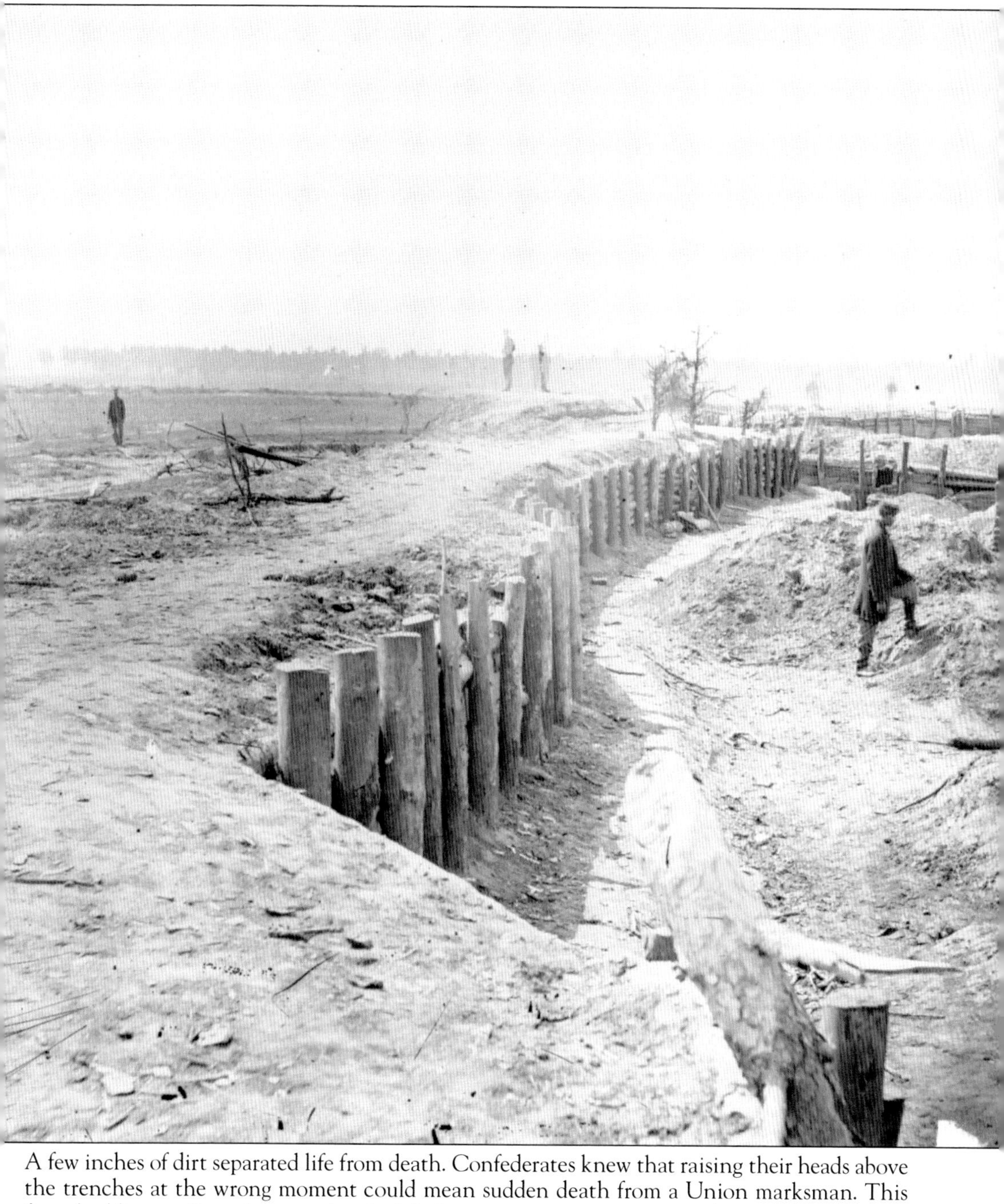

A few inches of dirt separated life from death. Confederates knew that raising their heads above the trenches at the wrong moment could mean sudden death from a Union marksman. This forced soldiers to dig underground to find shelter, as setting up tents was no longer practical. This photograph shows the ingenuity of the besieged Confederates, who excavated huts underground and went as far as to build chimneys to heat their damp living quarters.

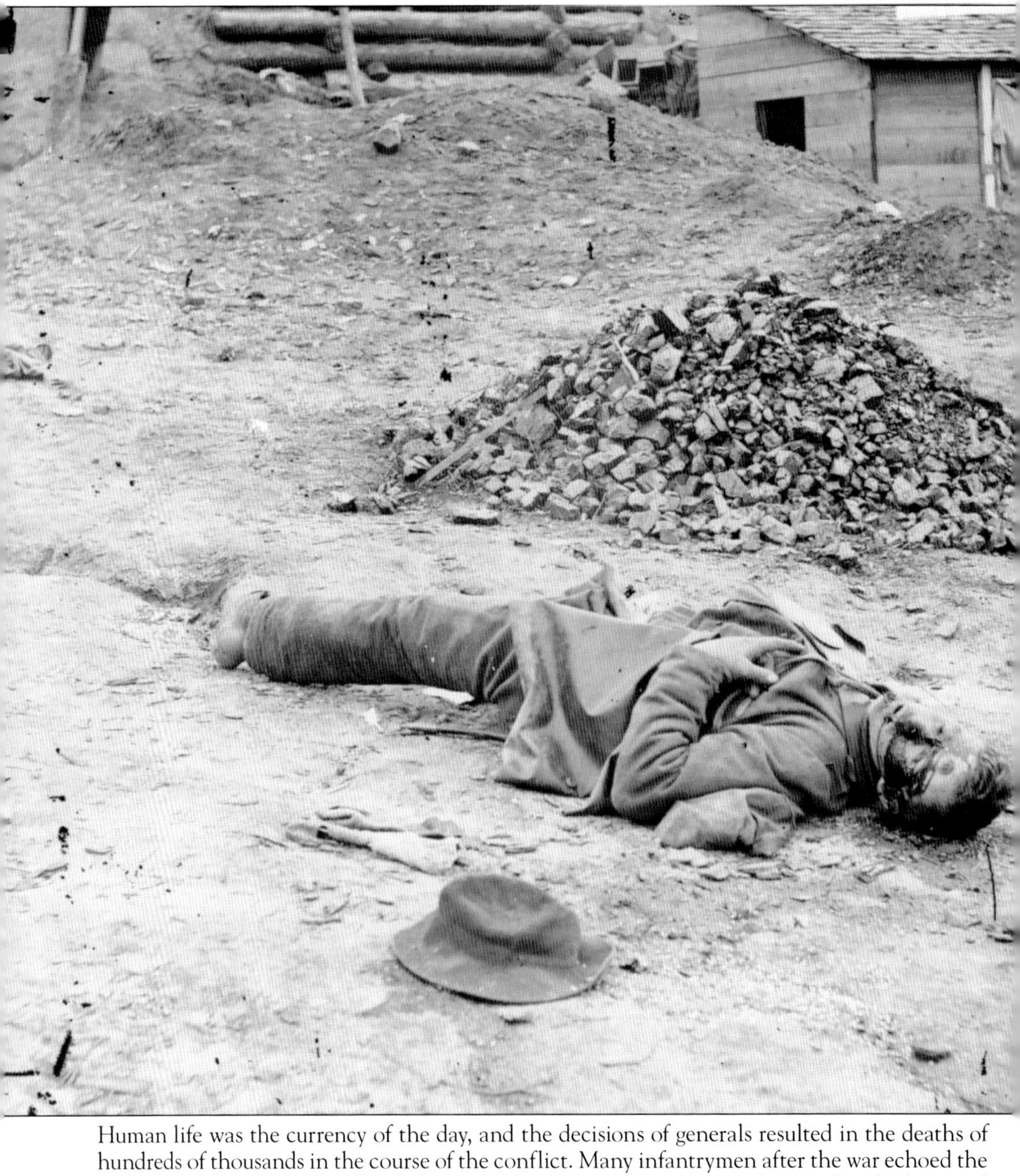

Human life was the currency of the day, and the decisions of generals resulted in the deaths of hundreds of thousands in the course of the conflict. Many infantrymen after the war echoed the sentiments of soldiers throughout the ages: what kept them going was the man beside them and the life-altering experience they shared. As the war raged on, units that contained thousands of men at the outset often comprised only a handful of men by war's end. These few survivors became increasingly close, and the loss of any one of them was often unbearable.

Many generals were profoundly affected by the tremendous weight of having ordered the death and destruction of the units they commanded. Generals like Lee and Grant did not take their responsibility lightly, and they were haunted by their decisions long after the war. Whether they wore blue or grey, they were all Americans, and no other struggle in the nation's history has accounted for the loss of more American lives. This tragic photograph shows a dead Union soldier and a Confederate casualty in the Virginia heat.

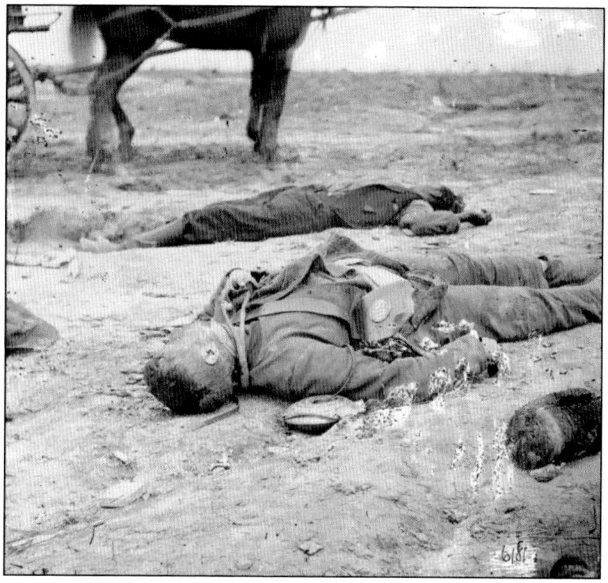

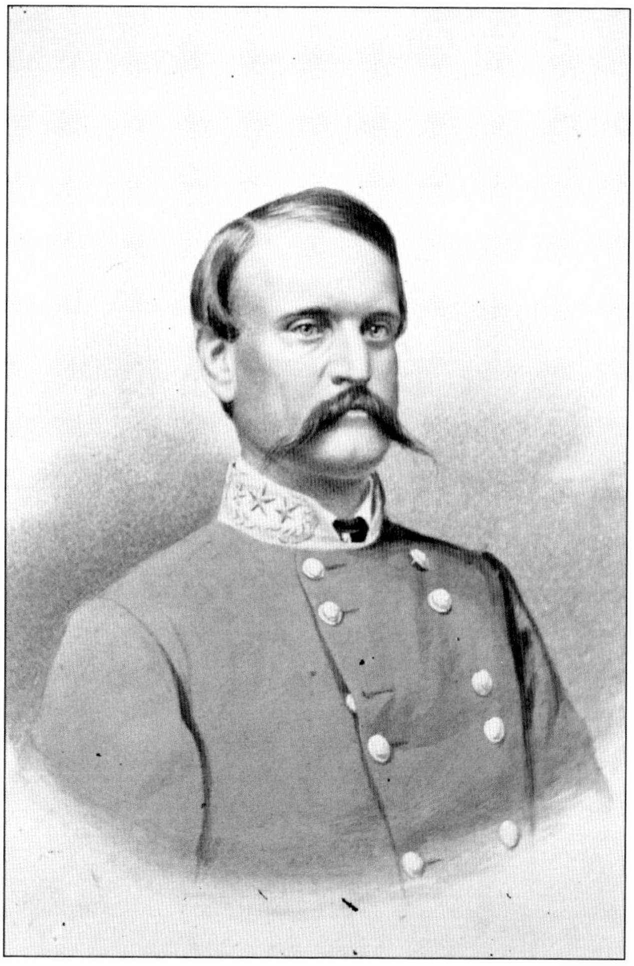

While the bulk of Lee's army was in a struggle for survival around Petersburg, a small independent force of under 6,000 Confederates achieved a dramatic victory in the Shenandoah Valley. Former vice president of the United States, now a Confederate major general, John C. Breckinridge rallied a ragtag army against Franz Sigel's Union force at New Market, Virginia. The battle made headlines throughout the country and is notable for the involvement of young cadets from Virginia Military Institute. Many of them were hardly old enough to fight, and the cadets were reluctantly sent into battle. Despite their youth, they performed gallantly and were instrumental in the Confederate victory. Upon sending the cadets into battle, Breckinridge uttered the famous words, "Put the boys in, and may God forgive me for the order."

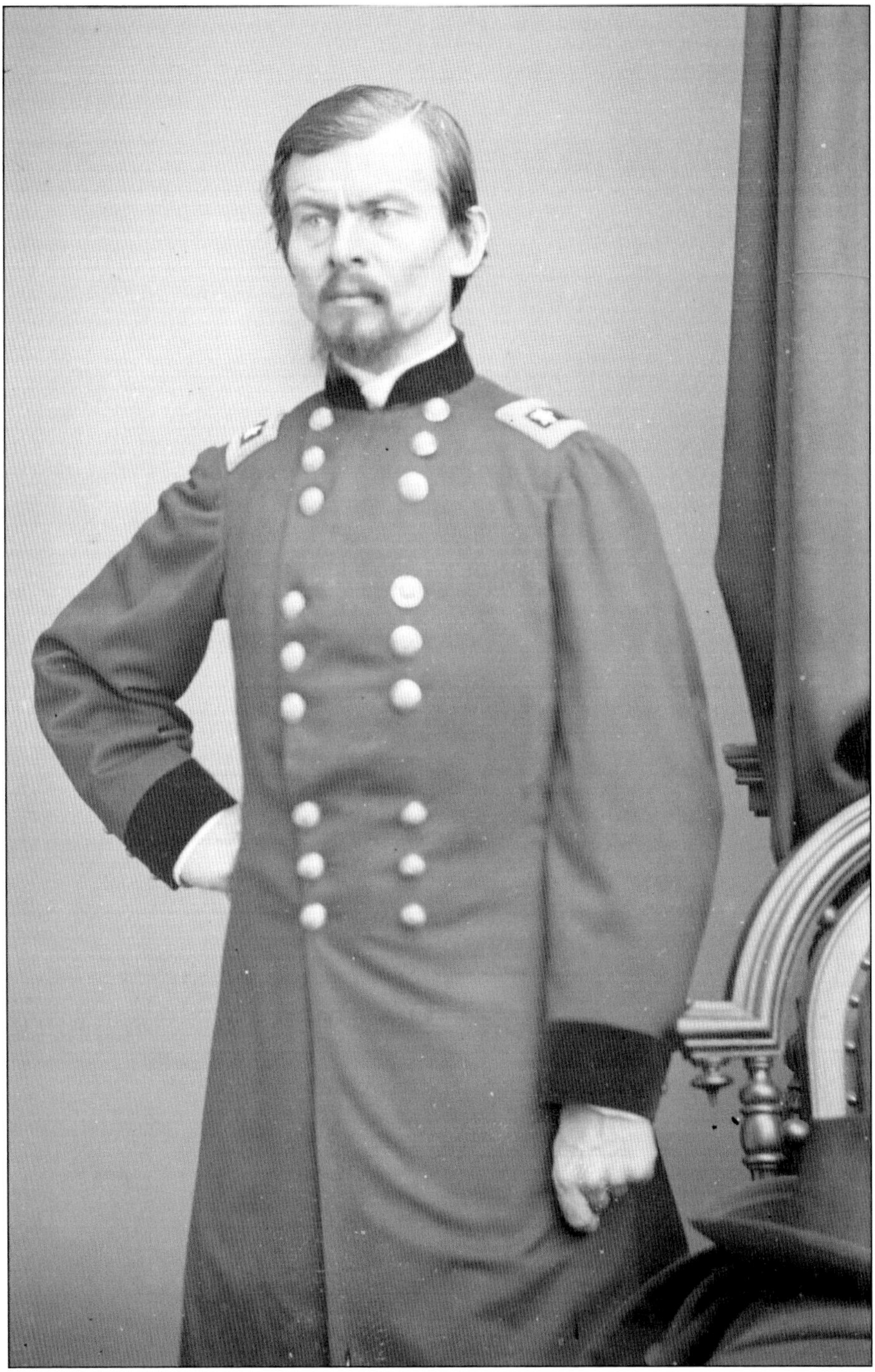

Breckinridge's opponent at New Market was Maj. Gen. Franz Sigel, who was born in Germany and immigrated to the United States before the war. It is important to remember that both armies had diverse ethnicities in their ranks up until the end of fighting. African Americans, Germans, Irish, and Native Americans served in both armies. In many cases, entire units were ethnically homogenous, such as the famous Irish Brigade, composed mostly of Irish immigrants.

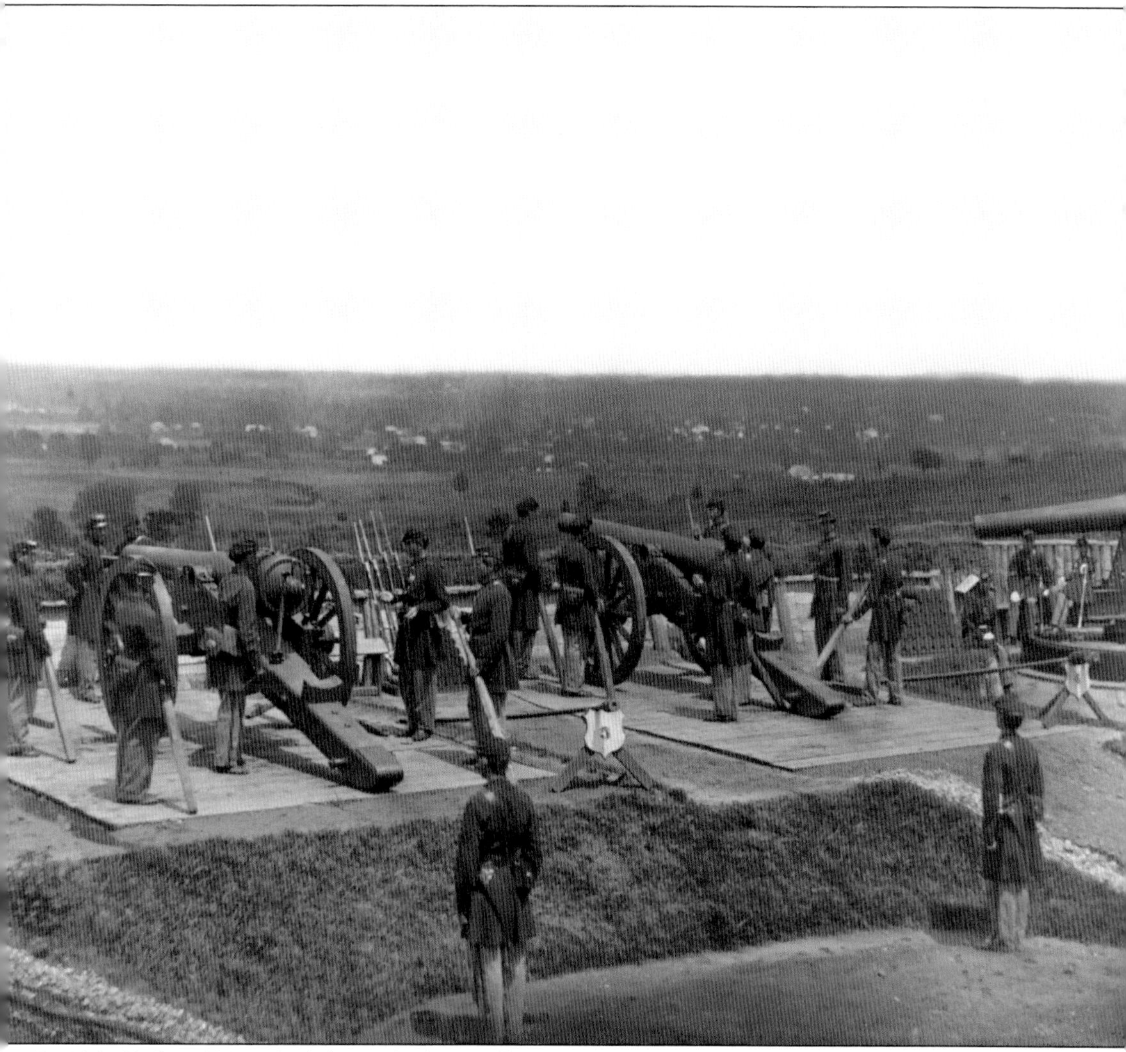

By 1864, Robert E. Lee had dispatched a small army under Gen. Jubal Anderson Early to disrupt Union operations in the Shenandoah Valley. It was hoped that this action would warrant the dispatching of troops by Grant from the siege at Petersburg to address the Confederate threat. Early did just that. By the late summer of 1864, he had worked his way up the Shenandoah Valley to the outskirts of Washington, DC, where he mounted an assault on one of the forts around the Union capital (pictured). This Confederate intrusion on the District of Columbia sparked harsh criticism from Union newspapers, which felt the US military was not doing enough to protect its citizens and end the war quickly.

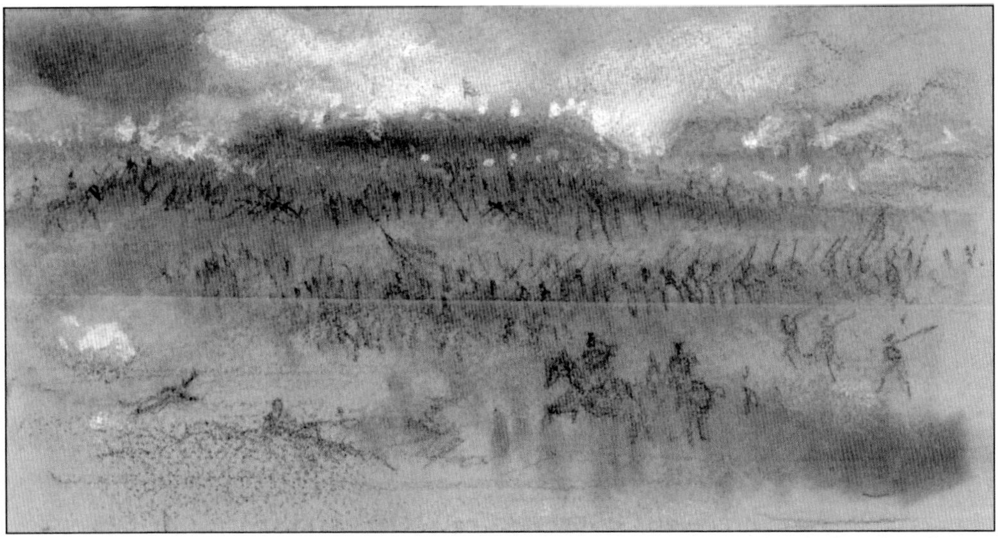

By the fall of 1864, Grant had dispatched one of his most talented generals, Phillip Sheridan, to the Shenandoah Valley to quell the threat of Early's marauding army. By September 19, Sheridan had cornered Early's force and forced him into a bloody fight at Winchester, Virginia. The fighting was so intense that it forced the Confederates to flee the field of battle in disorganized fashion. The retreat was so frantic that it was not stopped until approximately 15 miles south, where the two armies clashed a second time, at Fisher's Hill. During the fierce fighting outside of Winchester, Confederate colonel George S. Patton was killed. He is notable for being the grandfather of George Patton, who distinguished himself during World War II.

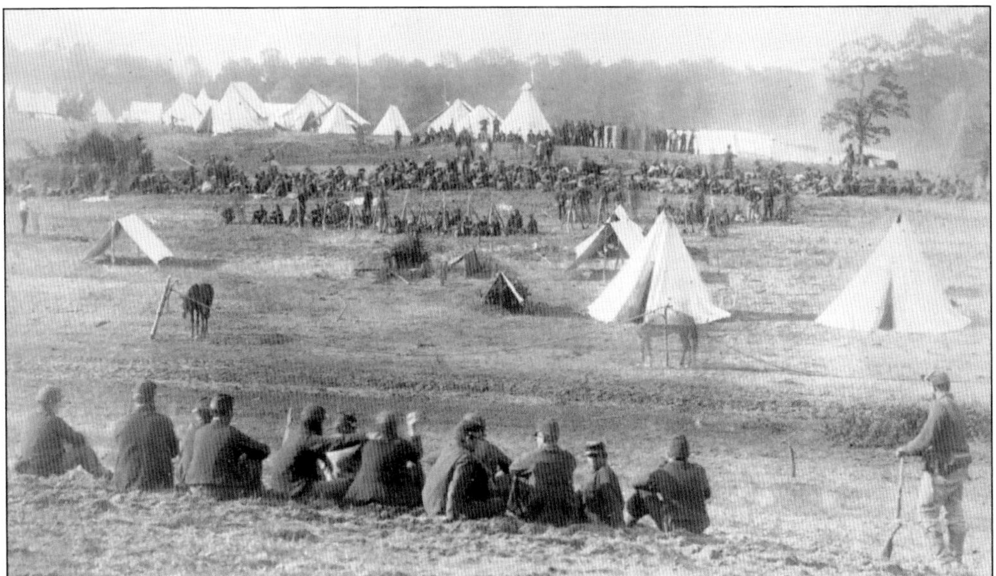

At Fisher's Hill, General Early was once again outmaneuvered by Sheridan, as the Union officer devised an elaborate plan to outflank Early's poorly positioned army. Early's high casualties further inhibited him from defending against the larger Union force. In late September 1864, Sheridan delivered another devastating defeat to the small Confederate army. The disaster at Fisher's Hill resulted in numerous Confederates being captured. Here, some of these unfortunate soldiers await transport to Union prison camps.

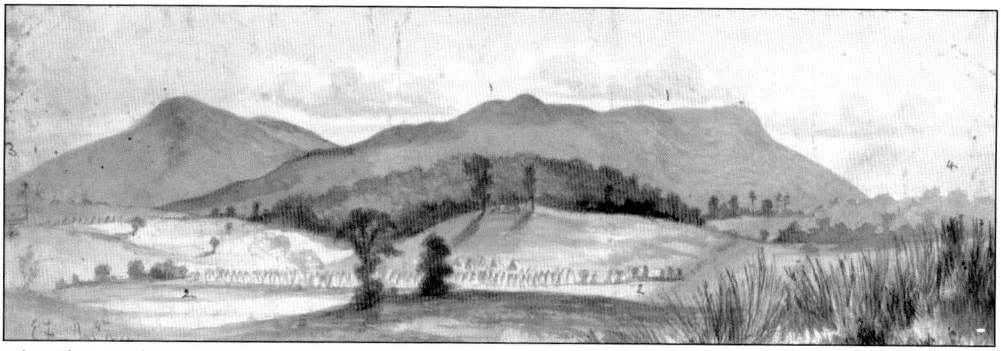

The Shenandoah Valley, flanked by the imposing Massanutten Mountain and the Appalachian range, was a valuable resource to Robert E. Lee's army operating in Virginia. The region was affectionately referred to as the "breadbasket of the Confederacy" for the crops and supplies produced in the valley. The Union recognized the Shenandoah Valley as vital to the Confederate war effort. In 1864, Washington dispatched Sheridan to burn and destroy thousands of acres of farmland, as well as barns, mills, and homes. This act of aggression on the civilian population is still the source of bitter sentiments to this day.

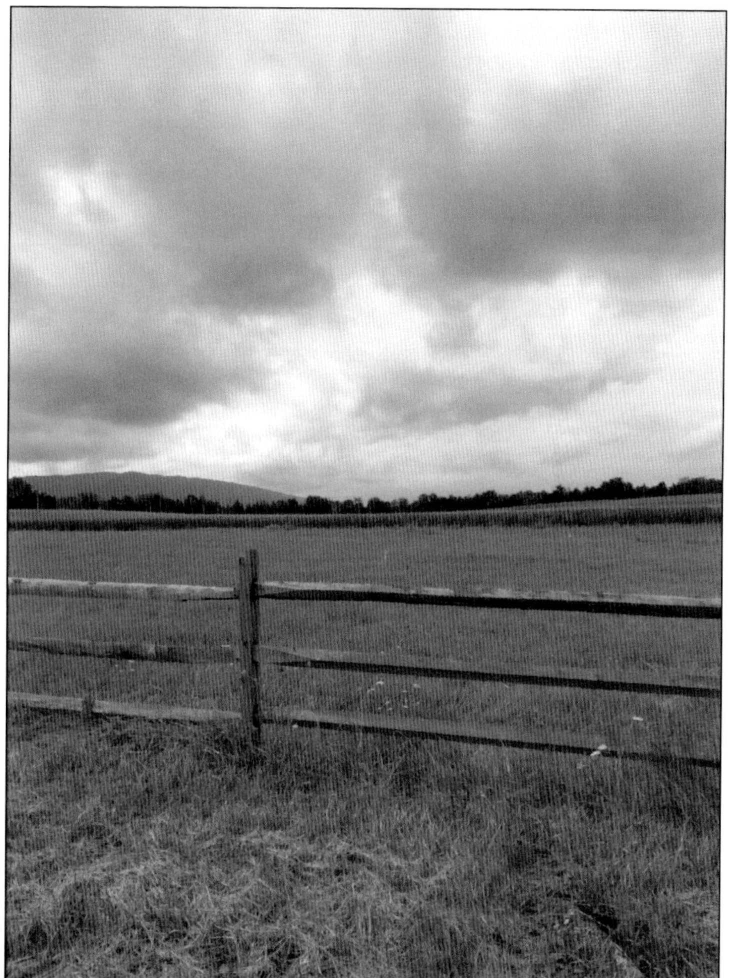

The final major battle in the Shenandoah Valley took place on October 19, 1864, when Gen. Jubal Early initiated a daring, yet precarious, surprise attack on Gen. Phillip Sheridan's position at Cedar Creek. Although the Confederate attack enjoyed initial success, it was soon repulsed and devolved into headlong retreat. Sheridan had an excellent cadre of subordinate officers at Cedar Creek, including George Armstrong Custer, William McKinley, and Rutherford B. Hayes. The latter two men would serve as presidents of the United States.

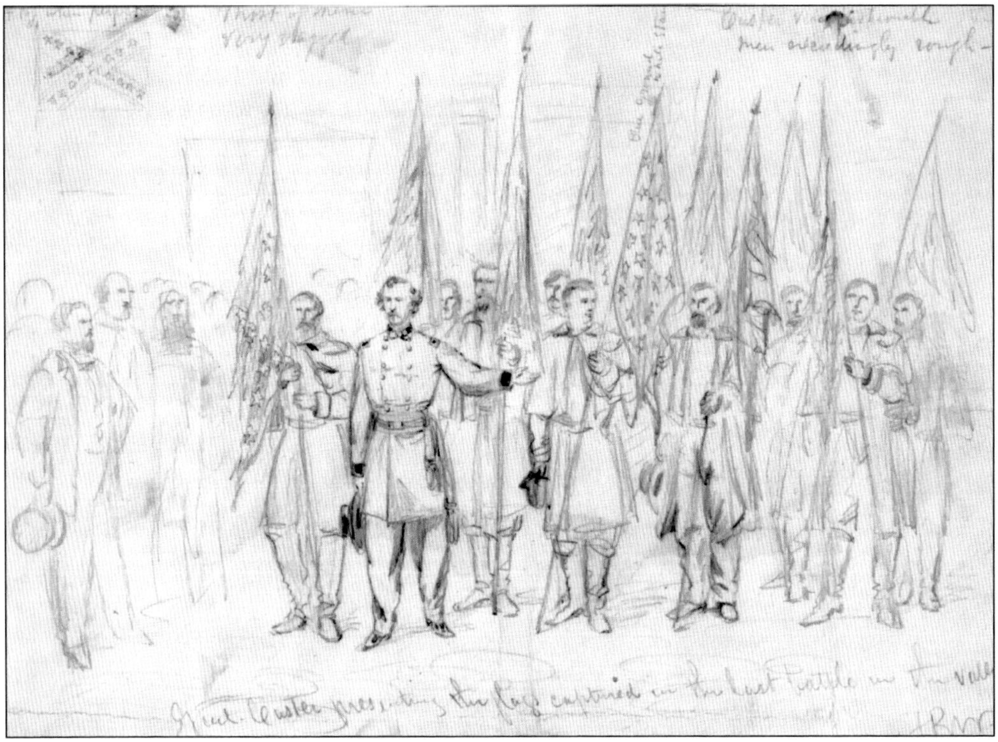

In this battlefield sketch, Gen. George Armstrong Custer presents Confederate flags captured during operations in the Shenandoah Valley. Throughout the war, each unit carried its own specific and often uniquely personalized flag. These flags were vital during battle, indicating the position of particular units. Furthermore, these banners had been imbued with sacred meaning by the troops over which they flew. The flags were to be protected at all costs.

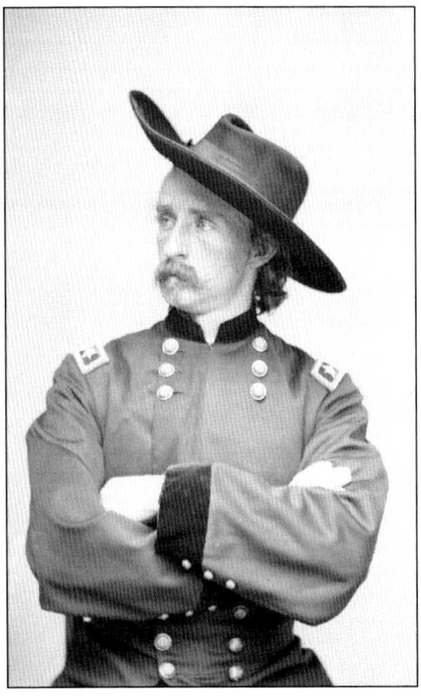

George Custer distinguished himself during the campaigns in the Shenandoah Valley as a valuable cavalry officer possessing the necessary courage to lead troops in battle. Even at this stage of his career, he was recognized for his flamboyance. At the Battle of Cedar Creek, one of his old friends, Confederate major general Stephen Dodson Ramseur, was mortally wounded and subsequently captured by the Federals. Upon hearing of this, Custer raced to Belle Grove Plantation, where Ramseur lay dying, to be with his friend. A few hours later, Ramseur was dead—one of the many casualties of the violent action at Cedar Creek.

Shown here is Belle Grove Plantation, where George Custer and Stephen Ramseur met during the Confederate general's final hours. The plantation figured prominently in the battle, serving as Sheridan's headquarters and located at the epicenter of the fighting. Today, the house still stands and is a popular tourist destination for its importance as a fixture on the battlefield, as well as the rich antebellum history it has to offer. (Author's collection.)

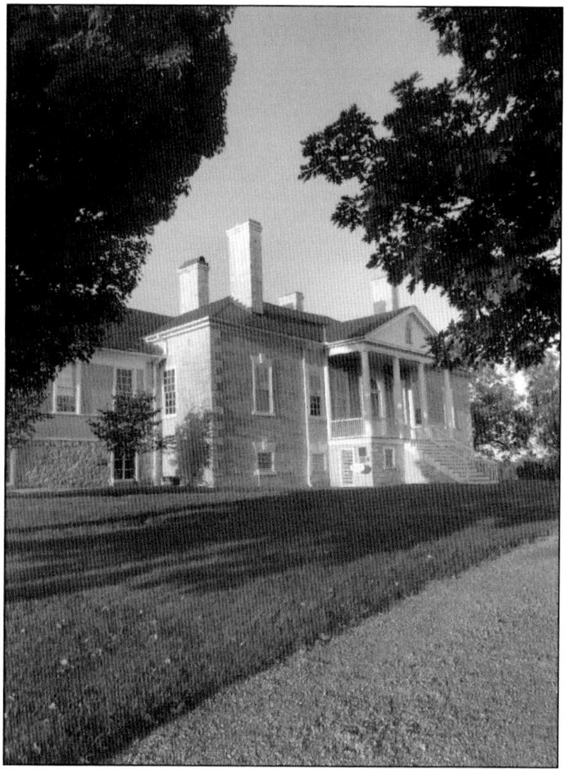

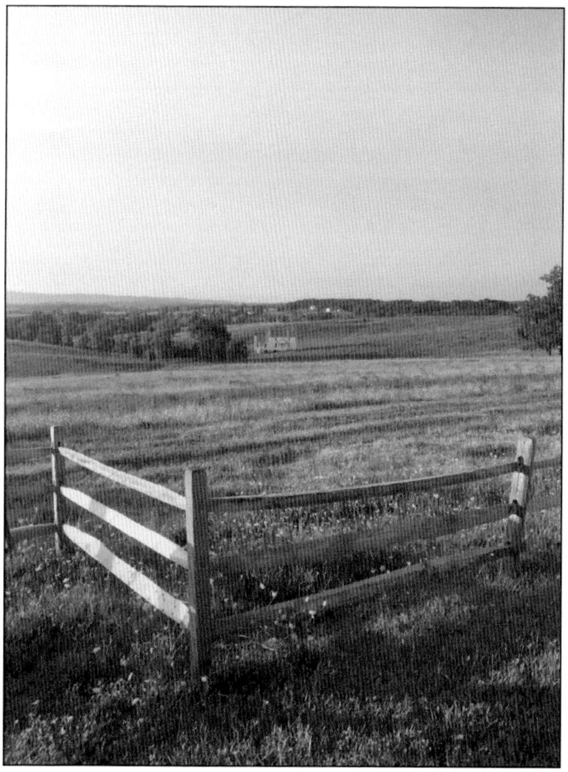

Although Belle Grove gets much attention for its role in the battle at Cedar Creek, the small house shown here saw significant action during the clash. During the engagement, both armies swirled around the structure as brutal fighting ensued. The house dates to the 1700s. It is amazing that it was not burned during the ferocious fighting. Today, the house is preserved by the Cedar Creek Battlefield Foundation and is an important feature in the park. (Author's collection.)

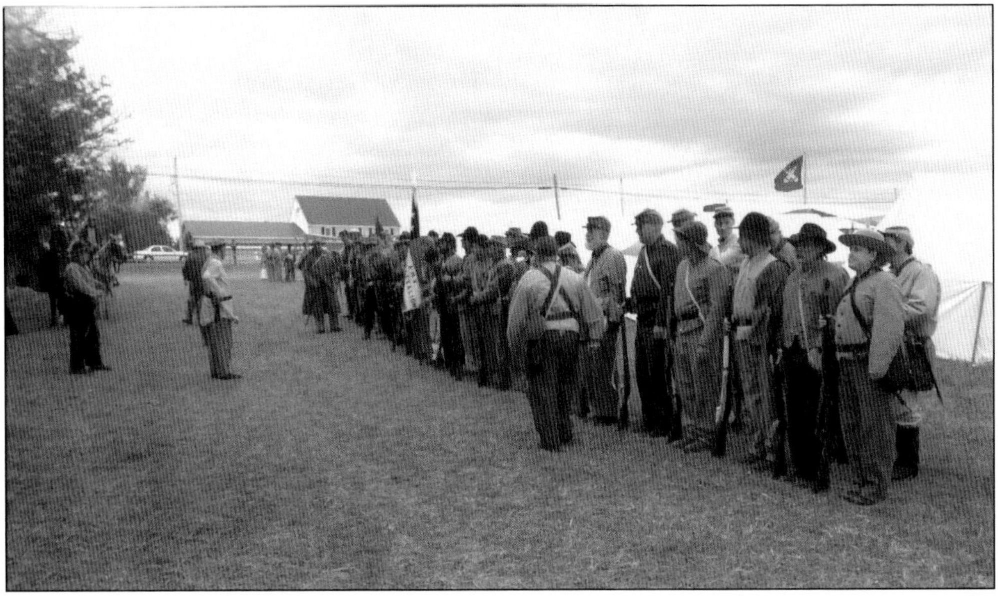

Every year, thousands of reenactors flood to Cedar Creek Battlefield to commemorate the final clash in the Shenandoah Valley. The significance of this battle draws thousands of living historians, as well as spectators. This event, and others like it, attempt to keep the memory of the war alive, so that new generations may learn, and appreciate, Virginia's rich history. Here, reenactors portraying troops from the 7th Louisiana Infantry form up before the simulated battle. (Courtesy of Hannah Berge.)

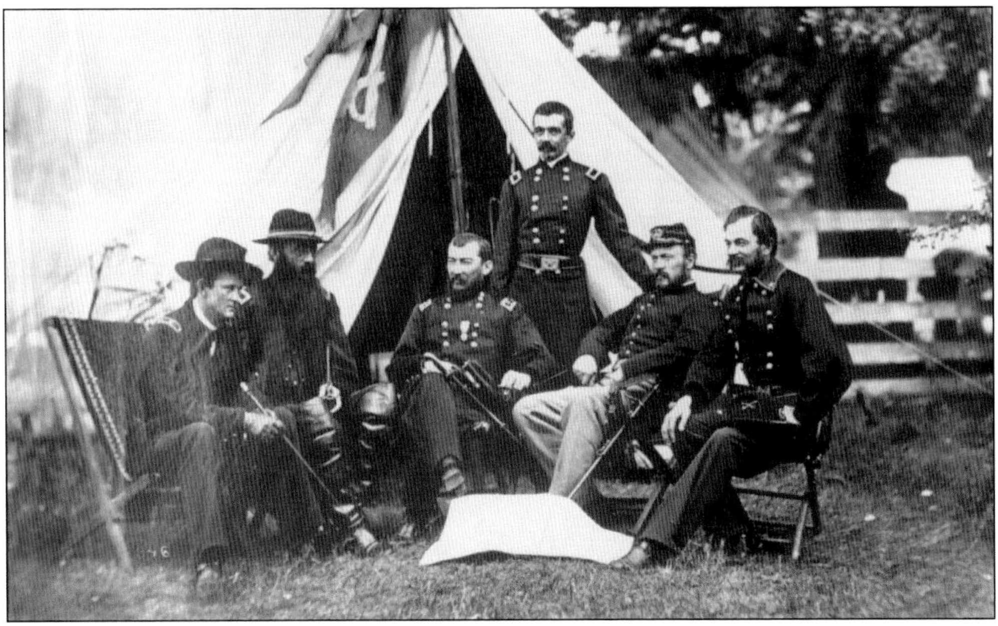

Gen. Phillip Sheridan (seated, center) relied heavily on his staff of skilled officers to manage elements of his expeditionary force in the Shenandoah Valley when he was unavailable. Furthermore, prior to the advent of modern means of communication, it was nearly impossible to micromanage one's staff. This forced Sheridan, and all generals of the time, to trust their subordinates to fulfill directives and, in many cases, engage the enemy without their direct supervision.

Here, Phillip Sheridan and his staff confer about their next course of action in the Shenandoah Valley. Although Jubal Early's army had been present in the region, the Federals occupied towns such as Winchester and, much to the displeasure of locals, set up their headquarters in homes and hotels. This type of interaction between Virginians and the Federal occupiers resulted in jeers and mistrust but rarely escalated into violence or open aggression.

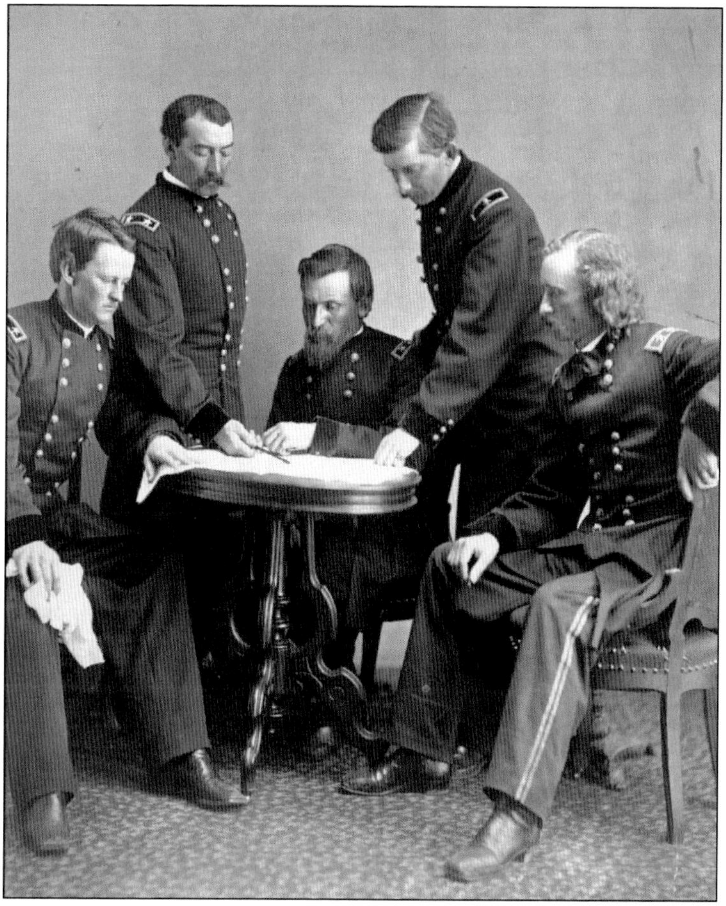

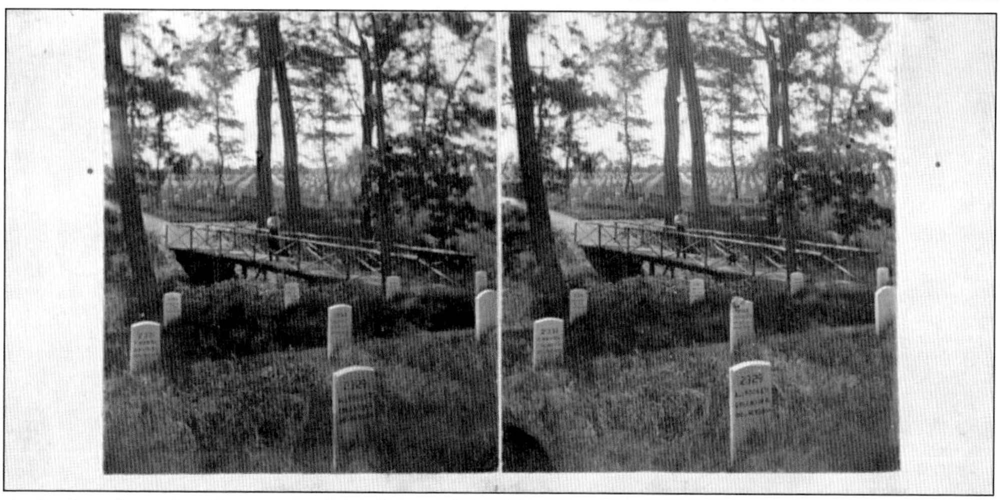

As bodies from the Shenandoah Valley and the bloody battles outside Richmond began to pour into the District of Columbia, Union officials considered where to bury the tens of thousands of dead. It was suggested that the property at Arlington belonging to Robert E. Lee be utilized as a cemetery. Many believed it to be a fitting insult for the Confederate general to have thousands of Yankees interred on his property.

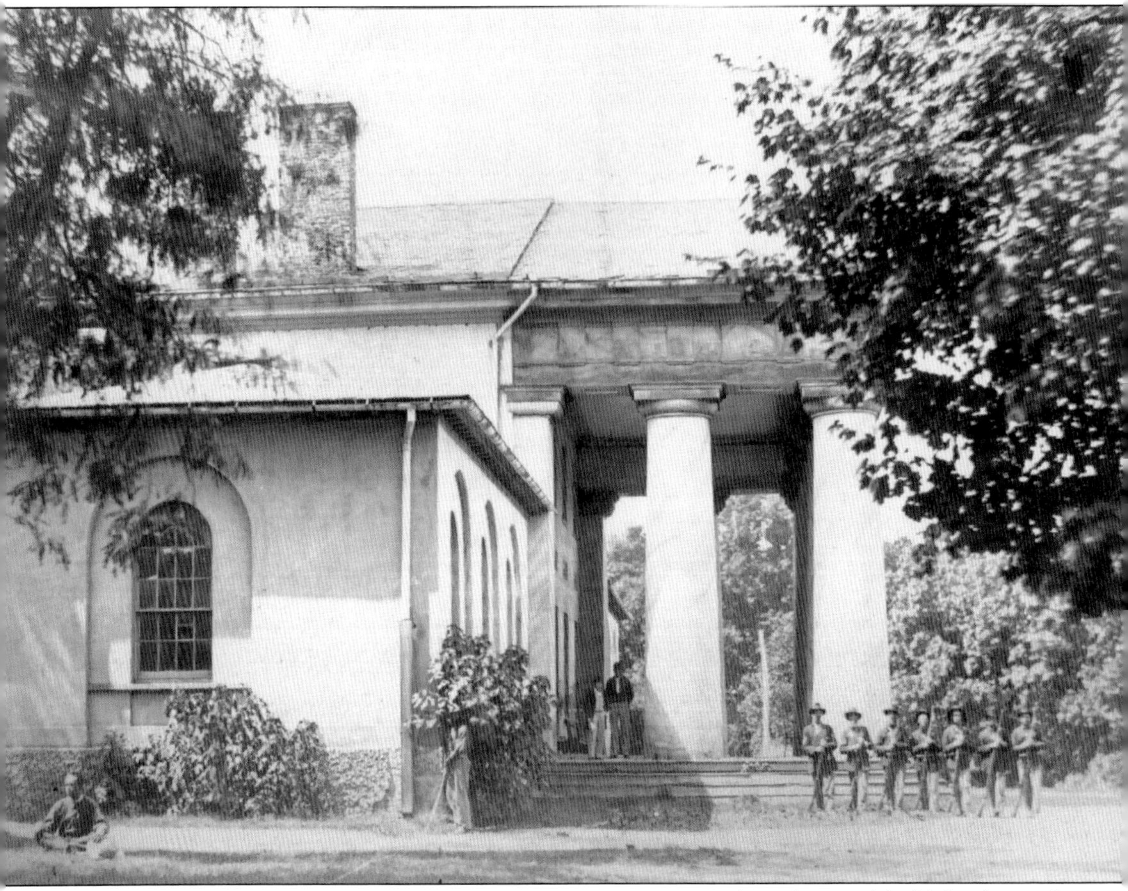

The Union officials' spiteful decision to use Lee's property as a burial ground for Federal casualties backfired, as the site has become hallowed ground. It is now considered the highest honor to be buried at Arlington National Cemetery. Today, thousands of soldiers from all wars are buried on the former Confederate general's property. Lee's house still stands, positioned at the epicenter of the sacred burial grounds.

Five

Virginia Reborn

By 1865, the entire Confederacy had been sliced in two and significantly diminished in size as marauding Union armies reclaimed lost territory. Robert E. Lee's army around Richmond had staved off Union advances for months and was on the verge of collapse. Lee, in a desperate attempt to preserve what was left of his beleaguered army, attempted to break out of the city. Although this attempt was well-meaning, it proved utterly futile, as the ever-tenacious Ulysses S. Grant relentlessly pursued the evacuating Confederates. Over the next few days, Lee's diminutive army would fight a series of escalating battles, which would eventually result in his force becoming so diluted that a continuance of the fighting would simply be a waste of human life. By April, Lee had decided it was time to conclude Virginia's struggle for independence, and, in orderly fashion, he surrendered his army to fellow West Point graduate Ulysses S. Grant. This moment marked the end of major hostilities in Virginia for the remainder of the conflict. Of all the civil wars that have occurred throughout the ages, the American Civil War is arguably one of the most unusual, in that the victors were remarkably magnanimous to the vanquished. There were no mass executions or severe reparations. Rather, a deeper brotherly love was established. This makes the struggle so profoundly fascinating. Lee's surrender set the stage for the rebuilding of America with a degree of unity and honor that set the foundations for the United States to become the leader of the free world.

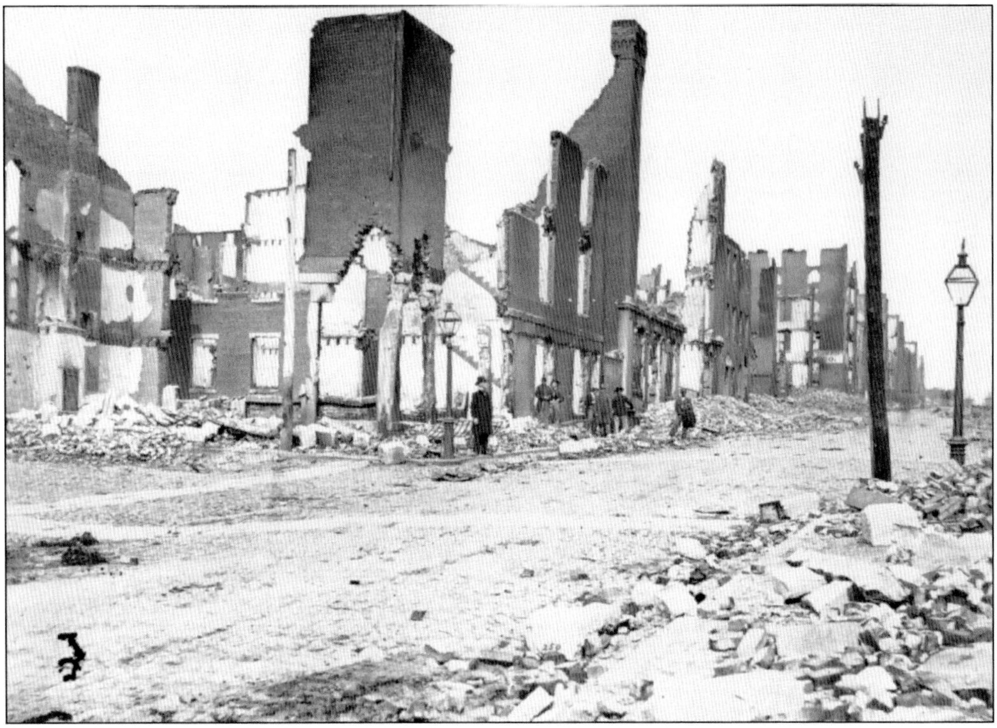

The mere skeletons of buildings line Carey Street in Richmond. The fractured remnants of the structures stood defiantly, like the Confederate soldiers—proud but defeated. By the time this photograph was taken, the majority of the streets had been cleared, but the rubble around the buildings had not yet been addressed.

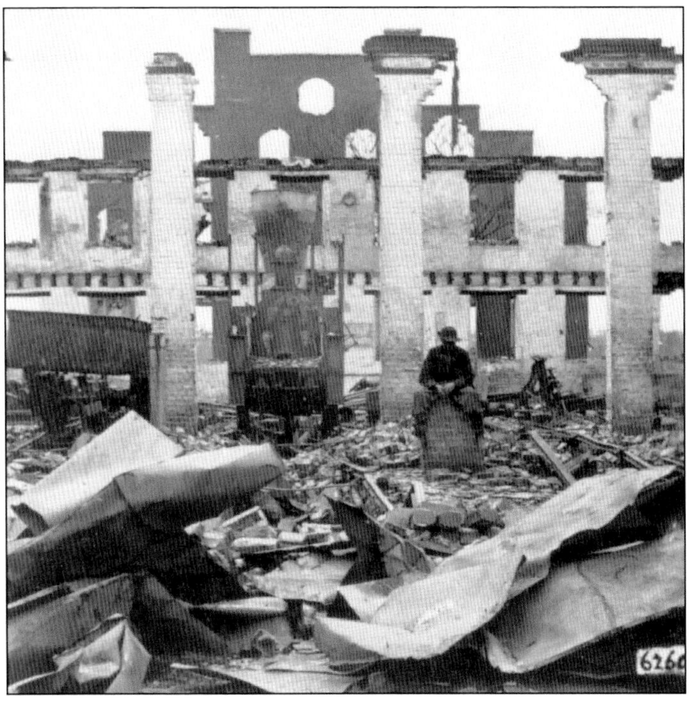

This picturesque photograph shows a freed African American amid the rubble of the Confederate capital. The ruins stand as a testament to the enormous effort it took to conquer the South. In the foreground are the remnants of a metal roof that once adorned these buildings. All that remains are a few walls and pillars.

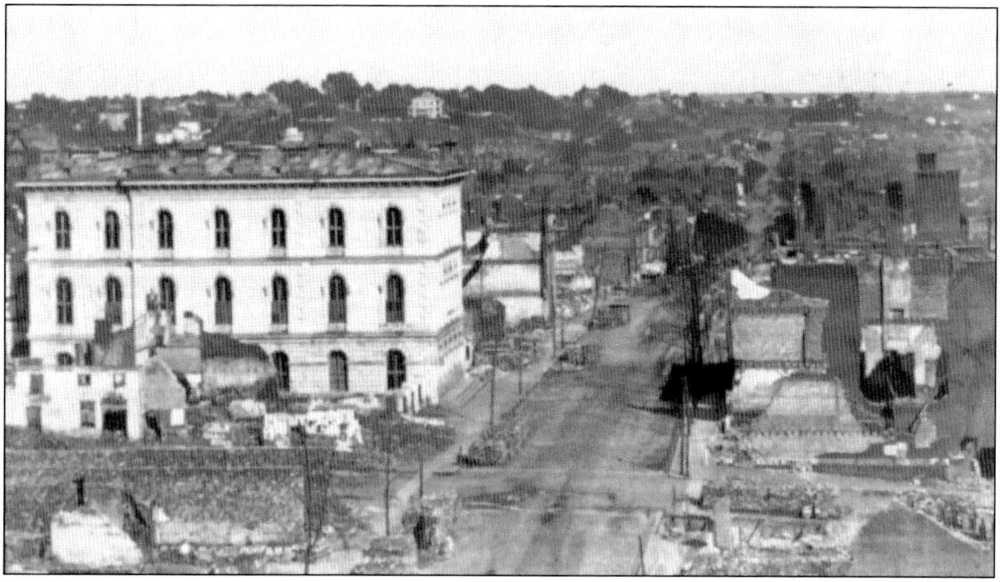

Here, an entire district of Richmond has been demolished. The ruins and destruction stretch far into the distance. The devastation certainly took its toll on the inhabitants of the city, as it made the routines of daily life nearly impossible. Despite the enormous destruction, it is clear that an effort has been made to preserve some infrastructure, as rubble has been cleared from the streets and stacked neatly into piles along the sides.

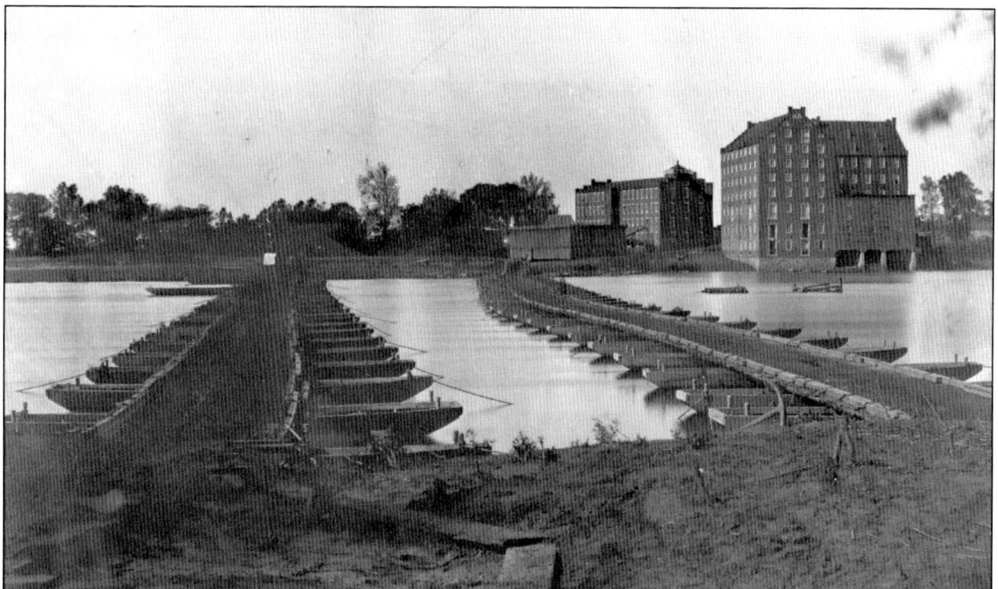

The mills at Manchester and nearby docks were vital to the Southern economy, as they were a gateway for tobacco, coal, and slaves. Coal was transported from Midlothian, Virginia, to Manchester; the industry solidified the port's role in Virginia's economy. Following the war, Manchester was eventually absorbed into Richmond and is now a neighborhood in the municipality. This photograph demonstrates the ability of Union engineers, who constructed this elaborate pontoon bridge across the James River.

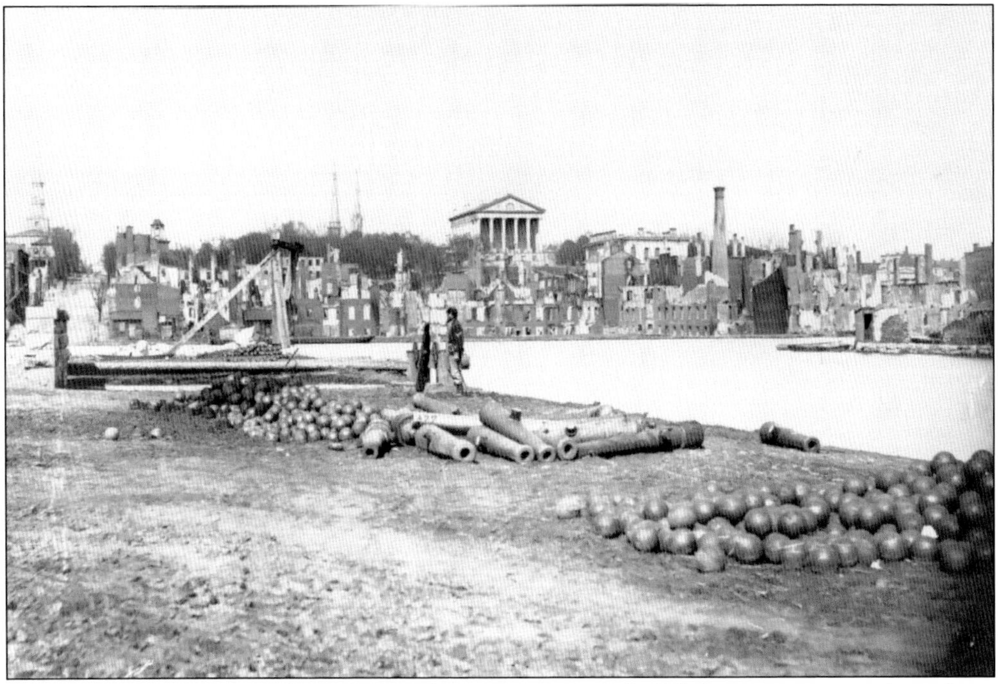

Iron and bronze cannon tubes, along with an assortment of solid shot ammunition, have been gathered after the war. This photograph accurately captures the absolute destruction that Richmond suffered in the last days of the war. The burned-out and destroyed buildings act as a metaphor for how thoroughly the Union troops defeated the Confederate army. Although many structures were utterly demolished, it should be noted that, as seen here, some buildings, such as churches and the former Confederate capitol (center), survived relatively unscathed.

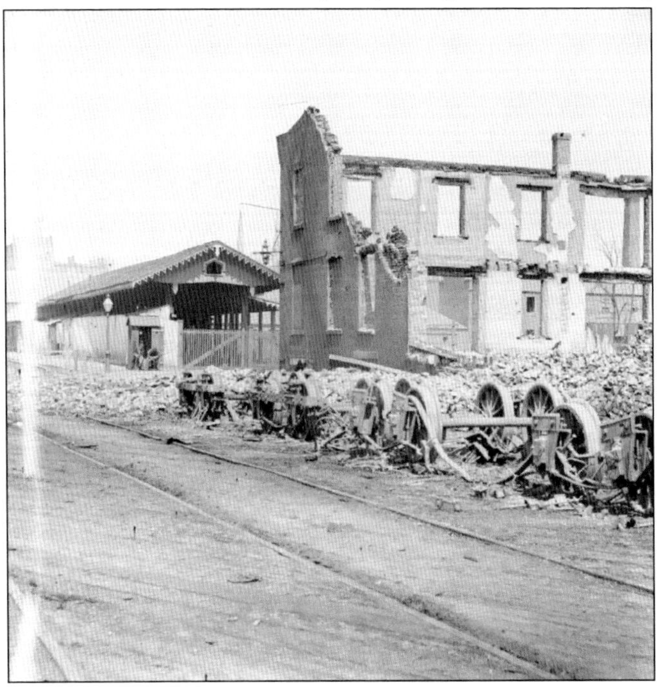

During the American Civil War, railways came into their own as a viable and rapid means of transporting troops and supplies. Throughout the war, generals on both sides shocked the world by quickly moving whole armies via rail to assault their unsuspecting enemies. Given the importance of railways, it is no surprise that the Union army targeted the Confederate railroad hub at Richmond. In the foreground are the iron remnants of burned-out train cars.

This photograph of the arsenal grounds at Richmond shows the immense firepower that was available during the siege around the city. The large solid shot in the foreground was effectively used against structures and other fortifications. Also visible are cylindrical canister shot, which contained smaller projectiles intended primarily for close-range use against human targets.

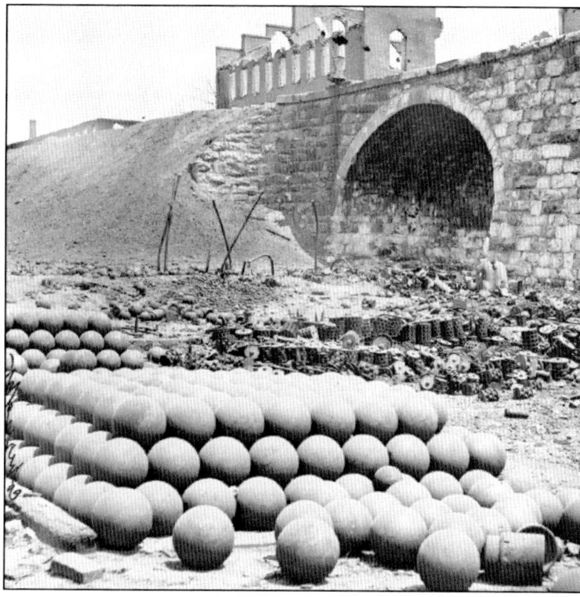

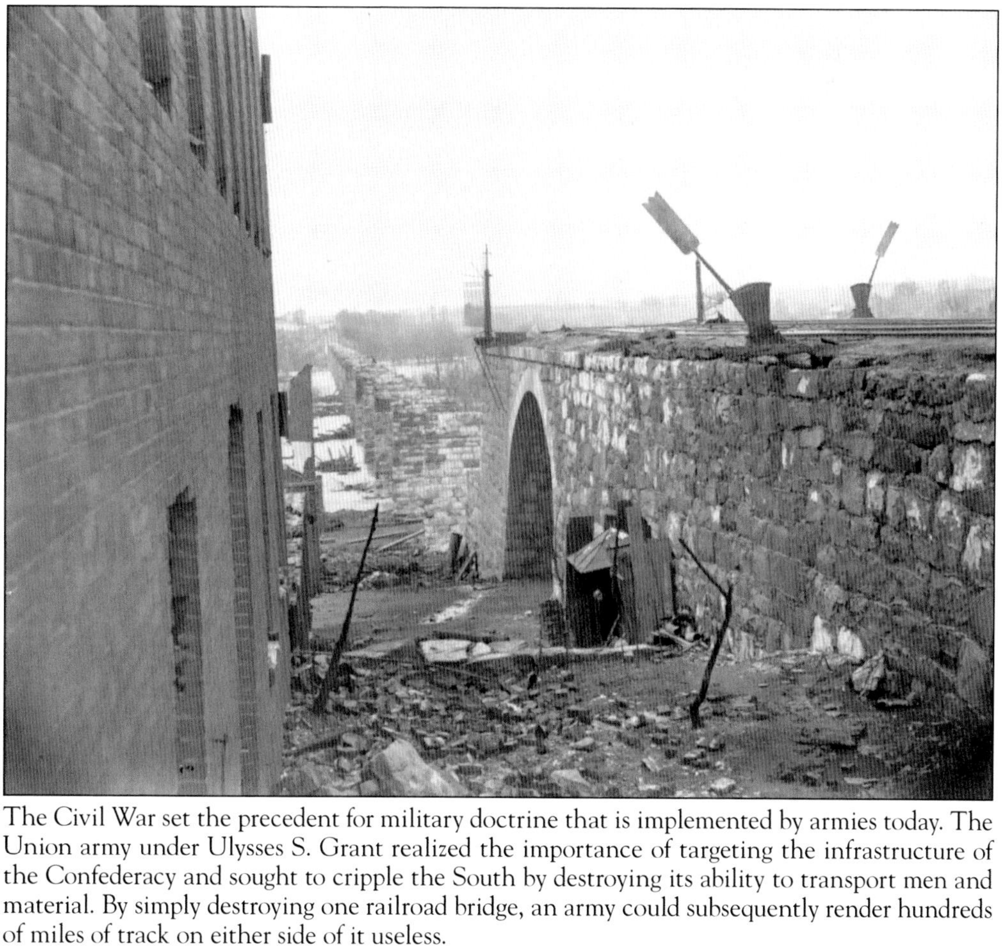

The Civil War set the precedent for military doctrine that is implemented by armies today. The Union army under Ulysses S. Grant realized the importance of targeting the infrastructure of the Confederacy and sought to cripple the South by destroying its ability to transport men and material. By simply destroying one railroad bridge, an army could subsequently render hundreds of miles of track on either side of it useless.

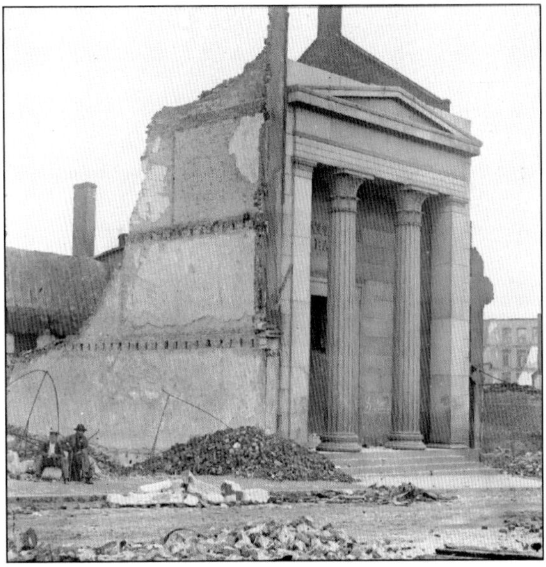

The formerly thriving economic hub of Richmond was reduced to little more than a facade of rubble. The ornate entrance to the Exchange Bank on Main Street is all that remains of the once-prominent structure. Although the bank's walls did not crumble until 1865, the currency it managed had been shattered years before. By 1862, the Southern economy was crippled and infested with counterfeit currency. Inflation progressively choked the Confederacy's ability to do business both domestically and abroad.

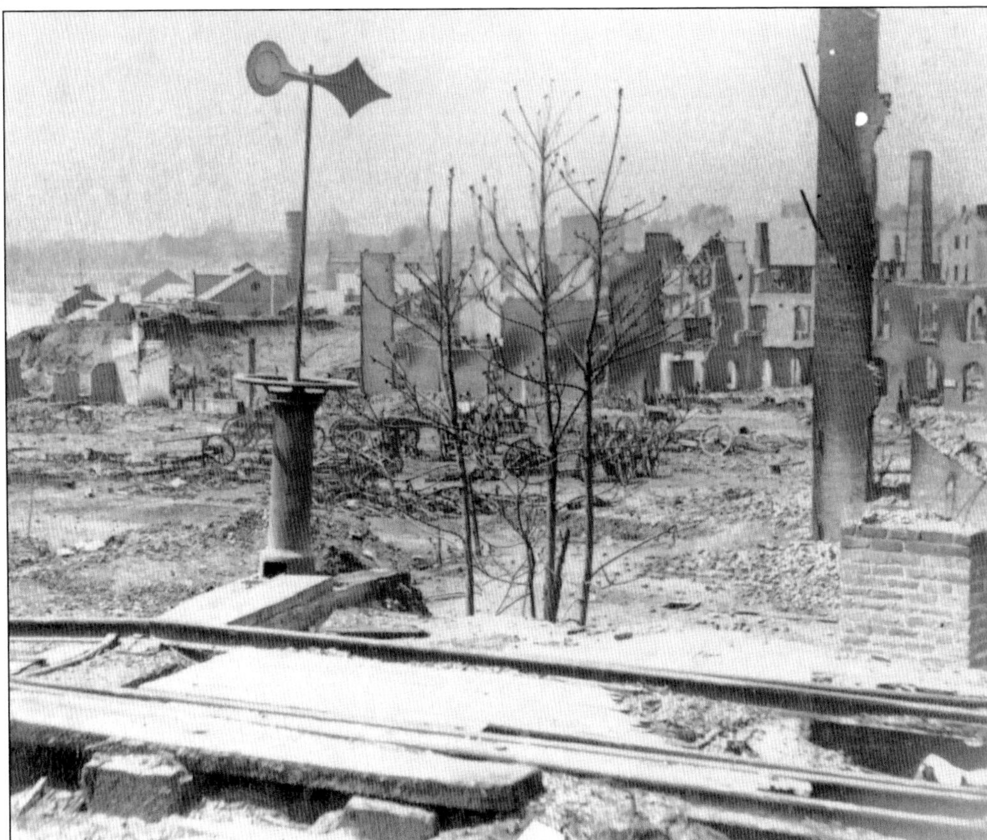

Pictured are the ruins of one of the Richmond arsenals. The arsenals were strategically placed near railways to facilitate the rapid distribution of ammunition and supplies to the front. The wreckage of limbers, caissons, and cannons are all that is left of this once-thriving military installation. In the distance, destroyed warehouses stretch to the horizon.

It is not clear whether this train engine was destroyed by the Confederates to prevent it from falling into the hands of the enemy, or if it was the result of a Northern effort to destroy the Confederates' means of transport. It is, however, an excellent example of just how thoroughly the city's infrastructure had been damaged. Regardless of the train's backstory, these Union soldiers seized the opportunity to be photographed atop what is left of the machine.

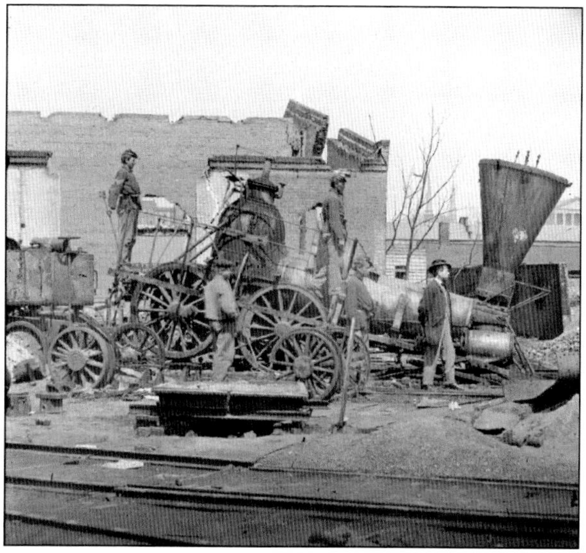

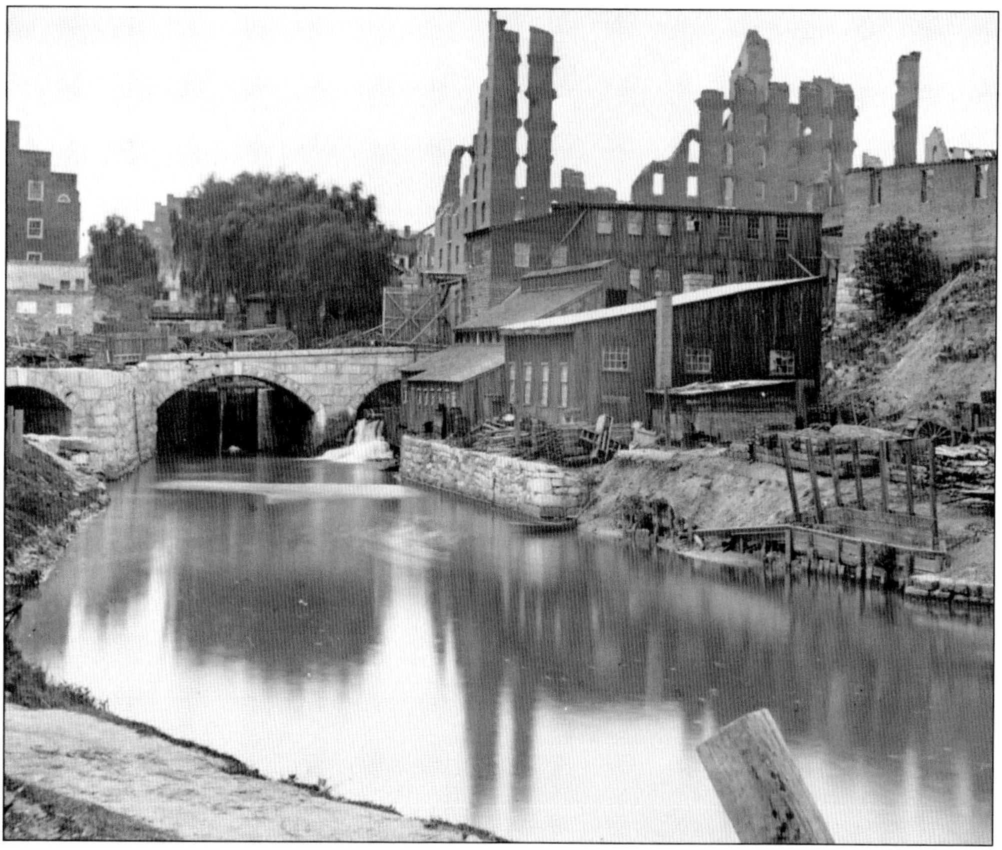

Pictured are the remains of the once-towering flour mills in Richmond. When Robert E. Lee's army evacuated Richmond, they set fire to numerous buildings, to deprive the enemy of their use. One set of buildings that the Southerners sought to burn was the Gallego Flour Mills. Although the fire achieved its intended goal, the blaze quickly became uncontrollable and spread to the rest of the commercial district, destroying much of the city with it.

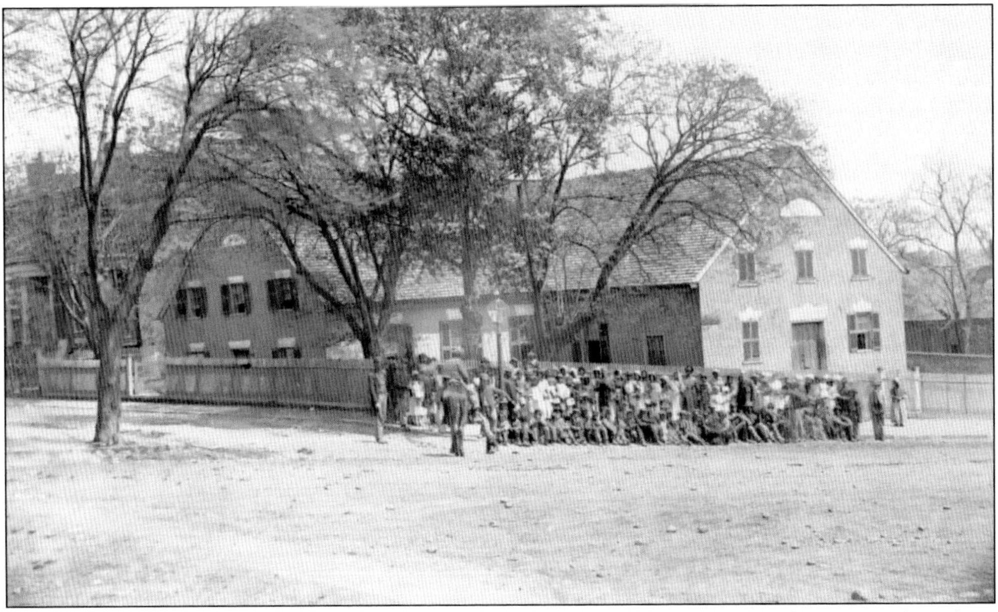

As the horrors of war raged around the Confederate capitol, people of all classes sought solace in their faith. Shown here is the congregation of an African American church in Richmond directly after the fall of the city. This district of Richmond remained relatively untouched, in stark contrast to the destroyed buildings of the commercial district.

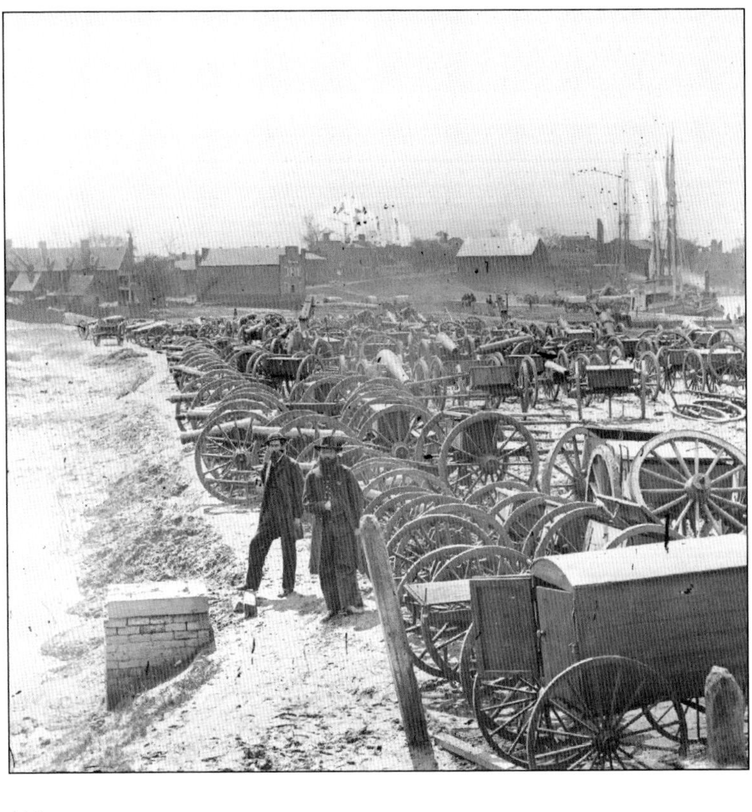

When the Federals captured Richmond, they also seized a large number of cannons and siege weapons from the fleeing Confederates. The cannons in the foreground are field pieces that would have been carried with the army on campaigns. The larger guns in the distance were used primarily in static positions, such as trench lines, and were too heavy for the retreating Confederates to retrieve before exiting the city.

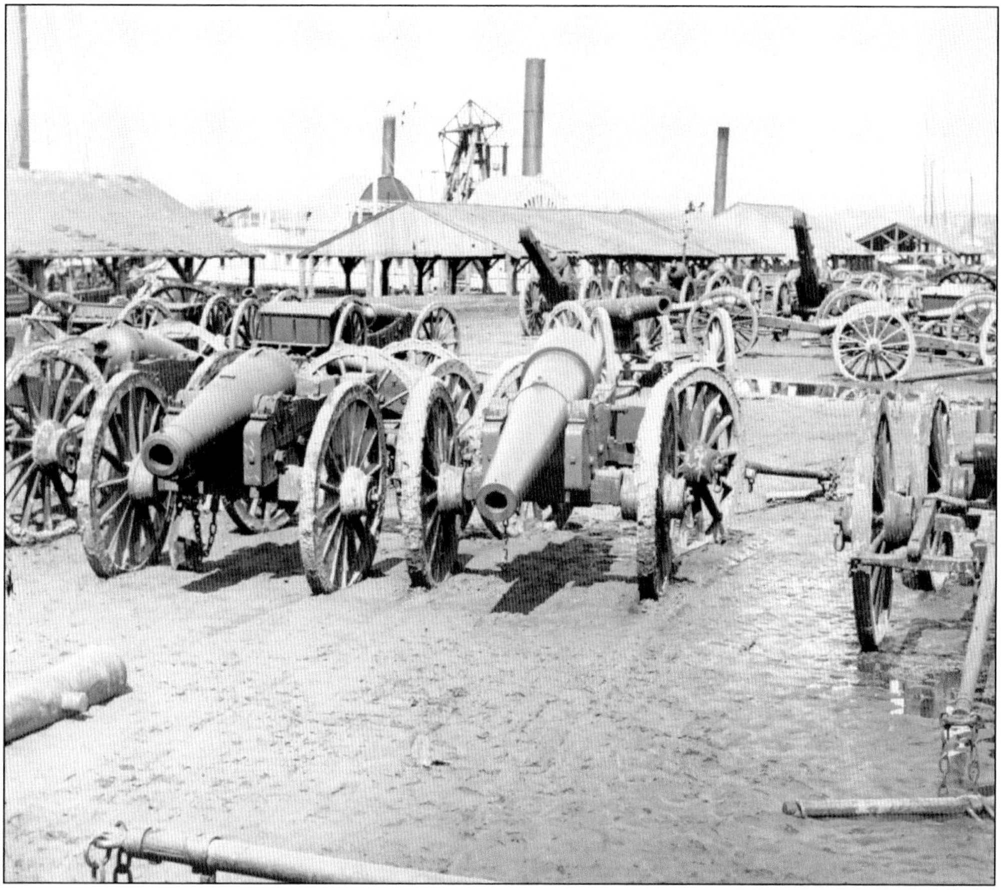

This photograph reveals the sheer size of the heavy artillery captured by Ulysses S. Grant's army. In the foreground is a Parrott rifle, which would have been emplaced in the trenches defending the capitol. The capture of these valuable weapons represented an important loss to Lee's army, as it severely inhibited the Confederates' ability to challenge Grant's force.

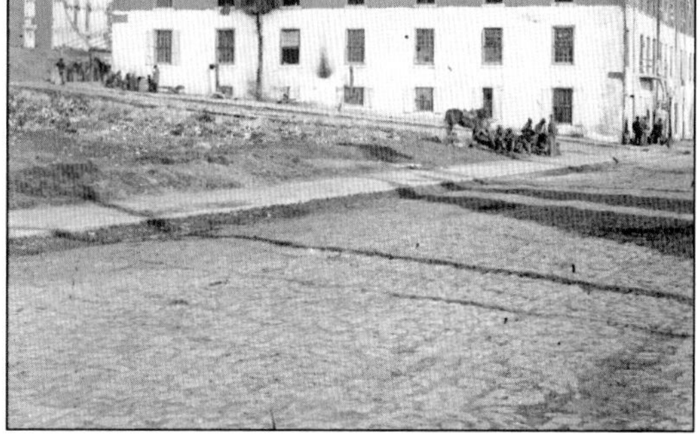

Through the duration of the war, both sides struggled with how to handle captured prisoners. Prisons on both sides were notorious for being overcrowded and disease-ridden. Libby Prison in Richmond was no exception; it became infamous for its deplorable conditions. The prison was one of the few buildings that survived the raging fire that devastated swaths of the municipality.

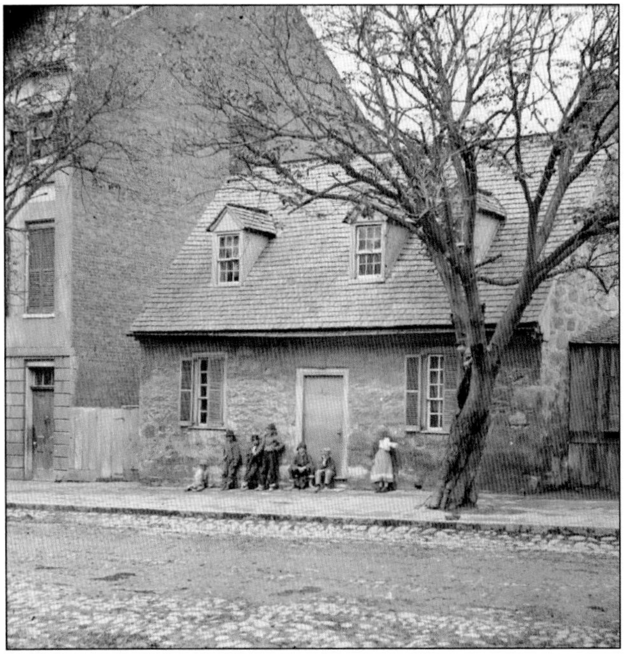

This house was purportedly Gen. George Washington's headquarters during the American Revolution. The assertion was later proven to be untrue, as Washington never used it. However, this myth did resonate with both Unionists and Confederates, as both sides idolized Washington and attempted to appropriate his mantle in their respective struggles against perceived tyranny.

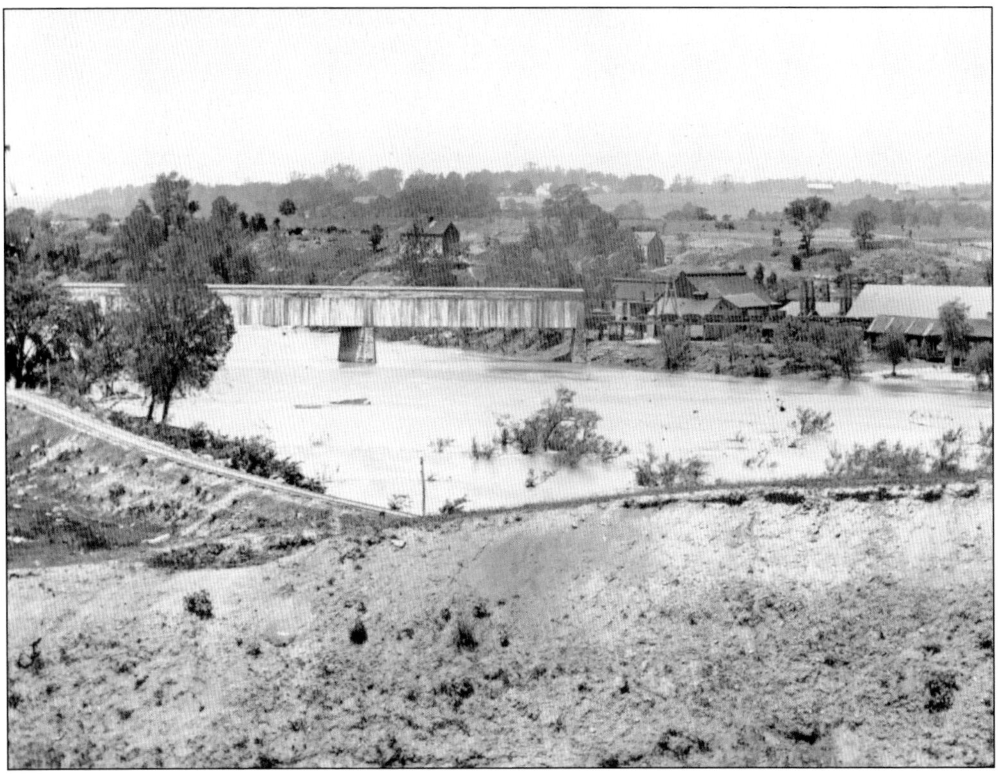

The production of iron was at the heart of the war effort for both the Confederacy and the Union. The material was essential to both armies, as it was required in the manufacture of railroads, steam engines, and artillery. Seen here is the railroad bridge to the Old Dominion Iron & Nail Works. This manufacturing base was an important target for Grant's advancing army.

These bronze and iron cannon tubes would have been mounted on wooden carriages with extensive iron components. They fired iron solid shot projectiles or shells with various timed fuses. This photograph demonstrates the extensive use of iron to create and support the artillery wing of the army. These cannon tubes were captured from the retreating Confederates as they left the city and headed toward Appomattox.

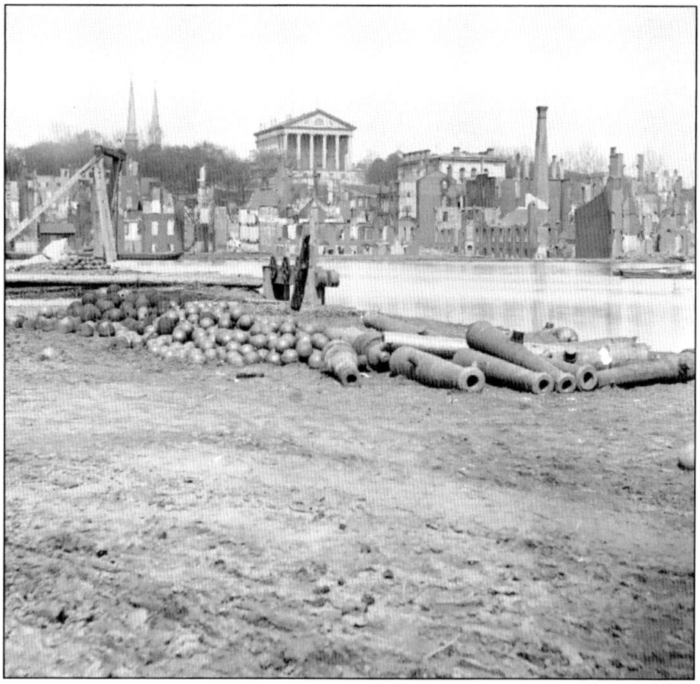

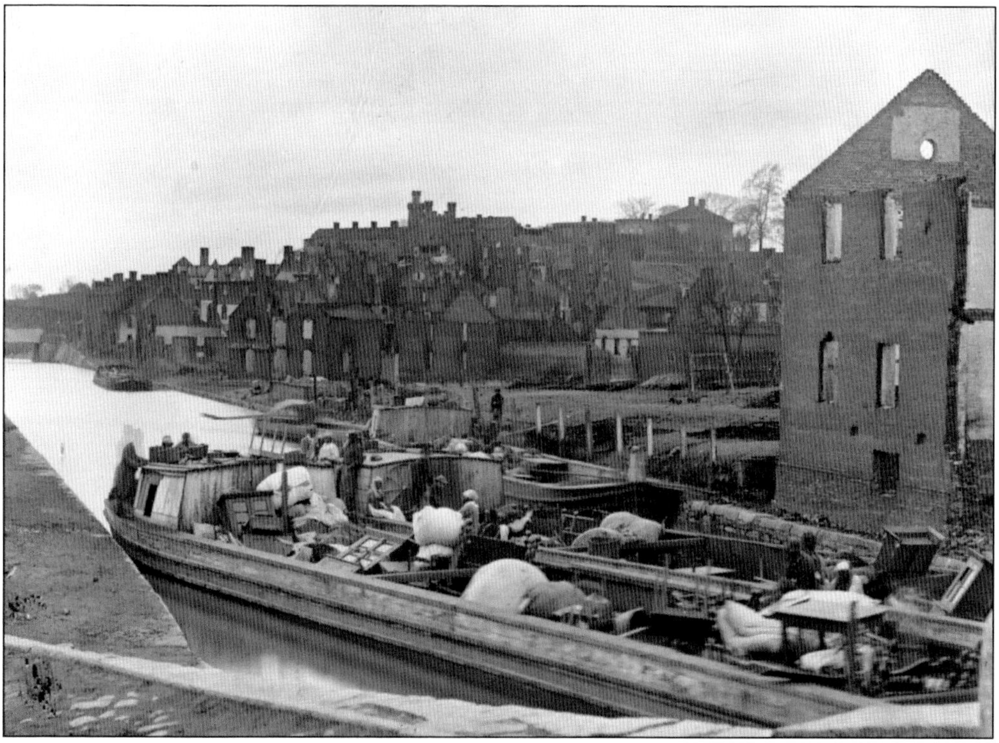

The canals throughout the greater Richmond area were integral in the transportation of goods to the larger ports on the river. Here, recently freed African Americans enjoy the mobility offered by the canal system. The extensive burning of Richmond did not spare this region of the city. Collapsed structures stretch to the horizon.

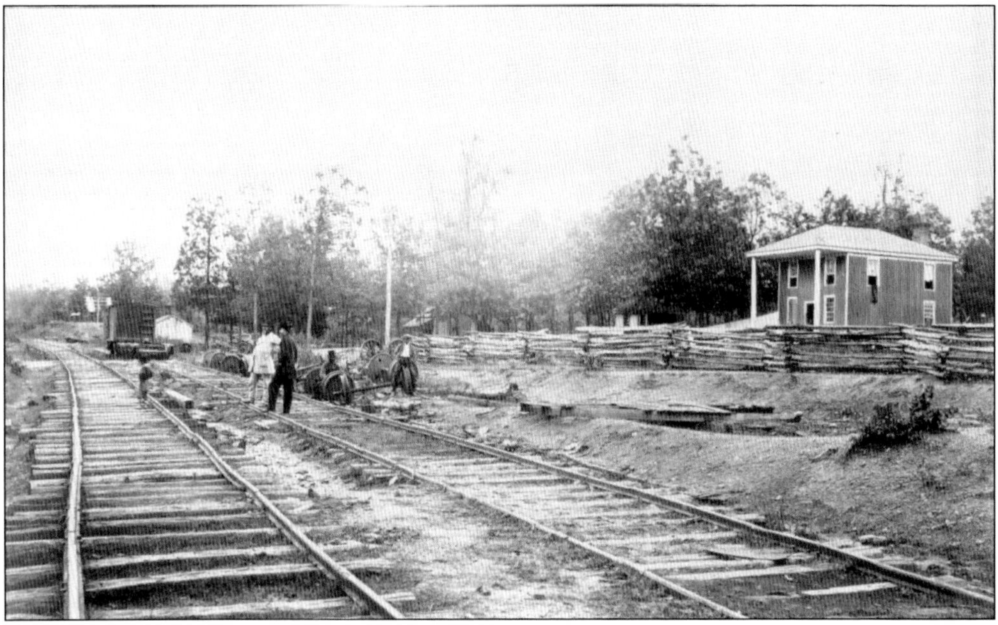

By the spring of 1865, what was left of Lee's battered army around Richmond desperately attempted to break out from the Union encirclement. As General Lee's force attempted to break contact with the enemy, Grant ordered his army to aggressively pursue the fleeing Confederates. This action signaled the beginning of the end of Lee's force. General Grant's tenacious tactics forced Lee into fighting numerous costly engagements over the next few days.

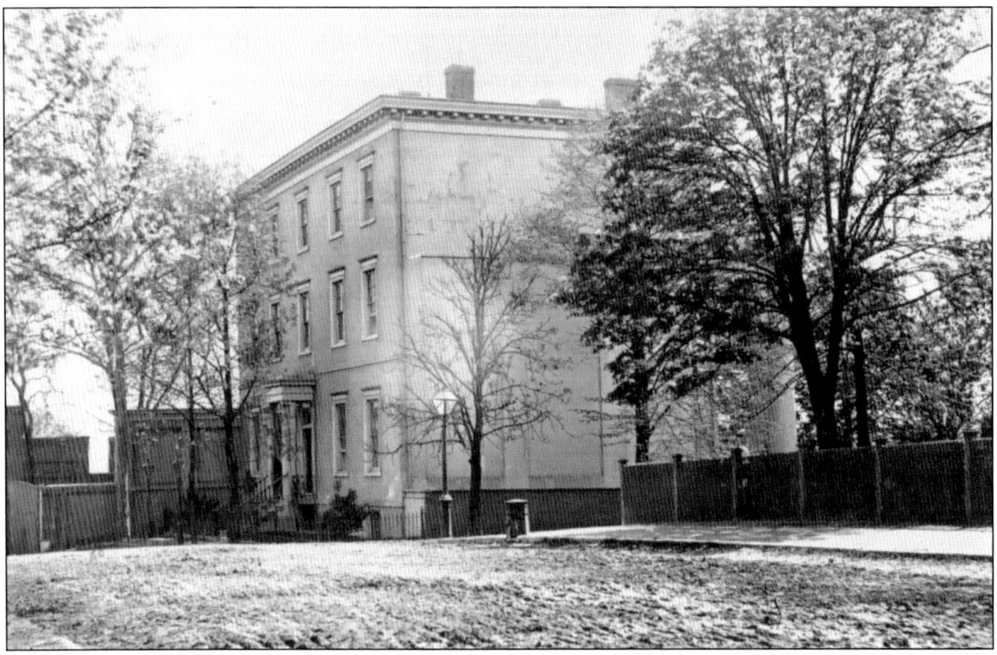

This Richmond home was formerly occupied by the Confederate president, Jefferson Davis. Like Lee's army, the government also evacuated the city. Davis and his administration attempted to set up proxy government facilities deeper south. This, however, proved quite tenuous, as marauding Union cavalry units harassed the fleeing government officials.

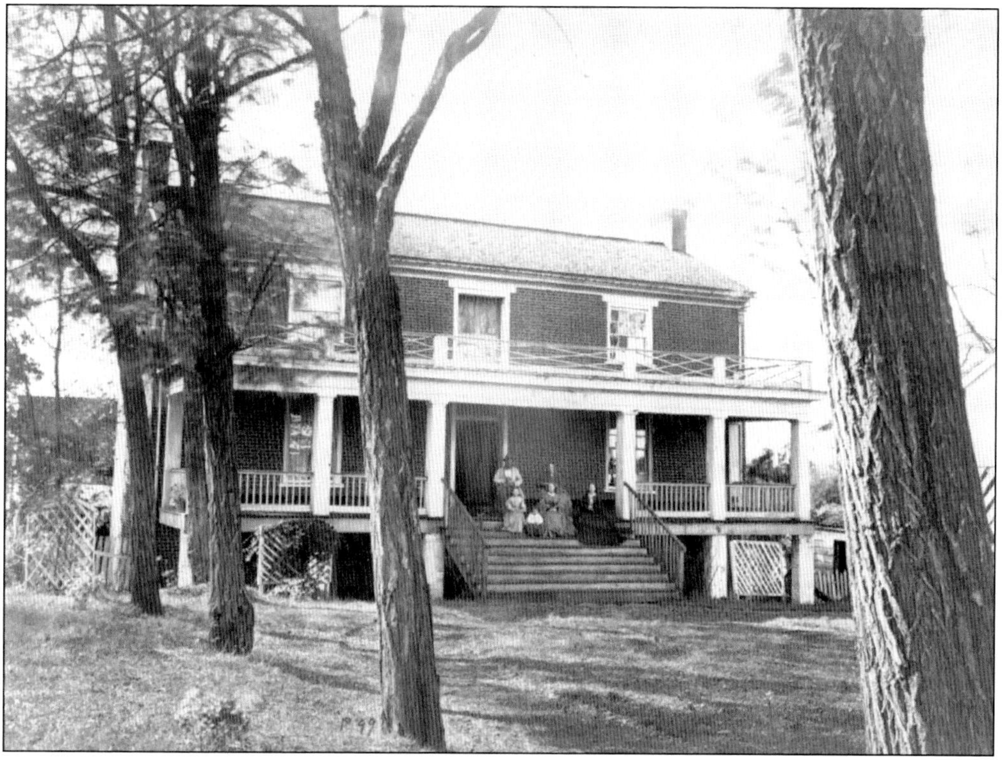

By April 9, 1865, Ulysses S. Grant had forced General Lee's troops into yet another bloody engagement. The Confederates had fewer than 30,000 men left at their disposal. The Federals, on the other hand, significantly outnumbered Lee's small force by more than three to one. Lee, seeing that continued resistance was merely a pointless continuance of the violence, made the tough decision to surrender his forces. The surrender was negotiated at the McLean House (pictured). Of interest, the owner of the house had also owned a dwelling on the battlefield at First Manassas and had moved following the battle to escape the war. Nonetheless, the war found him. It is often said that the war in Virginia started and finished on his property.

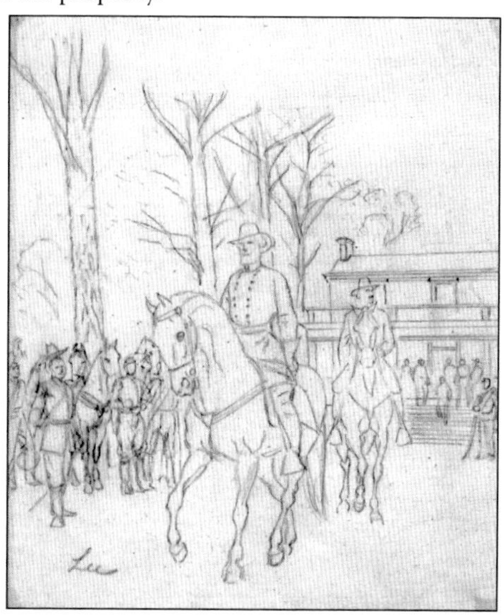

Lee and Grant discussed the situation like the gentlemen they were, and, at the conclusion of the talks, they had come to one of the most lenient terms of surrender in history. There were to be no hangings or executions. The Confederates were free to return to their homes, and the officers could even retain their sidearms. It is almost as if, in that very moment, the notions of Confederate and Federal were abolished and troops from both sides went back to simply being Americans. Following the surrender, both sides began making amends and immediately commenced sharing food and supplies as if brothers.

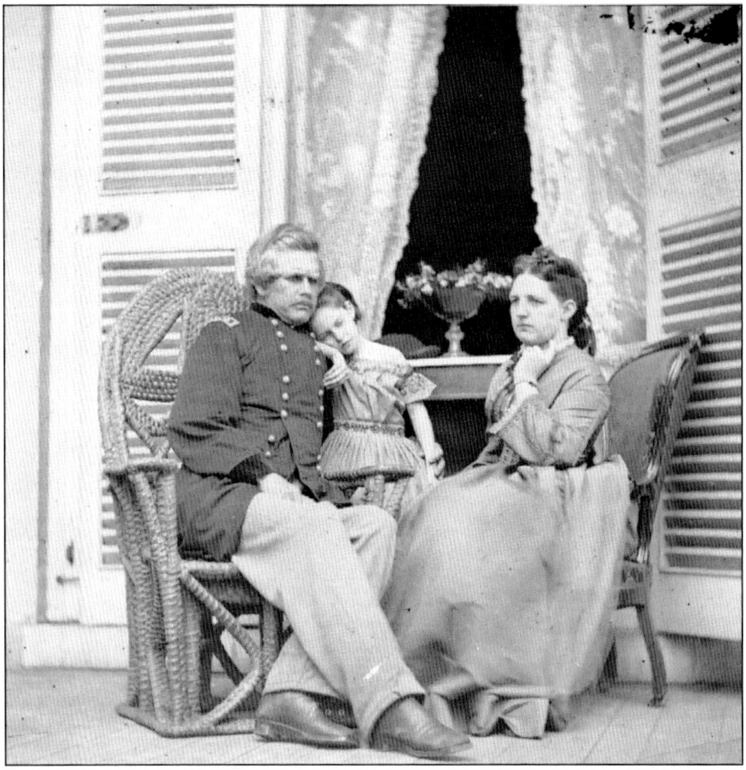

Following the iconic surrender, artifacts from the event became objects of curiosity for people throughout the world. Many wished to be photographed next to the table where the surrender documents were signed. Here, Gen. Edward O.C. Ord and his wife pose next to the piece of furniture in Richmond.

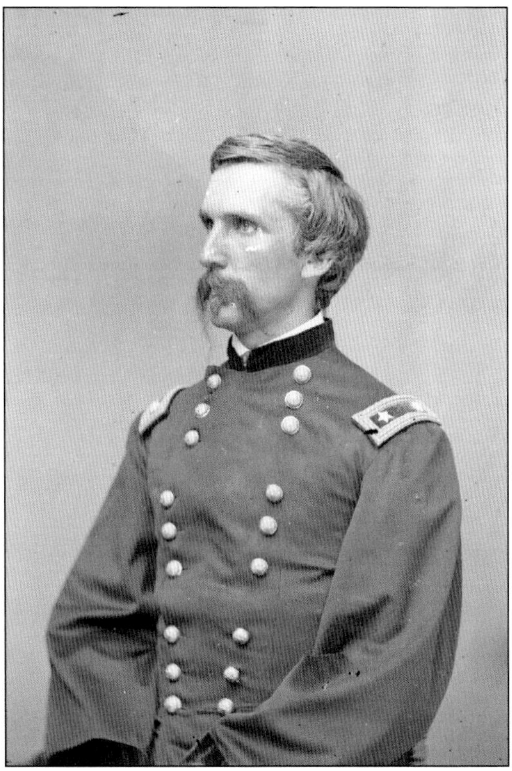

During the formal surrender proceedings, the Confederates relinquished arms to Maj. Gen. Joshua Lawrence Chamberlain. He began the war with no real formal military training, yet attained one of the highest ranks in the Union army by its conclusion. Chamberlain went on to become the governor of Maine. It is clear that the Civil War made Chamberlain the success he was.

The Confederate tasked with surrendering to Chamberlain was Maj. Gen. John B. Gordon, who, like Chamberlain, lacked formal military training. However, these men's performance on the battlefield spoke for itself. By the end of the war, Gordon was one of the highest-ranking Confederates at Appomattox. He was wounded countless times and was missing a significant portion of the left side of his face from wounds. However, Gordon and Chamberlain went on to respect each other immensely and recognized that, as warriors, they had much in common.

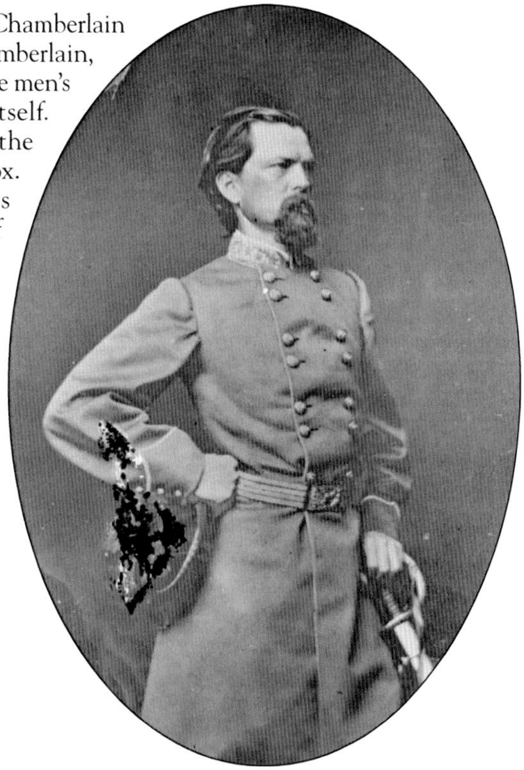

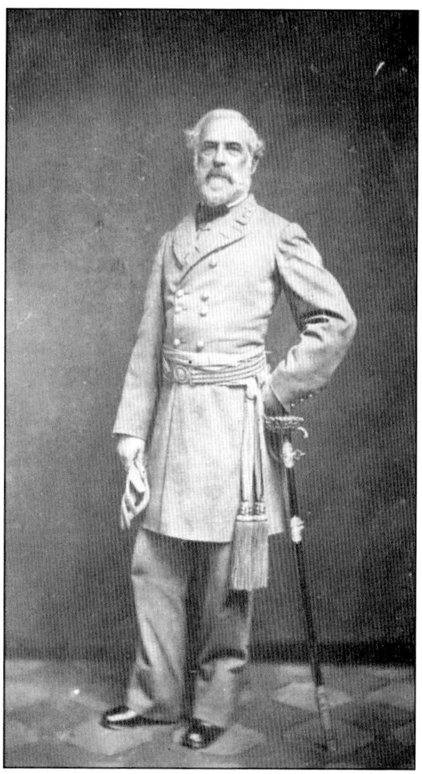

Sons of Virginia fought on both sides of the war, and none is more famous than Robert E. Lee. Following the surrender of his army, Lee became a hero in the South. To this day, he is venerated by Americans throughout the country. Following the war, Lee lived a quiet life and ardently supported the ending of hostilities and the reunification of America. He went on to become the president of Washington College, now Washington and Lee.

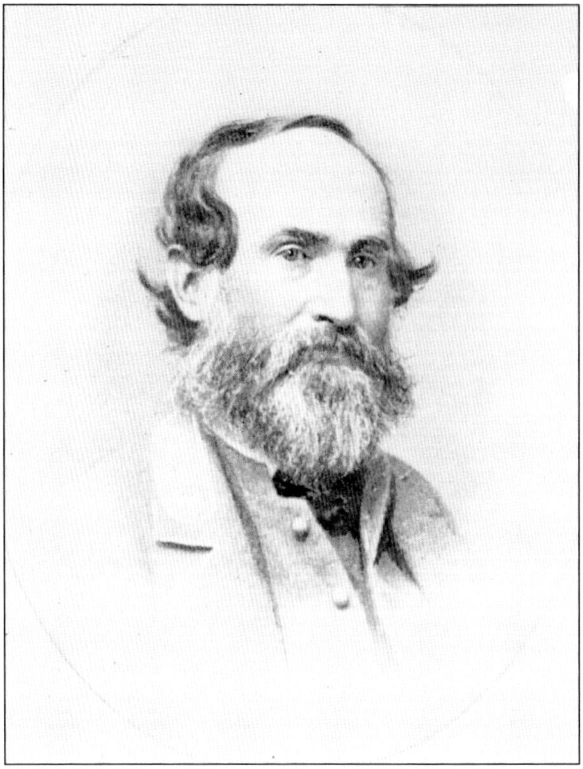

Another famous Virginian, Jubal Anderson Early, remained an unreconstructed Confederate to his death. He became one of the primary supporters of the Lost Cause and, despite being pardoned by the US government, felt that he was not truly part of the Union. After the war, he resumed his career as a successful lawyer, where his fiery personality and military discipline served him well.

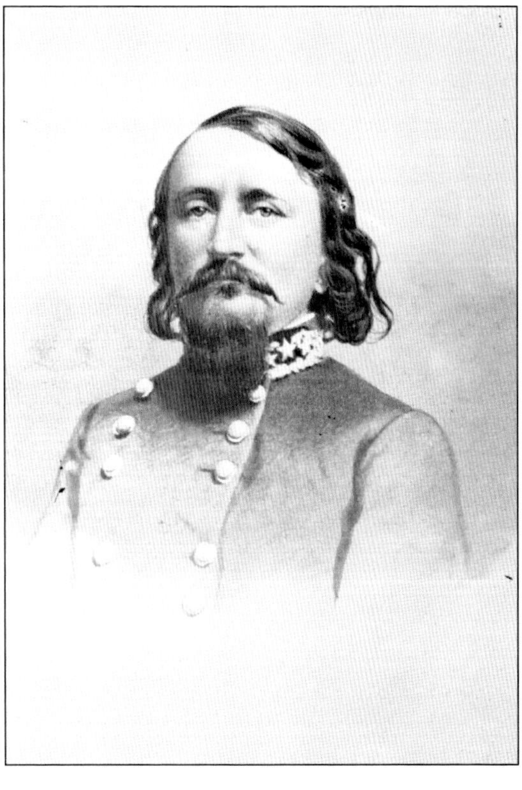

One of the most iconic Confederate officers from Virginia, Gen. George Pickett is most recognized for his fateful charge at Gettysburg, on which all of the hopes and dreams of the Confederacy rested. Following the war, Pickett sold insurance in Norfolk, but he never quite got over the horrendous loss of his precious division at Gettysburg. The loss of so many men under his command weighed on his mind into old age. When asked after the war why his charge was unsuccessful, he snidely replied, "I've always thought the Yankees had something to do with it."

Although Virginia was an ardently Confederate state, it was home to some distinguished Union officers as well. Adm. David G. Farragut was instrumental in organizing and managing the Union navy, which was involved in many crucial battles at ports throughout the South. Farragut coined the now iconic naval phrase, "Damn the torpedoes, full speed ahead!" He remained in the Navy after the war and went on to be the first US naval officer to attain the rank of full admiral.

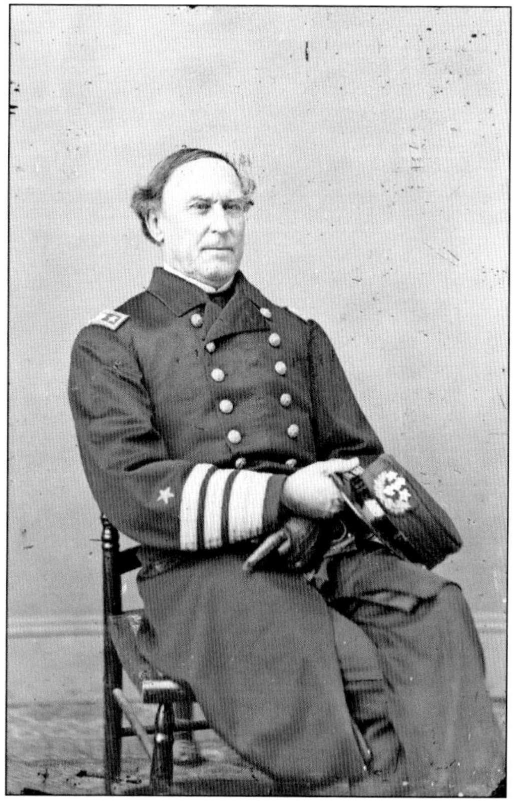

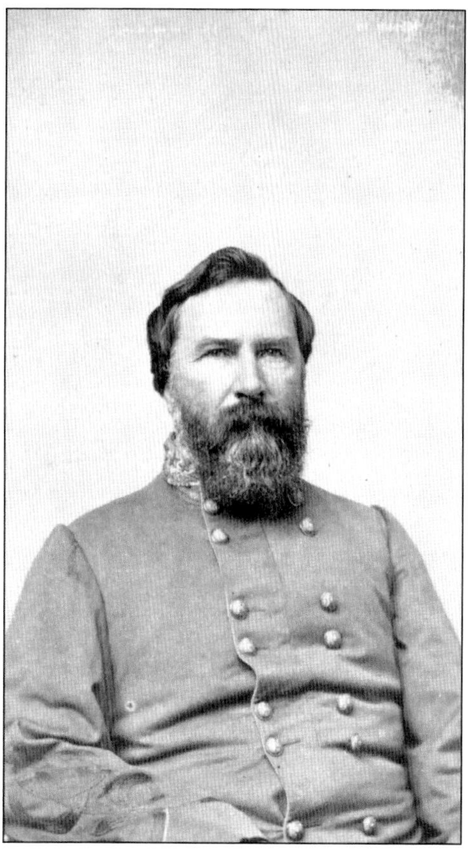

Lt. Gen. James Longstreet was much respected by General Lee, who held him in high esteem. Following the war, Longstreet put away his hostilities and got on with the business of living. He became a successful businessman and eventually was a prominent politician in New Orleans. He was a close friend of Ulysses S. Grant after the war and became the ambassador to the Ottoman Empire under Pres. Rutherford B. Hayes. Longstreet went on to serve under presidents William McKinley and Theodore Roosevelt.

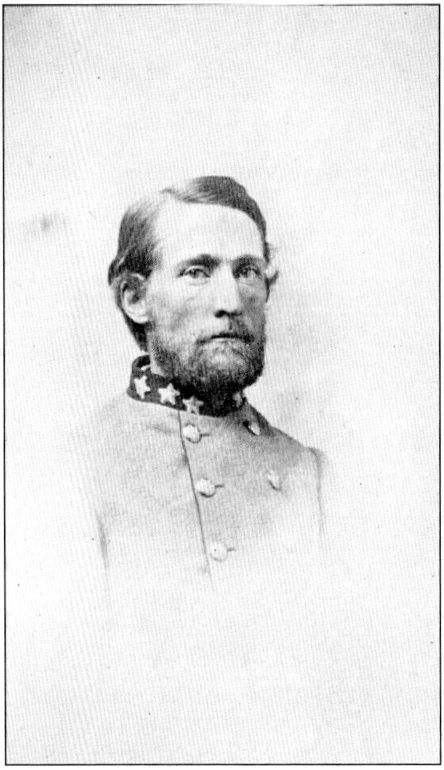

John Singleton Mosby, like Longstreet, put hostilities aside and worked to reunite the Union following the war. He went so far as to become a campaign manager in Virginia for Ulysses S. Grant's presidential race. Although these men were ferocious warriors for opposing causes, they quickly reconciled and worked to make the United States great after the war. In many respects, these men embody the higher ideals of what it means to be American, as they were capable of moving past their differences and working toward a better future.

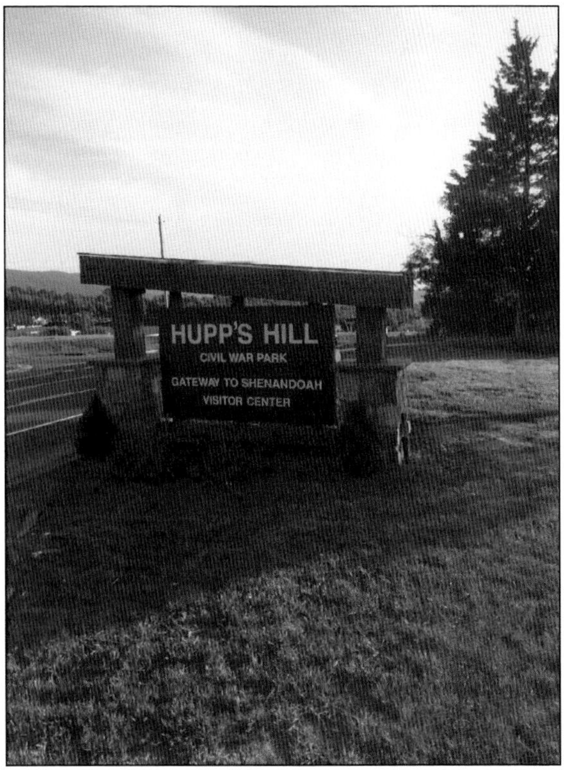

Although the war has long since ended, the mark it left on Virginia and the nation still exists. What makes history so powerful is that it allows people to reach back and touch the past. In doing this, people can begin to empathize with characters from the past as real people, not merely statues or figures in the pages of a textbook. Throughout Virginia, museums, historical societies, and parks strive to make the past approachable and accessible. Hupp's Hill Civil War Park is one such facility. (Author's collection.)

Many historians subscribe to the belief that, if people do not study their past, they are likely to repeat it. Thankfully, many organizations throughout the commonwealth work tirelessly to protect and preserve historically important land. Cedar Creek Battlefield Foundation, located near Middletown, Virginia, is a privately funded organization that works year-round to tell the story of the American Civil War and its effects on the Shenandoah Valley. In this sense, organizations like Cedar Creek are part of the continuing story of the Civil War in Virginia. (Author's collection.)

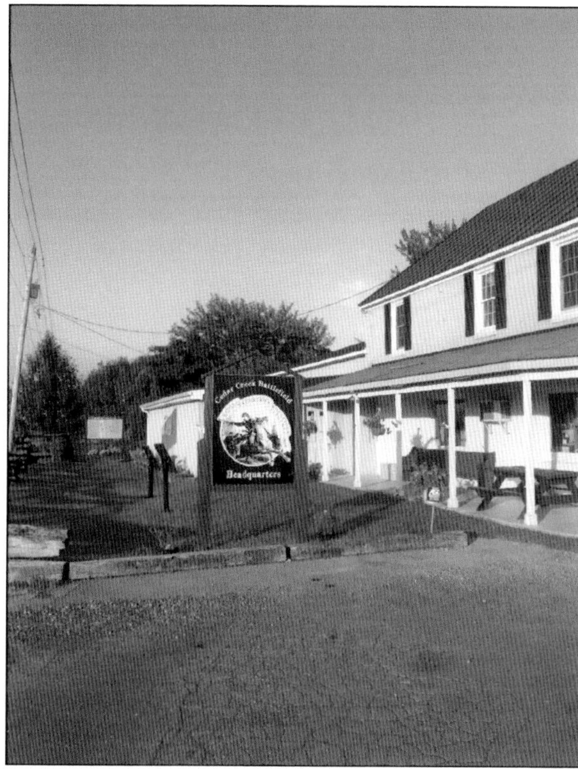

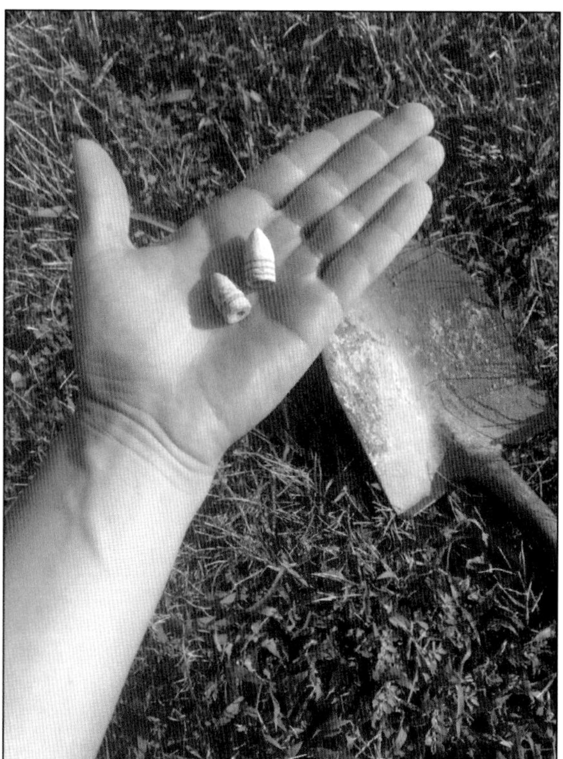

Many Civil War sites throughout the state have been subjected to residential and commercial development. Because of this, their importance to the war have been lost to the ages. However, archaeologists have discovered and examined thousands of other sites that played a role in Virginia's history. Seen here are Union and Confederate bullets that have been excavated from areas thought to have had no role in the war. All land is precious and has a story to tell. (Author's collection.)

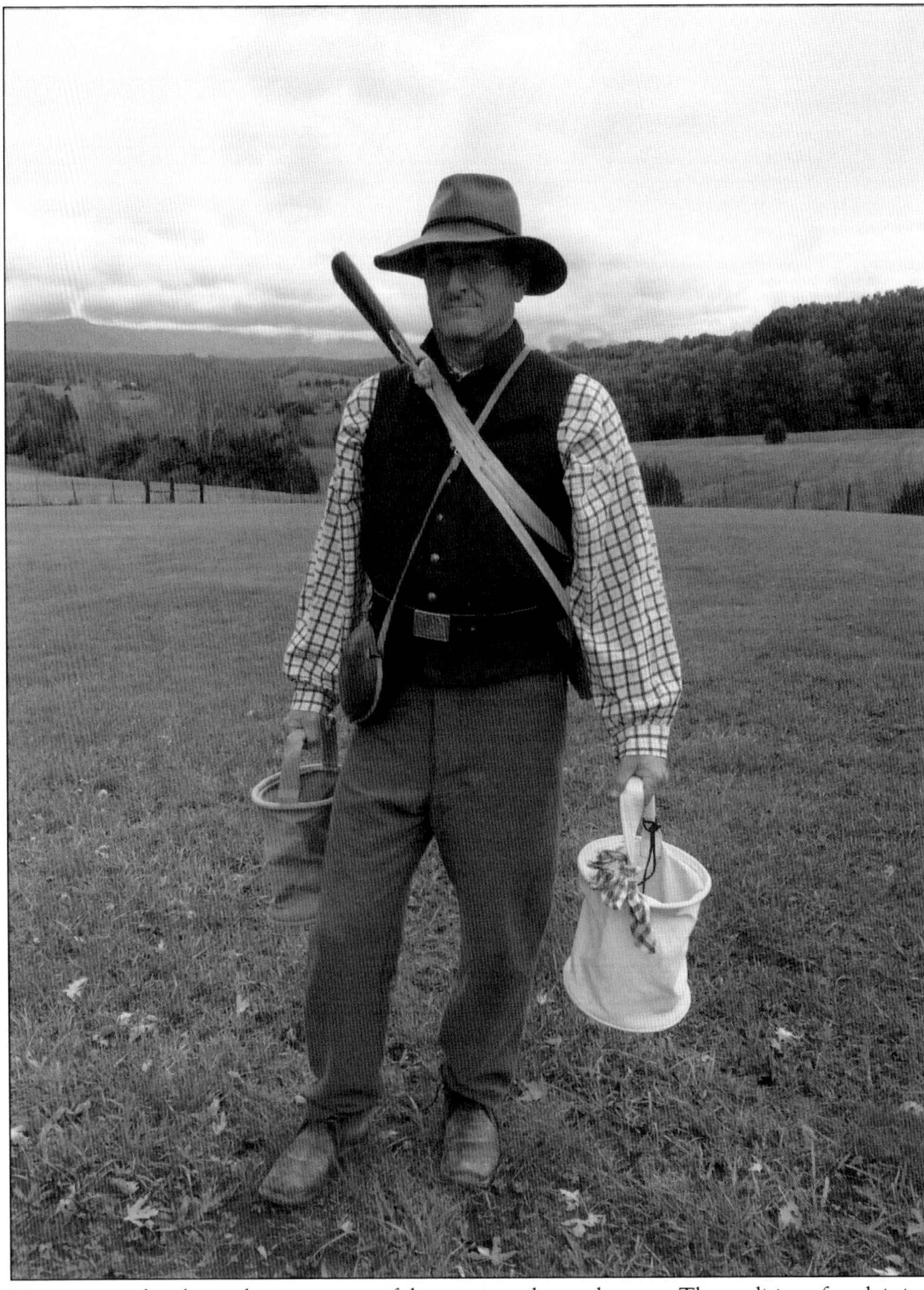

Historians work to bring the excitement of the past into the modern age. The tradition of explaining history in a lively, visceral fashion has been a part of Virginia's approach to the Civil War since the conflict's conclusion. To this end, reenactors and living historians attempt to convey the intense feelings, sentiments, and emotions experienced by the war's participants. Many parks and museums continue to host reenactments and other events, making history more accessible. (Courtesy of Hannah Berge.)

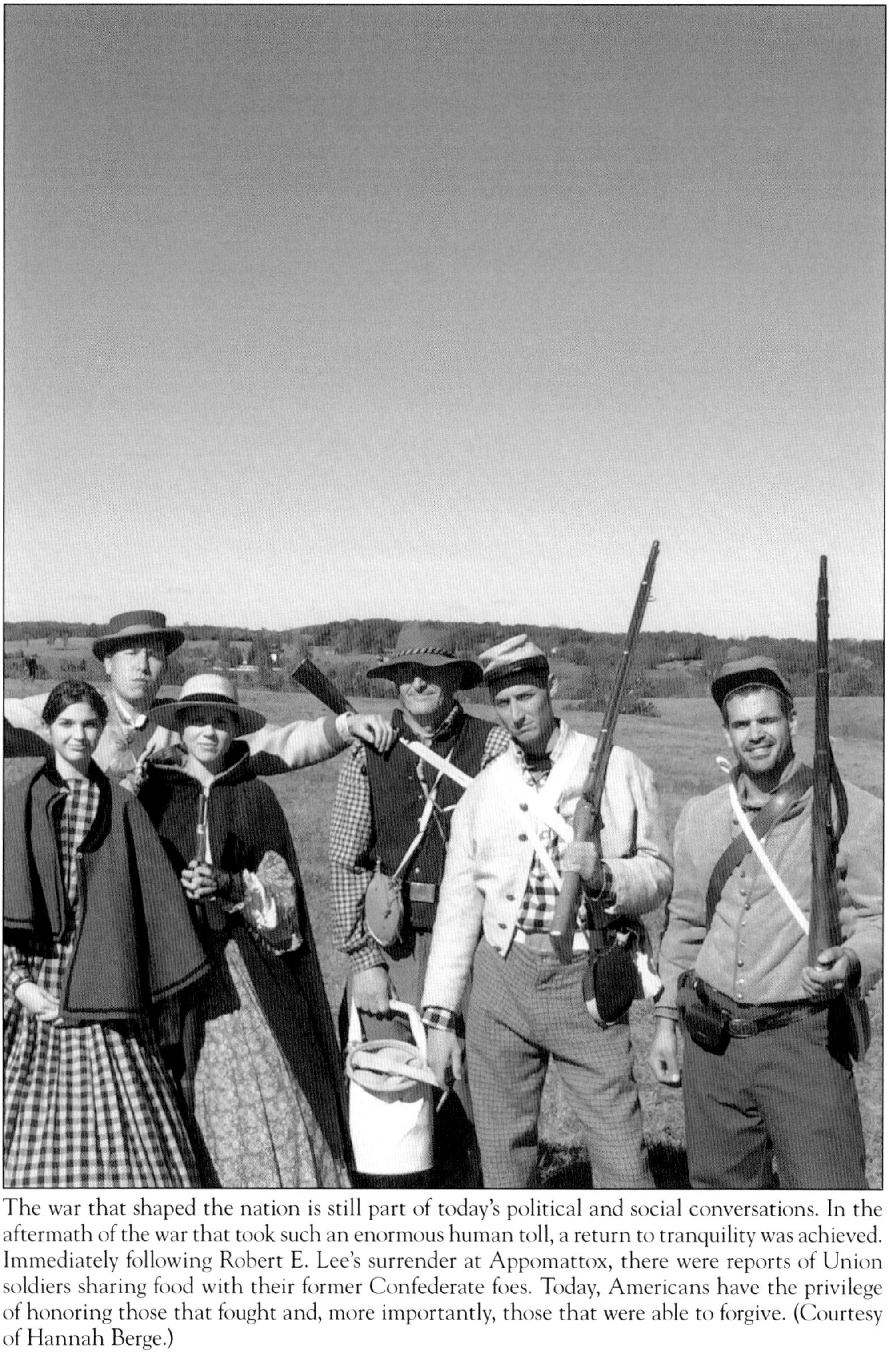

The war that shaped the nation is still part of today's political and social conversations. In the aftermath of the war that took such an enormous human toll, a return to tranquility was achieved. Immediately following Robert E. Lee's surrender at Appomattox, there were reports of Union soldiers sharing food with their former Confederate foes. Today, Americans have the privilege of honoring those that fought and, more importantly, those that were able to forgive. (Courtesy of Hannah Berge.)